GANDHI AND GRANT
Their Philosophical Affinities

GANDHI AND GRANT
Their Philosophical Affinities

Arati Barua

ACADEMIC EXCELLENCE
Delhi - 110 031 (India)

Published by

ACADEMIC EXCELLENCE
(Publishers & Distributors)
42, Ekta Apartments, Geeta Colony, Delhi-110 031
Phone : (011) 22445526, 22453953 / 09811892244
e-mail # books@indianacademicpublisher.com
www.indianacademicpubisher.com

GANDHI AND GRANT
Their Philosophical Affinities

Copyright Author

1st Edition, 2010

ISBN : 978-93-80525-08-2

[All rights reserved. No part of this book can be reproduced in any manner or by any means without prior permission of the Publisher.]

PRINTED IN INDIA

Published by *Rajkumar for Academic Excellence*. Delhi Laser typeset at *Graphic Era, Delhi and Printed at H.S. Printer. Delhi*

Foreword

During the past couple of hundred years, a particular view of understanding and organising the world has gained intellectual and political ascendancy. It developed slowly and was a product of the coming together of several different traditions of thought. Like all such comprehensive views, it involves ontology, epistemology and ethics, and has given rise to distinct theories of reality, rationality, relations between human faculties, what constitutes valid knowledge, the best ways of structuring personal and collective lives, and so on. Although this view of the world represents one phase in human history and one strand in human thought, it has come to be equated with modernity, a term that is used not just chronologically but to signify that it constitutes our inescapable predicament, represents the only rational way of understanding and organising human life, and that those not sympathetic to it are intellectually and morally backward. It exercises such a powerful spell over our imagination and has become such a central point of reference that all views of the world are judged in terms of it, and are categorised as pre-modern, modern, anti-modern or post-modern.

Modernity has not been without its critics. They fall into two broad categories. Some accept it but seek to define and combine its constitutive ideas, practices and institutions differently. Some others go further and challenge its hegemonic claims and seek to appropriate what they take to be its worthwhile features into a richer view of man and the world. Mahatma Gandhi belonged to the latter category. Both because he was a victim of the expansionist tendency of modernity and because he had available to him an alternative view of the world, he resisted the spell of modernity and was able to take a more objective and historical view of it. He appreciated its great strengths but also its profound limitations, and evolved a view that kept pace with modernity without being overwhelmed by it. His thought represents a creative and in parts unstable blend of ideas drawn from several pre-modern and modern traditions of thought, and cannot be easily classified as pre-modern, modern, post-modern or any of the other modernity-derived categories.

George Grant, a Canadian philosopher, was engaged in a similar exercise. Although his views are less widely known than Gandhis, he too was an important and influential thinker. His *Lament for a Nation, Technology and Empire* and other works challenged both an uncritical adulation and an equally uncritical rejection of modernity. He saw that technology, which lies at the heart of modernity, did not simply represent a way of controlling the world but also a particular way of thinking and living. It was not ontologically and epistemologically neutral, and both reflected and shaped the way human beings thought about themselves and organised their lives. He was highly critical of global American expansionism, and warned his countrymen against its insidious influence on them. Like Gandhi, he too refused to remain trapped within the inherited religious categories. While Gandhi, a Hindu, reached out to other religions especially Christianity, Grant did the opposite. He grew up within and valued the Christian tradition, but reached out to other religions especially Hinduism and tried to redefine both in the process. Like Gandhi, again, he sought to replace the currently dominant instrumental way of thinking by one that was more contemplative and meditative.

This volume represents a fascinating collection of high quality essays, exploring George Grant and Mahatma Gandhi both in their own and comparative terms. While some essays concentrate on either Grant or Gandhi, others set up a dialogue between them and look at each from the perspective of the other. They all collectively make a genuine contribution to our growing understanding of the sources and dilemmas of modernity.

Bhikhu Parekh
University of Westminster and House of Lords

Preface

George Grant was one of Canada's most original thinkers, and an important source of Canadian nationalism. He was a philosopher who taught in the department of Religion at Mc Master University, in Hamilton, Ontario, and in the Philosophy and Political Science departments of Dalhousie University in Halifax, Nova Scotia. In his major work *Lament for a Nation* (1965), that made him famous as a political philosopher, he argued that Canada was destined to disappear because 'the whole world was moving relentlessly towards a universal and homogeneous state' because of the impact of technology. For him the so-called modernity was not something to rejoice about because of its dehumanizing impact on our society and life. In yet another book *Technology and Empire* (1969), Grant expressed more intensely and vigorously his serious concern about the dangers of technology and modernism. These two works established Grant as a great patriot, an important political thinker, and an idealist philosopher of Canada. Grant's writings still influence Canadian politicians, political scientists, philosophers, religious thinkers, and scholars.

My exposures to the works of Grant was facilitated by the SICI (Shastri Indo-Canadian Institute's) Faculty Research fellowship which was offered to me in 2003 to work on "George Grant and Gandhi on technology and modernism: a comparative study" under the supervision of Professor William Christian of the Political Science Department, of the University of Guelph, Guelph, Ontario, Canada.

During the tenure of the award I also had the privilege to discuss Grant's thought with the late Professor Jay Newman, Department of Philosophy, of the Guelph University who is also a known Grantian scholar. On his advice I met James Gerrie who had then completed his Ph D on Grant, McLuhan and Innis. Further, Gerrie took me to the Mc Master University where I could meet Professor J. G. Arapura, an emeritus professor in Religious studies. He was a close friend of Grant who taught in Mc Master for 20 years when Prof. Arapura was there. Like Gandhiji, Grant's charismatic personality and profoundly original thought often created controversy and even sometimes antagonism. When I interviewed Professor John McMurtry at the University of Guelph and Professor Donald Weibe at the University of Toronto, they told me that Dr. Grant is often not given his proper status by other professors of philosophy in Canada, but he is very highly respected in the departments of religious studies, Canadian studies, and political science. This hostility from professional philosophers arose from an article Grant had written in 1951 in which he said: "The study of philosophy is the analysis of the traditions of our society and the judgment of those traditions against our varying intuitions of the Perfections of God". This understanding of philosophy lay at the core of his thought and was the reason why modern secular philosophers opposed him. But it was also the reason why his thought and Gandhiji's had such an affinity. It was quite sad for me to see the hostility he had faced from his fellow philosophers in Canada.

Again in 2004 I had been to Calgary to present a paper on Grant and Gandhi in an International Conference on Canadian Studies where I met Prof. George Melnyk who was the director of the seminar. On his invitation I went to his house for a dinner and there I found an Indian Laurel tree in his drawing room which he named after Gandhi and called it "Gandhi tree". It was so thrilling for me to see one Gandhi devotee in such a far off place like Canada. Melnyk told me the story that whenever he was disturbed he used to sit under that 'Gandhi tree' and used to do deep meditation to find out the solution and he said to me that he used to get it. What a true follower of Gandhiji in Canada!

Grant's work is not much known in India. In fact, many people have not even heard of him though his ideas are of much relevance in contemporary modern India. It is indeed a pleasant discovery to know that George Grant spoke in a language and tone having similar resonance with Gandhi's forceful argumentations against technology and modernism. The philosophical, logical, ethical and moral foundations of both the scholars are however significantly different from each other. This realization was in fact the turning point for me to think about working on a volume on Grant and Gandhi.

Gandhi's critique of technology and modernism first appeared in his masterpiece *"Hind Swaraj"*, which was published in 1909. And Grant's *"Lament for a Nation"* came to light in 1965. Thus, while there is a possibility for Grant to have known about Gandhi's views on technology and modernism, Gandhi certainly did not have that privilege. In fact, Gandhi formed his views quite independently, which came to us as a great revelation. George Grant knew Gandhi and admired him with great respect and compared him with Jesus Christ. It will not be wrong therefore to presume that Grant may have been influenced by Gandhi's views on *Ahimsa* and non- violence. This becomes clearer as one finds many similarities of Grant's views with Gandhi's, so much so that it may not be a travesty of fact if Grant is called – a Canadian Gandhi. As a matter of fact Grant is already known as one of the founders of modern Canadian nationalism. William Christian also talked about the similarities between the two, though Mrs. Sheila Grant, the wife of George Grant who lived in Halifax, feels that despite such apparent similarities, Gandhi's authority as an ethical preacher is immeasurably greater than her husband. She elevated Gandhi to a saint and her husband a moral philosopher. In her opinion a saint has much greater authority on humanity than a philosopher since "justice" is part of being a saint.

Our earth is finite and we live in finite time and space. Limitless technological growth and development is not feasible with finite resources as resources keep depleting with their increasing exploitation. The impacts of technological growth and modernization are increasingly felt on our limited resource base and environment. Thus, there is a need to put a halt on our increasing urge for raising wealth so that future generation will have enough resources to live with peace and harmony. This view of limiting growth and modernization stemming from scarcity of resources has of course a different logical foundation than the one which led Grant and Gandhi to talk about limiting growth. For Grant, modernization leads to homogenization of culture causing loss in cultural identity and human values and so he urged for limiting technological growth. On the other hand, Gandhi views technology in terms of its relation to man where man becomes increasingly subservient to the technology losing his soul and identity. As against outward expansion of human existence, Gandhi wanted a more inward development of life and soul. So he preached for limiting our wants. It is interesting to note that despite different logical and moral foundations for limiting growth in their analyses, the basic prescriptive idea stemming from their analyses converges with the modern economic rationality for limiting growth. It has become an increasing concern for us that the desperate surge for more and more wealth has posed a severe threat on our environment today posing a severe constraint on our life, survival and sustainability. It is in this context that we need to place the relevance of both Gandhi and Grant in the contemporary world. Both were pacifists who taught that the sacredness of life was primary.

With such a spirit of rediscovering the relevance of George Grant and Mahatma Gandhi in modern life, we had organized a seminar on George Grant and Gandhi at Jawaharlal Nehru University in 2006. It was an overwhelming experience for me that many scholars of repute had participated in the seminar with a lot of interest and enthusiasm and expressed their views that the papers presented at the seminar may be put together to bring out a volume so that the hard work will be of some permanent value. The idea of this volume in an embryonic form thus came out of that adventure. However, we did not have enough papers for a reasonable volume and therefore I invited papers from known Gandhian and Grantian scholars in India and abroad.

I am glad that I have received favorable responses from well known Grantian and Gandhian scholars of Canada like Ron Dart, William Christian, Peter Emberley, A. J. Parel and many others. In the same way, I have received enthusiastic support from many Gandhian scholars from India such as Professors Ramjee Singh, Anand Kumar, S. R. Bhatt and so on. Needless to say that without such support this volume would not have come to light.

A comparative study of Gandhi and Grant seems to me a timely and relevant theme for a discussion in the context of the present day world suffering from a lack of cohesive human existence in the face of growing individualism and enmity across people cutting across religion and castes and hatred and terrorism. It is expected that the younger generation may find in the works of such great minds plausible solutions towards construction of a better world free from those evils. With the above perspectives in mind I on behalf of the editorial board of the book wish to express sincere thanks to all the contributors in the volume for their support and guidance. I am especially thankful to Prof John Arapura, who was a colleague and a close friend of Grant and worked in the same university together for many years.

Arati Barua

Acknowledgement

I wish to thank Professor M. S. John, the Editor of *Gandhi Marg* for his kind permission to re-print Professor A. J. Parel's paper "Gandhi's Idea of Nation in Hind Swaraj" published in 1991, in *Gandhi Marg*, vol. 13, No. 3, October-December 1991, (pages 261 to 282) and for the article "George Grant and Mahatma Gandhi: An Interview with Sheila Grant" published in *Gandhi Marg*, vol. 26 number 4, January-March 2005 (pages 441 to 447) by Arati Barua to include in the volume.

I thank Professor Ron Dart, Editor to permit me to reproduce (pages 15 to 21) an article of Arati Barua "Mrs. (George) Sheila Grant on Gandhi: a live interview", from the Journal "*The Friend : The High Tory Review*" vol. 6# 3 Epiphany 2003 in this volume.

I am thankful to Navajivan Publishing House, Ahmedabad for permitting me to reprint pages - 36-7 (*Harijan*, 20-7-'35); p. 54 (Auto. p. 615); p. 130 (*Young India* 9-12-16). pp. 31-2 (*Harijan*, 13-6-'36); pp. 32-33 (Harijan, 29-8-'36); p. 33 (*Harijan*, 20-4-'34. pp.138-9 (*Auto.*, p. 615.) from the Book: *Truth is God* (Gleanings from the writings of Mahatma Gandhi bearing on God, God –Realization and Godly way) by M. K. Gandhi, Compiled by R. K. Prabhu, and published by Navajivan Publishing House, Ahmedabad-38001, in the volume.

I am very thankful to Professors William Christian, A. J. Parel, and A. Kumar for their guidance in organsing the notes of Grant and Gandhi in the appendix.

It is my pleasure to acknowledge that Professor Bhikhu Parekh, House of Lords and Professor in the University of Westminster and one of the world's leading Gandhi scholars accepted my request to write the "Foreword" to the book. He is so kind that in spite of his hectic schedule, he had very kindly agreed to read and comment on the manuscript. It is my pleasure to acknowledge my deep gratitude to him.

Lastly I thank Mr. Raj Kumar Gupta of Academic Excellence, (Publishers and distributors), New Delhi, India for bringing out the volume efficiently within a short period of time.

Arati Barua

Contents

Foreword	v
Preface	ix
Acknowledgement	xv
1. George Grant: Introduction to his life and Philosophy — William Christian	1
2. The Motive for coincidence between Gandhi and Grant — Ramjee Singh	12
3. George Grant and Mahatma Gandhi: On Pacifism and Technology — William Christian.	16
4. Gandhi and Grant: Deeper Nationalisms — Ron Dart	30
5. Gandhi and Grant on Empire and the Longings of the Soul — Peter Emberley	41
6. The Saint and the Professor: Integrating Nationalism and Religious Thought in the Writings of Gandhi and Grant — George Melnyk	70
7. Rethinking Democracy and Beyond: In the Back drop of Gandhiji's views — S.R. Bhatt	91
8. Gandhi, Heidegger and the Technological Times — R. Raj Singh	107
9. George Grant and Hinduism — Ron Dart	119
10. The New Sociological Imagination, Jnana Yoga and the web of life: Gandhi, Grant, Mills, Peirce — Johannes Bakker	131
11. Were Mohandas K. Gandhi and George Grant Neo-Luddite Nationalists? — James B. Gerrie	173

12.	Grant and Gandhi: A Live Interview with Mrs. Sheila Grant — Arati Barua	201
13.	George Grant on Order and Creativity — Andrew Kaethler	212
14.	Secularism – A Gandhian Perspective — Geeta Mehta,	222
15.	George Grant and his *Lament for a Nation*: With a Special Reference to M.K. Gandhi's *Hind Swaraj*: A Comparison — Arati Barua,	236
16.	Gandhi's Idea of Nation in *Hind Swaraj* — Anthony Parel	257
17.	Gandhi's Economic Philosophy — Joseph Prabhu	286
18.	A Tribute to Dr. George Grant — John Arapura	305
	Appendix	314
	Contributors	337
	Bibliography	345
	Index	

Dedicated

to the memory of

Sheila Grant (1920-2009)

1

GEORGE GRANT: INTRODUCTION TO HIS LIFE AND PHILOSOPHY

(William Christian)

During his life, George Grant (1918-1988) received many of Canada's highest honours. He was appointed to the Order of Canada, he was a Fellow of the Royal Society and received its distinguished Chaveau Medal, and he was awarded seven honorary degrees by Canadian universities. There are few professors of philosophy, political science, or history who don't know his name. He is included in every important reference book. His most important book, *Lament for a Nation,* has been named one of the hundred greatest Canadian books.

In spite of this fame in Canada, Grant is very little known outside his native country. Why? The simple answer is: He did not much care about being famous and, although he achieved great success, his success came because he was a great thinker, not because he coveted success.

That was not because he didn't understand the nature of success. Both his grandfathers were very eminent Canadians. His paternal grandfather, G.M. Grant (1835-1902), was a Christian clergyman in the Scottish Presbyterian tradition. He rose to national prominence, though as an educator. Canadian knew him as Principal Grant, the head of Queen's University in Kingston, Ontario. When he became its principal in 1877 it was a small, struggling, almost bankrupt college. At his death it was a vigorous, financially sound, and academically respected institution. Grant was also a political figure of note. He could count on assured access to the prime minister of the day. His journalism was influential and he was one of the best public orators of his era.

Grant's maternal grandfather, Sir George Parkin (1846-1922), was also an educator and a significant political figure. Like Principal Grant, he was a superb platform orator and, in the 1880s and 1890s, he traveled widely throughout Canada, Australia, New Zealand, and the United Kingdom arguing the case for maintaining close ties between the colonies. In 1896 he became head of the important Canadian private boys school, Upper Canada College, where he implemented progressive educational reforms. He is most famous for his accomplishments in the period from 1902 to 1920. He was responsible for organizing setting up and administering the Rhodes Scholarships, and it was for that accomplishment he was awarded his knighthood.

Grant's most famous relative was his uncle, Vincent Massey (1887-1967). Massey married Parkin's eldest daughter. He was Canada's first Ambassador to the United States, and served as High Commissioner to the United Kingdom for eleven years, including the critical period of the Second World War. However, he is best known as the first native-born Canadian to serve as Governor-General (1952-59). Another uncle was a cabinet minister and a third a famous inventor.

His family was not wealthy but he had a comfortable and privileged upbringing. His father, William Grant (1872-1935) was also headmaster of Upper Canada College. The position brought with it a significant salary, a house, servants, and free education for his son, who grew up with the children of many of the country's social and economic elite.

He studied history at his grandfather Grant's university, won one of the Rhodes Scholarships grandfather Parkin had helped established, and enrolled as a law student at Baliol College, Oxford, an institution with which Parkin, his father, and his uncle had close associations. But in 1940 all these forces that seemed to be guiding him toward worldly success were shattered.

His whole family were imperialists. They believed that the destiny of Canada lay within the British Empire and that, when England was in danger, it was the duty of the Empire to come to its aid. That meant, in their eyes, that it was George Grant's duty to enlist as a fighting man and do his duty for his King and Country. Grant could not do this. He was a pacifist. He had decided that war was morally evil and that spiritually he could not take part. He recognized that there might be serious repercussions, including the disapproval of his family, but he was sure that he could not fight. He first trained to join and ambulance unit, then served as an Air Raid Precautions warden to help those who suffered from the German bombing of London. In December 1941 he had an intense religious, perhaps mystical, experience, that confirmed his faith in the divine.

When the war finished Grant returned to Oxford. To the strong opposition of his family, he abandoned the study of law and began to attend to philosophy and theology. In 1947 he accepted an appointment to teach philosophy at Dalhousie University in Nova Scotia on Canada's Atlantic Coast. He remained there until 1960. He was a gifted teacher and formed close friendships with some of his students, some of which lasted until his death.

Three aspects of Grant's philosophy immediately set him apart from the mainstream of the Canadian philosophic tradition. The first was that, although he had some exposure to the Oxford school of analytic philosophy of Gilbert Ryle and A.J. Ayre, he found it arid and rejected it. He was one of very few Canadian philosophers who turned to continental European philosophers for inspiration. In the 1950s he encountered the French philosophers, Simone Weil and Jean Paul Sartre, and the Germans, Leo Strauss and Martin Heidegger. Heidegger and Weil exerted an influence on him throughout his life.

Second, Grant's philosophy was very rarely 'academic.' He was not a philosopher who tried to address other philosophers. For the most part he wrote in a way that was accessible to well-educated men and women who were not professionally trained philosophers. Even more unusual was the subject matter he addressed. He didn't deal with language, truth, or logic, or publish books with titles like *Tractatus Logico-Philosophicus*. His first important book bore the title *Philosophy in the Mass Age*, and talked about the difficulties modern men and women faced in a world where they were no longer confident that the morality they had inherited from their older tradition of meaning was any longer valid now that freedom had become the dominant value in the modern world.

The phrase 'the older tradition of meaning' points to Grant's third, and sharpest, break with other Canadian philosophers. Many of them were not believing Christians, and even those who were did not think that philosophy and Christian should have anything to do with one another. Grant utterly rejected his position: 'The study of philosophy is the analysis of the traditions of out society and the judgement of those traditions against our varying intuitions of the Perfection of God.' This sentence was virtually a declaration of war against secular philosophy, and Grant waged it without regret until the end of his life.

In 1960 he moved to a newly created university, York, in Toronto, Ontario. After he accepted the position, he discovered that a required text for the first year philosophy text was one that he considered debased philosophy and demeaned Christianity. He refused to use this book and resigned. The next year he became a professor of religion at McMaster University in Hamilton, Ontario. When he became head of this department in 1964, he was determined that he wanted to shape it in a particular way. Most departments of religions approached the study of religions from the perspective of the various social sciences, especially sociology, psychology, and anthropology. Grant was determined that his students would learn from scholars who believed in the truth of their religions, but who would not try to 'convert' their students. One of these professors, John Arapura, author of *Radhakrishnan and integral experience; the philosophy and world vision of Sarvepalli Radhakrishnan* (1966), *Hermeneutical essays on Vedāantic topics* (1986), and *Gnosis and the question of thought in Vedeanta : dialogue with the foundations* (1986) became close friends with Grant. Over the years they met often to talk about religion and philosophy. Grant often described himself as standing on 'the extreme Hindu wing of Christianity.' He had a deep knowledge of Hinduism and expressed deep admiration for Lord Krishna. When Dr Arapura sent him a copy of *Gnosis and the question of thought in Vedeanta*, Grant replied that it had helped to lead him away from some unwise interpretation of the Bhagavadgita that he had formed from his one study. 'your conclusion was wonderfully helpful for philosophy seen only from the western tradition, as indeed are the last sections of I & II, particularly I, because it is so immensely free from what the western tradition became, although through that conclusion (of II) I think I had a glimpse of the foundation of certain things that are very obscure to me in Plato'.

Christianity recognizes both the vita activa and the vita contempliva. Grant held in deepest admiration those like Gandhi who had lived the vita activa to the fullest, had accepted the will of God, and had become Love and Justice. Grant did not reject the demands of the vita active. He was a pacifist, and he was prepared to accept whatever suffering was necessary in its cause. But the divine had not called him to live that life to the fullest. His vocation was a philosopher. For him it was not just necessary to believe; he needed to think the meaning of his beliefs. In the words of the Christian philosopher St Anselm, *Credo ut intelligam*, I believe in order than I might understand.

His need to understand came to a focus in 1963. The United States wanted Canada to allow nuclear warheads to be fitted to certain Americans weapons stationed on Canadian soil. Although the Progressive Conservative government led by Prime Minister John Diefenbaker had earlier agreed, his assessment of the strategic situation changed and he no longer believed they were necessary. US President Kennedy disagreed and a grave diplomatic crisis arose between the two countries which led to the downfall of the Diefenbaker government and the election of a Liberal government led by Lester Pearson, a Nobel Peace Prize winner, who had committed his government to accepting these weapons.

Grant was outraged that any Canadian government would allow nuclear weapons on Canadian soil. He thought that the episode signalled the effective end to Canada's existence as an independent sovereign nation in North American. He reflected on the historical forces that had brought this change about. The result was *Lament for a Nation*, a short book that had as powerful an effect on Canada as *Hind Swaraj* did on India. The book was a best-seller and instantly Grant became a immensely popular national figure. Although the philosophic premise of his book was that, ultimately, the forces of technological modernity would destroy any essential differences between Canada and the United States, Canadians, especially younger Canadians, felt that he expressed with eloquence and profundity a love of Canada that they shared and that he had defied the United States at a time when Canada's politicians and businessmen were timidly accepting American dominance.

In the mid-1960s he had a strong following among Canadian university students and anti-Viet Nam activists. In his mid-forties, he was a charismatic personality. Deeply intense, with a rich, melodious voice, an extraordinary intellect and a fierce commitment to social justice, Grant galvanized a generation of politically sensitive young people. Some were uncomfortable with his deeply held religious beliefs, but they shared his fear that technological modernity was destroying the possibility that human beings could live decent lives.

Grant struggled understand the nature of the modern world and develop a language with which to discuss it. He knew that public discussions of God made people uncomfortable in a secular country like Canada, so he talked about Good and Justice instead; but he meant the same thing. His first collection of primarily philosophic essays was *Technology and Empire* (1969), which collected work of the past decade. About the same time, he delivered a series of lectures on the Canadian Broadcasting Corporation, *Time As History*. These talks were extraordinary for two reasons. They were, I think, the first time, that any Canadian thinker had seriously engaged with ideas of Friedrich Nietzsche in a public forum. More important, Grant said that this German writer, who many in the English-speaking world had previously dismissed as an obscurantist and proto-Nazi of little philosophic importance was instead the founder of modernity whose thought it was consummately important to understand. In five short but persuasive lectures Grant challenged Canadians to encounter Nietzsche's dangerous thoughts.

In 1974, Grant delivered the Wood Lectures at Mount Allison University in Sackville, New Brunswick. Their central theme was the question of justice in liberal society. The American Supreme Court delivered its judgement in Roe v. Wade in 1973 which in effect struck down all laws prohibiting abortion. The core of their argument was that the foetus was not a person and therefore deserved no protection in law. Grant was shocked by this line of reasoning. If the foetus was not a person, he asked, what was it? And if persons were not souls before God, then what was it about them that made them deserving of justice? What demand did justice have on any human being if freedom to make our own destiny was the ultimate value, as Nietzsche taught?

In the 1970s politics held Grant's interest less as he tried more and more to recover a vision of the Good. His works during this period make greater demands on the reader. Previously he had tried to express his thoughts in a language that was accessible. As the thoughts he was thinking in the 1970s and technological modernity converged even further, the gap between his writings and his audience's ability to understand them widened. At the same time, though, his insight deepened and his critique of modernity became more profound. He carefully studied Martin Heidegger's four volume study of Nietzsche, which appeared in translation in 1982, and he continued to read the writings of Simone Weil, whose writing he first encountered in 1951. The result was his last collection of essays, *Technology and Justice* (1986). It contained 'Thinking About Technology' and 'Faith and the Multiversity,' two of his deepest meditations. 'Faith and the Multiversity' represents, in my view, the pinnacle of his thought to that point, an argument that the technological way of being is fundamentally inadequate because it excludes love. At the time of his death, he had just begun his most ambitious essay, an attempt to explore the inadequacy of Heidegger's account of Plato.

Since his death, his philosophical stature has continuously increased. *Lament for a Nation* has celebrated its fortieth anniversary in print, and all his other books are in print. His collected works are close to completion and a major scholarly biography appeared. Numerous books have been written about various aspects about his thought and theses from the honours to the doctoral level have been written in all parts of Canada.

It is strange that, in spite of the magisterial quality of his thought, he is still little known outside of Canada. There are certainly scholars in the United States who know and admire his writings, but considering their universal themes, it is amazing that he is not better known. If he had a choice for his thought to be known anywhere, it would be India. After he married and had six children, he rarely travelled outside Canada, but he felt a great affinity for the philosophy and religion of India. When I had the privilege in early 2006 to speak to Indian audiences about Grant's thought, they were very receptive. I want to thank Dr Arati Barua for giving me that opportunity, and also to acknowledge her considerable wisdom in creating this book.

George Grant's Biography

18 December 1916	William Grant, (father), becomes principal of Upper Canada Colllege
13 November 1918	George Parkin Grant (GPG) born
6 September 1920	Sheila Veronica Allen (wife) born
25 June 1922	Sir George Parkin (grandfather) dies
3 February 1935	William Grant (father) dies
1939	wins Rhodes Scholarship, enters Balliol College, Oxford, studies law
1940	awarded BA by Queen's University, Ontario
Summer 1940	as a pacifist, refuses military service. Trains with an ambulance unit. Serves as an Air Raid Precautions Warden during the German bombing of London
October 1941	attempts to join merchant marine, reject on health grounds
February 1942	returns to Canada
February 1943	begins work with Canadian Association of Adult Education

1 July 1947	marries Sheila Allen
September 1947	appointed to Philosophy Department at Dalhousie University, Halifax, Nova Scotia
1950	awarded D.Phil. degree by Oxford
1952	Vincent Massey (uncle) becomes Governor-General of Canada
1959	publishes *Philosophy in the Mass Age*
1960	appointed to and resigns from York University, Toronto, Ontario
1961	appointed to Religion Department, McMaster University, Hamilton, Ontario
1 February 1963	Maude Grant (mother) dies
1964-7	chairman of Religion department
1964	made Fellow of the Royal Society of Canada
1965	publishes *Lament for a Nation*
1969	publishes *Technology and Justice*
1971	awarded honorary degree, Trent University, Peterborough, Canada
1972	awarded honorary degree, Mount Allison University, Sackville, New Brunswick, Canada
1974	delivers Wood lectures at Mount Allison – later published (1978) as *English-Speaking Justice*
1974	honorary degree, Dalhousie University, Halifax
1976	honorary degree, Queen's University, Kingston
1979	honorary degree, University of Toronto, Toronto, Ontario, Canada

1980	honorary degree, University of Guelph, Guelph, Ontario, Canada
1980	honorary degree, Thorneloe University, Sudbury, Ontario, Canada
1981	award Chaveau Medal by the Royal Society of Canada
1981	made Officer, Order of Canada
1986	publishes *Technology and Justice*
27 September 1988	George Grant dies in Halifax (pancreatic cancer)
1993	University of Toronto Press publishes *George Grant: a Biography*.
2000-5	U of T press publishes first three volumes of *Collected Works*

ಬ ಛ

2

THE MOTIVE FOR COINCIDENCE BETWEEN GANDHI AND GRANT

Ramjee Singh

Indeed it is a thrilling experience to go through Dr Arati Barua's brief note about her original research on a comparative study between Gandhi and Grant. Had I not been handicapped with my vision I would have loved to go through the entire writings of George Grant especially his *"Lament for a Nation"* and *"Technology and Empire"*. The similarities between Gandhi and Grant are not only amazing but vital to introduce new dimensions to study Gandhi. As a humble student of philosophy I am not so much interested in protological and descriptive points of similarity between these two great men of our era. I am more interested in the quest for finding out motivations for this coincidence of their ideas.

To me truth is monopoly of none- neither of Gandhi nor of Grant. It is of universal dimension. It is therefore that there has been immense similarity between the central vision of great saints and seers from Socrates to Gandhi.

We cannot deny that there are differences in their views but the basic motivation and expressions are almost the same. Socrates was a martyr of truth and justice. Martyrdom of Jesus and Gandhi has been to uphold the claims of truth. Similarly almost all religious prophets from Buddha and Mahavir to Jesus, Mohammed and Nanak speak almost in the same vein about the general principles of morality. It means they think alike presumably because the situation is the same. Humanity though it appears to be multiverse but indeed it is a unity. Hence saints and seers like Gandhi and Grant do not belong to a particular nation or a particular religious faith. Socrates had earlier proclaimed that he was neither an Athenian nor a Greek but a citizen of the world. Similar are the expressions and exhortation of all other saints in different parts of this globe and in different times. The reason for this has been that the humanity faces the same problems everywhere of course these forms may differ. The mission of these saints and seers is to unify the humanity and place the universal truth for safe guidance and happy living. It is no wonder that Gandhi in the east, Tolstoy, Ruskin and Thoreau or Grant in the west have the same concern for the dangerous phenomena of this modern civilization. No doubt, modern civilization has bestowed upon mankind many a blessings through science and technology but it is also true that it has brought on the brink of a disaster which can wipe out and annihilate not only the entire mankind but all the living beings. Hence unfettered and unguided growth of science is a danger for humanity. The great scientist Einstein has been constrained to observe, "Science without spirituality is blind and spirituality without science is lame". Hence Gandhi in his *Hind Swaraj* and Grant in his "*Lament for a nation*" may apparently look to be anti-science or anti-technology but these are in fact the saviours of civilizations.

They advocate the growth of science for human happiness and not making weapons for mass destruction. Similarly they are not against technology but they want technology for man not man for technology bringing alienation and dehumanization. Unless human values are associated with the goals of science and technology, we are bound to face a doomsday sooner than later. Similarly neither Gandhi nor Grant is against modernity if it stands for rational thinking. They are against all superstitious orthodoxies and outdate in human social and moral customs. But if modernization means unbridled growth of human needs and requirements it is again unproductive and anti - civilization. Our civilization and culture aim at total and balanced development of man—physical, intellectual, moral and spiritual. The present civilization must be accused of dividing humanity into West and East, North and South and the developed and the developing nations. A civilization based on the basis of unlimited wants and ever-growing craze for pomp and luxuries, extravagant and immoral pleasures, it is bound to face an unprecedented derailment. Toynbee had rightly shown that though civilizations which have been grown on the basis of immorality have wiped out of their existence.

Gandhi also quotes, that such civilizations like Sodom and Gomorra have been completely wiped out. Hence morality and ethics are not superstitious spiritual conundrums but essential for existence and happiness. Alexis Carrel the Great Nobel Laureate in his book *'Man the unknown'* has seriously made efforts to develop a 'Science of Man'. What is the standard if civilization where there is plentitude for only a fourth of humanity and the rest thrice fourth living in abject poverty, illiteracy, disease etc. Similarly the ideal of hedonistic pleasure is not only illusory but also self defeating. Hence we need a civilization where we can properly discriminate between the material and the spiritual and pleasure and happiness. We need not discard the demands of material and physical body but we must remember that there is no limit to our sensual pleasure. Even the concept of 18th century nationalism has become out dated. It is almost like tribalism which has engineered savagery in human history. If humanity is one the world should be one and there should be a world government. If I think Gandhi is hundred percent for a world government and a world culture, I hope, Grant would also share this idea. Secondly, the concept of personal religion has also become outdated and destructive for the growth of universal fraternity. Human History has shown that more than six thousand small and big wars have been fought both in the name of nationalism and personal religion. Hence if humanity is one there should be one world and Science is universal, religion must be universal. Hence Gandhi has laid great emphasis upon equal respects for all religions as a practical dynamics towards reaching the ideas of universal religion. In fact if spiritual is an essence of religion there should be absolutely no difficulty in evolving the concept of universal religion based on inner voice and conscience.

Gandhi has been eulogized as Jesus of modern times. He may be compared with Lord Buddha or other such saints and seers but I think it would be unfair to limit Gandhi to be called only as a saint and much less only as an academician and theoretician. He was both a saint and warrior. Though his method was different, he had invented moral and spiritual equivalent of war called Satyagraha. He not only preached sermons on the morality and spirituality but also demonstrated the efficacy of moral power in mass action. Gandhi no doubt was an ardent pacifist. But his pacifism was not for peace of the graveyard. He fought against social injustice and political enslavement because according to him peace and non-violence are not only idological and much less utopian but it is a practical action for liquidating and minimizing all sorts of structural and institutional violence in social, political, economic and educational life. I think both Grant and Gandhi should meet on the level of idea and action.

ಬ ಲ

3

GEORGE GRANT AND MAHATMA GANDHI ON PACIFISM AND TECHNOLOGY

(William Christian)

A few days after Gandhi's death on 30 January 1948, Canadian philosopher George Grant wrote in a letter to his mother. 'Gandhi's death was a blow - but his being was of the quality that makes it possible for less clear lights like us to know where to go'.[1]

Grant always distinguished between those he called the 'great thinkers' and 'saints'. A great thinker was someone whose thought was 'remarkably open to the whole'. A saint was on of those 'rare people who give themselves away'.[2] Many people describe Mahatma Gandhi as a man of great moral courage. For Grant this description does not encapsulate the essence of his reverence for Gandhi. Christ said, 'Happy are those who hunger and thirst for justice's sake'. (Matthew 5:6) That was, in Grant's view, exactly what Gandhi had done. He had had given himself away and made himself the instrument of God's will for the sake of justice.

As Christ said on the Cross: 'Not my will, but thine, be done' (Luke 22:42). (In saying this, I am not suggesting that Grant thought that Gandhi was a Christian, only that there is little that separates the Christian truth and the Hindu truth. Grant often described himself as standing on 'the extreme Hindu wing of Christianity'.)

For Grant, Gandhi's thirst for justice was not something abstract or theoretical. Gandhi had not merely thought the meaning of justice: He was, in the language of the west, a saint. Simply put, he had made it flesh: he had become justice itself. Justice is often something that eludes human understanding. It rolls around, in Plato's words, in the shadows. It escapes our attention. It is an easy thing for us to be distracted from justice, but there are certain moments in history when an awareness of justice forces itself on us, and those moments are most compelling when justice is supremely absent, as it was when just human beings such as Socrates, Christ, and Gandhi were killed. At that moment our hunger and thirst for justice is almost unbearable, because we know that justice was completely absent in those killings.

In Grant's opinion, Jawaharlal Nehru, Gandhi's protégé, was far more of a political figure, and he did not understand that Gandhi fundamentally was not political. For Nehru, civil disobedience was primarily a brilliantly successful political act that led to Indian independence. As Grant understood, and Gandhi makes clear in his autobiography, he, unlike Nehru and many of the other members of Congress, did not hate the British Empire. On the contrary, he knew that, for the most part, the British were just, firm, caring and used the bayonet sparingly. As Grant said in a later work, *English-Speaking Justice* (1974), Satyagraha was successful in leading India to independence because the British exercised restraint in their imperial adventures. Gandhi had to negotiate with Lord Halifax, not with the Nazi Heinrich Himmler or Lavrenty Beria of the Soviet NKVD.[3] However, it is not guaranteed that even saints can hold back the forces of their age or hold back a civilization, though

Gandhi at times seemed to suggest that the force of love and justice might be enough to transform not just one person or several, but entire countries. Grant feared that, whatever individuals did, the world was preparing for nuclear warfare that would spread the civilization of Hollywood, and that no individual, group, or state would be able to withstand the forces driving in that direction.

Grant's position confused people, as did Gandhi's. Both were deeply sincere pacifists who had a profound understanding that they lived in a world of himsa. To understand the underlying coherence and its philosophical origins of Grant's thought we have to look at one of the thinkers who had the greatest influence on him, the fifth century Christian philosopher, St Augustine. One of Augustine's most powerful images was the contrast between the two cities in which a human being could choose to live, the city of God and the city of man.

All human beings were born into secular political units, and force was a primary determinant of relations within states and, even more, in conflicts between states. However, the Christian had a choice. He or she could choose to become a citizen of the city of God. This city did not exist on earth, but it was nonetheless real. Ultimately, if there were a serious clash between moral and political claims, the Christian had to follow Christ. Each world was driven by its own imperatives: the one by force, the other by love. In Grant secular words: 'I am not a Tory, but I see less & less logic in any position that is not either Tory or Christian pacifist'.[4] Tories accepted the world of force without regret and happily lived in the city of man. Gandhi put is in this way: 'Kings will always use their kingly weapons. Force is bred into them'. Christian pacifists chose the heavenly city as their habitation. Liberal progressive or socialists, in his view, did not understand that salvation was not possible in this world, but they tried to achieve it anyway, often with disastrous consequences. Grant understood Gandhi's spiritual resistance as an example of his participation in Saint Augustine's heavenly city. He agreed with the position that Gandhi set forth in *Hind Swaraj* that 'Real home-rule is self-rule or self-control and that the way to it is passive resistance: that is soul-force or love force'.[5] The heavenly city was one that every human being could and should join and in that city there would be no need of force.

In 1960 Grant was part of group of intellectuals invited to contribute essays to *Social Purpose for Canada*, a work that was meant to contribute to the philosophical basis for a new social democratic political party and give it a solid intellectual foundation. Grant's contribution concerned itself with the issue of equality.[6] Grant's Augustinianism permeated its principal conclusion. The only equality that really mattered was the equality of souls before God and any political, social or economic equality could find a true ground in that basis. The foundation for equality is essentially religious. 'Such a foundation will seem to the unbeliever too limited a basis for social principle. It must be insisted, however, that the idea of equality arose in the West within a particular set of religious and philosophical ideas [Christianity and Kantianism]. I cannot see why men should go on believing in the principle without some sharing of those ideas'.[7] If people did not believe that what was fundamental about human beings was their equality as souls before God, why would they embark on the immensely difficult social practice of treating each person as important?[8]

There were people other than politicians who thought that they knew how to improve the world, but they too had lost sight of the fundamental basis of human equality. Freudian psychoanalysis was one example. It claimed to understand the truth about human beings, and to bring them to full freedom, but it was ambiguous about the relationship between modern science and its impact on man. In its own techniques it implicitly accepted the ideal of controlling nature, but it simultaneously understood it as the cause of alienation in modern man. Freud's later writings made this paradox ever clearer. His treatment of the death instinct led to therapeutic pessimism: man could never live freely with his instincts; at best he could sublimate them.

After Freud's death, psychoanalysis was assimilated to the model of American medicine. The medical profession accepted without question that the goals of modern science were good. Psychotherapy took over the leading rôle of providing mental health in a mass society as an extension of the practical 'do-goodery' of liberal Protestantism. 'Psychotherapists adjusted themselves to the needs, desires, and interests of the industrialized, democratic, capitalist society. Finally, as responsibility for the mass society grows, the very immediacies of practicality push the profession farther and farther away from clarity about its ends.[9] Yet as it gained power, the weakness of its position became more apparent. It lacked any understanding of human health other than that of adjustment, and since the dynamism of contemporary society led to constant change, so it undermined any stable understanding of what a healthy personality required. Because psychiatry saw life as pleasure through adjustment, it cut itself off from elemental aspects of the human condition. 'If the Christian is to be in true repentance before the Cross, human beings must face some of their past acts as sins'. Christianity's incomparable truth was 'never to forget that suffering and death must be included in health as much as life and gratification. Nowhere has modern psychotherapy more mirrored and influenced our society of progress than in the way it disregards death or looks at it with stoicism'.[10]

Social work suffered from a different, but comparable, failing. In its origins, social work sought to achieve little more than to improve living conditions for the poor. Now it was more ambitious; it aim at social engineering. That ambition, to be effective, relied on social science, and once the writings of Max Weber took hold in North American, it was value-free and hence rudderless. The bureaucrats of the new mass, imperial culture had for decades drawn strength from the great myths of Protestantism that were taught in the small towns across the continent. For decades it had been thought good that they be emancipated from these myths, which stood in the way of progress, and hence were old fashioned. But the disappearance of one source of meaning in life gives rise to the attempt to discover others. Many found comfort in pseudo-myths; others tried to live in the ancient myths. For social workers, the task was not easy. They had to deal with the problems thrown up by contemporary mass society, while trying to attain a state such as bliss or *ananda*.

However, it was not possible for us to meet the immoderation of technique with an immoderate retreat from society. 'Man is by nature a social being; therefore it is a kind of self-castration to try to opt out of the society one is in'. What could you do if fate had destined you to live in a tyranny, as it had destined us? And Grant made it quite clear that he thought that the technological era was going to be a tyranny'. The answer was twofold. At the practical level, you could try to limit it. That was what he was doing by teaching about ancient religions and ancient philosophy at McMaster University in Hamilton, Ontario. The other was that you had to live through it, but how you lived through it was important. 'At all times and in all places it always matters what we do', was his mantra. If we could not prevent our fate, it was still possible to cultivate the virtue of openness. This quality is the exact opposite of control or mastery. Mastery tries to shape the objects and people around us into a form which suits us. Openness tries to know what things are in themselves, not to impose our categories upon them. Openness acts on the assumption that other things and people have their own goodness in themselves; control believes that the world is essentially neutral stuff which can only be made good by human effort. Openness is a virtue most difficult to realize in our era as it requires daily the enormous discipline of dealing with our own closedness, aggressions and neuroses, be they moral, intellectual, or sexual. To be open in an age of tyrannical control above all requires courage.

One of Grant's most profound essays is called simply 'A Platitude'. A platitude is a commonplace remark, especially one solemnly delivered. This writing was as far from banal as possible. The title was ironic. The argument was lucid, elegant and profound, at one level as far from the banal as possible. However, the truths he now spoke were so obvious in the older, suppressed tradition that there was nothing original or meritorious in his remarks. Our vision of ourselves as freedom arose only after our ancestors' systems of myth, philosophy and revelation had decayed. Whatever you might call what man has lost - superstitions, taboos, sacred restraints - did not conceal that there had been some loss, some deprival. The desire to overcome chance so that freedom might prevail depended on the destruction of the old tradition; it had prevailed so mightily that what was lost could only be understood even as deprival only with great difficulty.

Grant's greatest work was a slim volume, about the same length, as Gandhi's *Hind Swaraj*. *Lament for a Nation* is one of the most celebrated books about politics written in Canada, and like *Hind Swaraj* it arises out of a particular time and situation, but transcends it. The immediate cause was the fall of the John Diefenbaker Progressive Conservative Government in 1963. In the 1950s the Diefenbaker government had agreed to accept certain American nuclear weapons on Canadian soil to combat the manned bomber threat against North America from the USSR. By 1963 Diefenbaker had decided that these weapons were no longer necessary. President Kennedy disagreed, but Diefenbaker insisted that Canada, as a sovereign nation, had the right to make the final decision. American pressure was intense.

As we have seen, Grant distinguished between pacifism for individualism and for nations. For individuals, it was a moral obligation of the highest order, no matter the price, and Christ and Gandhi had shown how high the price might be. With regard to nations, he thought that their obligation was high, but not absolute. A nation should commit itself to as tactical pacifism, that is, internationalism. This view said that negotiation and diplomacy should be the core of a state's foreign policy: Force must only be used with the greatest reluctance, and in the very last resort. This was not only morally correct; it would prove an effective policy.

He titled his book *Lament for a Nation* because, in his view, the Conservative government had been trying to use Canada's sovereignty in the interests of this moral and inherently practical stance. 'Diefenbaker's nationalism was taking the form of a new kind of neutralism, a simple refusal to accept any demand from the present imperialism'.[11] Diefenbaker himself was 'no pacifist, no unilateralist, nor was he sentimental about Communism. If nuclear arms were necessary for North-American defence, Canada would take them'. What so distressed Grant was that there seemed to be an alternative for Canada to accepting these hideous manifestations of technological destructiveness, but that no one other than Diefenbaker and his Foreign seemed to see the significance of the choice. 'Green's appeal to a gentler tradition of international morality had little attraction for the new Canada'.[12]

To explain why Diefenbaker received so little support from his fellow country against the United States, Grant turned to the writings of the French philosopher Alexandre Kojève, who argued that the world was moving steadily towards a universal and homogeneous state. Grant's reading of the German-American philosopher Leo Strauss had convinced him that this coming civilization would be a terrible tyranny. In his essay, 'In Defense of North America' he pointed out that North America is the dynamic heart of modernity, the leader of technology in the western world, and describes the increasing difficulty we experience in our attempts to think outside of technology. Canada shared the continent with this dynamic heart of modernity and it was necessary for Canadians, more than the citizens of any other nation, to think through the implication of such proximity.

In the mid-1960s Grant's attention was drawn increasingly to the Vietnam war. The pursuit of peace was his highest political goal. He wrote many articles denouncing the war and gave a memorable address to anti-war activists at the University of Toronto. If his concerns could be summed up very briefly, it might be in a letter he wrote to Kenneth McNaught in 1966: 'For whatever motives, it seems to me that the USA has got into a position where it is massacring masses of Vietnamese. Canada is more and more implicated in this, and the thought of us being implicated in a long and growing war between Asia and North America is too terrible to contemplate'.[13] It was necessary to understand why Canada was being dragged into this dynamic empire.

In 1966 he encountered the writings of the French social theorist Jacques Ellul, who in *The Technological Society* presented the character of modern technology in disturbing detail. Grant now understood much better the apparent meaninglessness of society. He was particularly struck by Ellul's account of how technique is self-augmenting and autonomous. 'Technical progress tends to act, not according to arithmetic, but according to a geometric progression'.[14]

For Ellul, technique was still a 'thing', however dominant it had become. As Grant pondered the writings of the German philosopher Martin Heidegger he saw more clearly what he had previously only intuited: technology had become a mode of being. Grant developed these thoughts in a speech he was invited to give to the Royal Society of Canada. His paper, 'Knowing and Making' was addressed to the scientists who were the vanguard of technology. He warned them that they were quite likely creating a monster. A new relation had arisen between the arts and the sciences. Making, or art as it used to be called, had been transformed by the methods and discoveries of modern science. The interdependence (Grant called it co-penetration) of knowing and making had led to important scientific discoveries, but at the same time had made these discoveries quite outside any consideration of human good. They claimed to be value free. The problem that was driving Grant, and that he painfully tried to answer, was how it was even possible to think about goodness when the language with which we had invoked it had been taken from us. Bio-technology was a classic example of the feebleness of the language of good or justice in the modern world: through it human beings were transforming human nature itself. Where was the standpoint from which we could assess this change, know that it was good - or evil? In this address to Canada's most distinguished scientists, Grant's appeal was passionate, because it was inspired by a real and growing fear.

Grant saw the origins of the Western predicament as follows. Natural law philosophers such as Saint Thomas Aquinas, following the tradition of antiquity, taught that there were moral laws beyond space and time that were absolutely and universally binding on all human beings. However, in the seventeenth century a British philosopher, Francis Bacon, envisaged a radically new scientific project: in future science was to make human beings the masters of nature. Their moral authority for this dominion was enhanced by the eighteenth century philosopher Immanuel Kant, who maintained that the essential characteristic of human beings was their freedom and that they were bound only by moral rules to which they had freely assented. All three of these views were widely held in the modern world. Each seemed, by itself, true and necessary for the human well-being. Yet they were, both in principle and in practice, incompatible. Grant's philosophical contribution was to reveal the implications of these contradictions and alert his contemporaries to the need for a resolution. Gandhi argued that certain instruments of western civilization such as the railways beyond dispute propagated evil.[15] He also argued, even more controversially, that western medicine resulted in a loss of control over mind and that hospitals were institutions for propagating sin.[16]

Grant, by contrast, was genuinely perplexed. As his early writings show, he understood technology as the dominance of human beings over nature, but the machines it created - the automobile, the washing machine, penicillin - led to genuine improvements in the human condition and in human freedom. Jesus had said: Feed my sheep (John 21:17) and he had made the lame walk and the blind see. Surely it was incumbent on Christians to follow his example to the extent they could. Yet the same technology had also brought the holocaust and the atomic bomb. He laid out these contradiction is his first important work, *Philosophy in the Mass Age* (1958), but offered no resolution.

One quality of modern technology, he came to understand, lay in its tendency to impose uniformity. Grant accepted Kojève's thesis that the whole world was moving relentlessly towards a universal and homogeneous state. For Kojève such an outcome was desirable, since it was a prelude to a universal peace where war between classes or nations no longer existed. In *Lament for a Nation* Grant accepted this understanding of the impact of technology, but for him it was not a cause to rejoice. He maintained that Canada's geographical position next to the dynamic centre of technological modernity, the United States, would lead to its eventual disappearance as a independent country, since Canadians and Americans shared the same commitment to technological modernity. '[Canada's] culture floundered on the aspirations of the age of progress', he wrote. [17]

In *Technology and Empire* (1969), Grant's concerns about the dangers of technology became more intense. Science, he now argued, no longer limited itself to the domination of non-human nature; it now increasingly attempted the domination of human nature as well. Some critics of technology that it is was something 'out there' that people could control, should they so choose. This, I think, was Gandhi's view. Grant thought that technology had so permeated society that society as a whole could not reject it. He agreed that it was possible for individuals such as Gandhi to choose to live outside the assumptions of his age.

For him, technology was no longer something outside most of us that we could choose to use for good or ill. We lived in a society in which society (and increasingly a world) in which technology determined all existence. 'For it is clear that the systematic interference with chance was not simply undertaken for its own sake but for the realisation of freedom... [but] how do we know what is worth doing with that freedom?'[18]

The predicament of modernity was that those men and women who were the driving forces behind technological modernity believe that their project promotes 'the liberation of mankind'.[19] The older tradition of Plato, Aristotle and Aquinas believed that there were some things that it was absolutely wrong to do and perhaps even wrong to contemplate. By contrast, Grant often attributed to Robert Oppenheimer, a nuclear scientist, the words: 'When you see something that is technically sweet, you go ahead and do it'. In other words, technology knows no limits outside itself.

When asked whether computers were neutral instruments, he observed that their existence required the work of chemists, metallurgists, mine and factory workers; algebra and other mathematics; Newtonian and other physics; electricity and a society in which there are many large corporations. Such a society contains an elite trained to think in a particular way and excludes other forms of society. Technology can never be neutral because of its historical, social and conceptual preconditions.

Technology for Grant, then, was not just a way of making things or even a way of doing business. It was a way of thinking and it was becoming a way of being. So when the American Supreme Court handed down its historic decision in Roe v. Wade (1973) a case that legalized abortion, he was profoundly worried. The account of justice given there, influenced as he thought by technological modernity seemed to put into question what it was to be a person. Consequently, modern liberalism seemed unable to answer the question: 'What is it about any members of our species that makes the liberal rights of justice their due?'[20]

Grant never denied that science had delivered the goods it promised, but in doing so it destroyed something of infinite value. 'Brilliant scientists have laid before us an account of how things are, and in that account nothing can be said about justice'.[21] But above all justice mattered. In his last book, *Technology and Justice* (1986), he argued that the technological understanding of the world was fundamentally flawed. Love was primary fact of human existence; modern human beings 'cannot hold in unity the love they experience with what they are being taught in technological science'.[22]

Gandhi put this thought into words with which I think Grant agreed. At the end of his *Autobiography* he wrote: 'The little fleeting glimpses, therefore, that I have been able to have of Truth can hardly convey an idea of the indescribable lustre of Truth, a million times more intense than the sun we daily see with our eyes. In fact, what I have caught is only the faintest glimmer of that mighty effulgence. But this much I can say with assurance, as a result of all my experiments, that a perfect vision of Truth can only follow a complete realization of Ahimsa. To see the universal and all-pervading Spirit of Truth face to face one must be able to love the meanest of creatures as oneself....God can never be realized by one who is not pure of heart'.[23]

Notes

1. GPG to Maude Grant (MEG), early February 1948
2. GPG, 'In defence of Simone Weil,' (1988), *The George Grant Reader*, ed. William Christian and Sheila Grant (Toronto: University of Toronto Press, 1998) 257
3. Grant, *English-Speaking Justice*, (Mount Alison University: Sackville, N.B., 1974) 64
4. GPG to MEG, 1949
5. M.K. Gandhi, *Hind Swaraj or Indian Home Rule* (Ahmeddabad: Navajiva Publishing House, 1938, 2001)
6. For a longer discussion, see William Christian, *George Grant: A Biography* (Toronto, 1993) 211-4
7. George Grant, 'An Ethic of Community', in *Social Purpose for Canada* ed. Michael Oliver (Toronto: University of Toronto Press, 1961) 21

8. Grant, 'An Ethic of Community', *Reader* 21
9. Grant, 'Conceptions of Health,' *Reader* 339
10. Grant, 'Conceptions, *Reader* 344
11. Grant, *Lament for a Nation*, (Toronto: McClelland and Stewart, 1965) 23
12. Grant, *Lament*, 31
13. GPG to Kenneth McNaught, 11 February 1966, copy provided by Professor McNaught
14. Jacques Ellul, *The Technological Society*, trans. by John Wilkinson (New York, Knopf, 1964) 59
15. Gandhi, *Hind Swaraj*, 40
16. Gandhi, *Hind Swaraj*, 51
17. Grant, *Lament*, 54
18. Grant 'A Platitude', *Technology and Empire* (Toronto: House of Anansi, 1969) 138
19. Grant 'In Defence of North America', 1969, *Reader* 27
20. Grant, *English-Speaking Justice,Reader*, 110
21. Grant, *Technology and Justice*, (Toronto: House of Anansi, 1986) 60
22. Grant, *Technology and Justice*, 67
23. Gandhi, *Autobiography or, The story of my experiments with truth*, (Harmondsworth, Middlesex: Penguin, 1982) 504

☯ ☪

4

GANDHI AND GRANT: DEEPER NATIONALISMS

Ron Dart

The greatest figure of our era, Gandhi, was interested in public actions and in political liberty, but he knew that the right direction of that action had to be based on knowledge of reality-with all the discipline and order and study that that entailed.

George Grant

Masterpiece is not a word to use lightly, but Lament for a Nation merits it. In it Grant distilled his years of study of theology and philosophy, together with his knowledge of history and his acute attention to the daily passage of political events. The former adult educator put it all into a book that was instantly accessible to the broad reading public, but rewarded repeated reading by academic philosophers.

William Christian

Preamble

I have, sitting before me in my library, on one side, framed pictures of Mohandas Gandhi and Leo Tolstoy. I have, on the other side, framed pictures of Stephen Leacock and George Grant. The letters between Tolstoy and Gandhi are legendary, and both Gandhi and Leacock were pilloried and mocked by Sir Winston Churchill. When Leacock went to England in 1907-1908, he held high the Canadian nationalist way and dared to question the dated and waning English empire. The youthful Churchill called Leacock's comments 'offensive twaddle'. When Gandhi arrived in England in 1931 for the Round Table Conference, the older Churchill said, in the crudest terms, that he was revolted by 'the nauseating and humiliating spectacle of this one time Inner Temple lawyer, now seditious fakir, striding half-naked up the steps of the Viceroy's palace'. India and Canada have taken their rhetorical and literal punches and beatings from the English. We both have much in common.

George Grant, unlike Churchill, had a great respect for Gandhi and Indian thought, and there is a good book waiting to be written on Grant and India. The motherlode is there. Spade must be taken to earth to reveal the gold, though. Grant's grandfather, Principal George Munro Grant (1835-1902) of Queens University, wrote one of the first books in Canada on religions other than Christianity: *The Religions of the World* (1895). In short, George Parkin Grant came from a family with larger interfaith concerns. The Religious Studies Department (at McMaster University) where Professor George Grant taught for 20 years in the 1960s-1970s had one of the best undergraduate and graduate programmes in North America in Indian thought. When I studied at McMaster in the 1980s, the interest in both Peace Studies and Gandhi was high. In fact, there is an annual 'Gandhi Peace Festival' each year in Hamilton supported by the McMaster Centre for Peace Studies. There is no doubt Grant's impact lingered long after he had returned to the Maritimes on the East Coast of Canada.

A former professor of mine in my undergraduate days in the 1970s was quite a specialist in Gandhi/Tagore, and his charming missive on these two eyes of modern India was published in the 1980s: *Gandhi and Tagore: Visionaries of*

Modern India (1989). When I returned to British Columbia in the 1980s on staff with Amnesty International, I was fortunate to spend lingering hours with the aging Mildred Fahrni (1900-1992). Mildred had spent many a day and hour with Gandhi in 1931 when he was at Kingsley Hall in London, and the recent biography of Mildred, *No Plaster Saint: The Life of Mildred Osterhout Fahrni* (2001), speaks much about Canadian-Indian relations and the role of Gandhi in bridging these two distant lands and cultures.

It should come as no surprise, therefore, that there is a growing interest in both Canadian-Indian relations and Grant-Gandhi. The best thinkers and activists in India and Canada have thought deeply and broadly about the meaning of nationalism, and it is to the wise insights of Gandhi and Grant we now bend our listening ears.

Nationalisms: Gandhi and Grant

We live at a period of time when nationalism tends to live with a bad and worrisome name. Many of the more thoughtful shake the dust from their feet when such ideas emerge. Others genuflect uncritically to such a notion and ideology. The aggressive nationalism of the Germans, Italians and Japanese in WW II has not warmed many to the idea of nationalism. The ethic cleanings in the Balkans and Rwanda have left the language of nation and nationalism with a bad taste in the mouth of many. The patriotism and nationalist impulse in the USA pre-post 9-11 make many wary and hesitant about bowing the knee to some unquestioned and questionable good. The rise of militant Islamic nationalism makes many moderates within the Muslim community gun shy, and many non-Muslims keen to bury the body of religious and nationalist impulses. Violence and brutality, ideology and mindless commitments often walk hand and hand with the politics and language of nationhood. The reaction to such a way of understanding the nationalist urge is, often, to spurn any notion of nationhood and celebrate the pluralist rights of the liberated and free thinking individual. But, will not this either-or approach merely take us to a political and cultural cliff's edge and cul-de-sac?

Is there a saner and sounder notion of nationalism that veers far from the Skylla of a violent and authoritarian nationalism and avoids the Charybdis of a narcissistic and indulgent individualism? And, more to the point of this paper, what can Mohandas Gandhi and George Grant tell us about a deeper, wiser and more just way of approaching the nationalist issue?

M.K. Gandhi (1869-1948) and George Grant (1918-1988) never met, of course. Grant was only a stripling of thirty years of age when Gandhi was killed by a Hindu with deranged nationalist aspirations. There was a tragic irony to Gandhi's nationalism. Gandhi was a contemporary of the well known Canadian Stephen Leacock (1869-1944) and James Shaver Woodsworth (1874-1942). Woodsworth was the founder of the Cooperative Commonwealth Federation (CCF) party in Canada, and some solid work is waiting to be done on Gandhi, Woodsworth and the CCF. Woodsworth had many an explicit affinity with Gandhi, and some of the early CCF platform in the 1930s were indebted to Gandhi's ideas. Mildred Fahrni (who was with Gandhi in 1931) took many of his ideas, and joined J.S. Woodsworth to found the CCF in the spring of 1933. The CCF was the main leftist party in Canada that by the early 1960s gave birth to the New Democratic Party (NDP). George Grant had some involvement with the CCF-NDP in the 1950s, hence the Gandhi-Grant connection can be made on a variety of significant levels. What, though, can M.K. Gandhi and George Grant tell us about a way of being nationalist without being ideological? There are four areas I will all too briefly light but not linger on in discussing the nationalisms of Gandhi and Grant.

First, both Gandhi and Grant were not ideologues. The realm of politics could never become an end it itself for them. There had to be something deeper, more profound, more transformative, more ultimate that shaped political theory and action. In short, there had to be a more demanding spiritual vision that defined and animated, disciplined and corrected the political impulse when it became too pragmatic, too given to power, victory and the polls, too quick to bow before political realism and a Machiavellian approach. There is no doubt that Gandhi and Grant viewed politics as a necessary but not sufficient approach to the good life. Both men were ever on the lookout for a deeper theological and philosophic, moral and spiritual grounding and underpinning for the political. This meant that the politics of nationalism should never become an end in itself. There are ultimate, penultimate and antepenultimate commitments and concerns in life, and in the priorizing of such commitments, there is the need for an ordering of such standards and virtues. There must always be interaction between the ultimate, penultimate and antepenultimate issues, but it is the former that feeds, nourishes and is the root of the latter. So, at the outset, it is essential to recognize that Gandhi and Grant held high the importance of the political and nationalism (in opposition to those who retreated from the public fray), but they understood that politics, nationhood and nationalism must be inspired, informed, shaped, defined and disciplined by a more demanding standard than the political. It is from such an ultimate standard or mountain peak the political can be judged, evaluated and rerouted. What, then, are some of those peak virtues or standards that Gandhi and Grant held high and would not budge from? The answer to this question takes us to the second area of affinity between Gandhi and Grant.

There are three notions that are foundational to Gandhi, and we can see the same notions (in a different language and context) at work in Grant. There is no doubt Gandhi was fully committed to the ideas of *Satyagraha, Swaraj* and *Ahimsa*. It is virtually impossible to read the life and writings of Gandhi without being faced and confronted, again and again, with these ideas. *Swaraj* had to be informed and guided by the deeper notions of *Satyagraha* and *Ahimsa*. The decolonization process for India, and the liberty of the Indian people, if not informed by something deeper, could erupt into violence or political realism. This is part of the struggle Gandhi had with the Indian National Congress. Nehru pulled the Indian Nationalist movement in a direction Gandhi argued lacked depth at times. Tagore tended to hold high a more aesthetic, moral and spiritual notion of nationhood. Gandhi found himself poised and positioned between Nehru and Tagore, and he tried, in many ways, to walk the trying tightrope. Gandhi, Nehru and Tagore agreed on the importance of *Swaraj*, but they tended to disagree on how it should be defined and lived forth in India.

Gandhi insisted that *Swaraj* had to tempered and softened by such notions as *Satyagraha* and *Ahimsa*. What do these ideas mean in both theory and practice? *Satyagraha* presupposes there is an order in the universe, and it behooves us to both know and attune ourselves to such an order. At the heart and core of the order is being *(Sat)*, and it is our task to reach from our inner being to the Being of the universe. *Satyagraha* can also mean 'clinging to truth', and the Ashram Gandhi founded in 1915 at Ahmedabad was called Satyagrahashram. We are to hold tight, to cling to truth, to the very Being of God. Nothing should deflect or divert us from such a journey. It is Being (*Sat*) that informs and gives shape to all else, and to ignore Being is to slip into Non-Being. It is to such ultimate ends that Gandhi turned to understand how nationhood and politics should be lived and understood. Because Being (*Sat*) pervades all things, all is sacred and not to be hurt or harmed. This leads to the notion of nonviolence (*Ahimsa*). These ideas of Gandhi were carefully thought through and spelled out in *Non-Violent Resistance*. This collection of Gandhi's essays tells it all. Many of these essays were written for Gandhi's magazine, *Harijan*, and the weighty tome is carefully divided into ten sections: 1) What Satyagraha Is, 2) Discipline For Satyagraha, 3)Non-Co-Operation and Civil Disobedience, 4) Vykom Satyagraha, 5) Kheda and Bardoli Satyagraha, 6) Salt Satyagraha, 7) Indian States Satyagraha, 8) Individual

Satyagraha Against War, 9) Miscellaneous, 10) Questions and Answers and 11) Conclusion. There is no doubt that Gandhi thought deeply, at the level of theory and practice, about the meaning and significance of Satyagraha for his notion of Indian nationalism. The integration of *Swaraj, Satyagraha* and *Ahimsa* cannot be missed, and Gandhi's well thought out *Non-Violent Resistance* attests to such a fact.

How, though, does Grant see such ideas? How do he and Gandhi walk the same path? Let me turn to the opening passage of this paper. Grant stated, in the clearest manner, that he was most impressed by Gandhi's notion of liberty, but he also realized, as many did not, that Gandhi's notion of liberty was informed by a commitment to a view of the nature of reality, discipline, order and study. Liberty, for Gandhi, like *Swaraj*, needed deeper roots. Grant shared this idea with Gandhi. Grant never made politics or nationalism an end in itself. This meant that Grant climbed to the peaks of theology and philosophy to see more clearly how the world of politics and nationalism should be ordered in the valley of Canadian life. Grant, of course, never wrote a book on nonviolence in the depth or detail that Gandhi did, but Gandhi was much more involved in the trenches and political fray than was Grant. Grant was engaged with political parties in Canada, and his commitments were never in doubt, but his practical and daily political calling was somewhat different than Gandhi's. But, both men did insist that politics and nationalism needed higher standards to steer the ship across the water of time.

Grant had a passion for the national good of Canada from his earliest years. *The Empire—Yes or No?*, 'Have We a Canadian Nation?' and a book review of Violet Anderson's *Canada and the World Tomorrow* between 1943-1945 attest to Grant's concerns for the larger nationalist questions. Grant, like Gandhi, had to deal with the waning English empire, but Grant, unlike Gandhi, had to confront, as a Canadian, the waxing of the American empire, an empire much greater than Rome or the disappearing British empire. Grant sought to articulate, in the clearest possible manner, his concerns as a Canadian about the American experiment to the south of Canada. Grant's subtle commitment to the Canadian way was articulated in an exquisite manner in *Lament for a Nation: The Defeat of Canadian Nationalism* (1965). This 'masterpiece of political meditation' did much to stir and awaken a new generation of Canadian nationalists, although many did not fully understand Grant's more nuanced approach to Canadian nationalism in this evocative missive and political tract for the times. Grant, like Gandhi, had to deal with empires, and both had to articulate a nationalist way in opposition to the empire that threatened to colonize them. India and Canada faced the same problems.

Lament for a Nation begins with the 1963 federal election in which the conservative nationalism of John Diefenbaker went head to head with the liberal integrationist tradition of Lester Pearson. Canadians voted for Pearson and the integrationist tradition (with the USA), and Grant saw this as a defeat of Canadian nationalism. But, Grant's argument went much deeper and was more profound than merely a political argument. Grant took the argument in *Lament for a Nation* to both a philosophic and theological level. He probed the problems of the American addiction to liberty and individualism, and the way such principles, when fleshed out, undermined the commonweal. He questioned the way the USA uncritically genuflected to the modern liberal spirit and how they were the prime evangelists for such a tradition. Grant probed and probed, dug and dug ever deeper into the modern liberal way, and clearly articulated why the USA had to be brought before the dock on many of its theological, philosophical and political traditions. Grant's nationalism was multilayered and had much to do with being open to a larger reality and attuning the soul and mind to such an order. Grant made it clear that when we banish or marginalize the importance of God, we set ourselves up for much hurt and harm. But, he also made it clear that God and the Good/Justice could not be severed or separated.

God and the Good, for Grant, transcend the ideological politics of the right, centre and left.

Many of the New Left in Canada were drawn to Grant's pacifism (which he shared with Gandhi) and nationalism in the 1960s-1970s. Grant made it clear that he had little patience for the aggressive American policy in Vietnam and the military industrial complex and 'power elite' in the empire. The New Left was keen on Grant, but they did not fully understand that his brand of nationalism did not square with the leftist liberal nationalism that was emerging. The differences became more obvious by the 1970s-1980s. Grant's turn to Plato as interpreted by Simone Weil highlighted his commitment to a deeper understanding of the soul and nationhood than most of the New Left could grasp. What were some of these deeper approaches to nationalism, in thought, word and deed that Grant and Gandhi pointed to? The answer to this highlights the third point of affinity between Grant and Gandhi.

Both Gandhi and Grant, given their deeper and more significant ethical and spiritual roots, had questions about the political tribalism of the left. right and centre. Grant and Gandhi saw good in each clan, but they had enough wits and critical insight to also see the limitations of these political tribes. Both men could appear on the left on some issues, and they could appear on the right on other issues. Both men would question the breakdown of the family and the pro-choice movement (which would put them on the right), and both men were critical of empires, corporate wealth and militarism (which would put them more on the left). Gandhi dipped his bucket deep and often in the evocative Indian Classic, *The Bhagavad-Gita,* while being sensitive and alert to the teachings and life of Jesus in the Sermon on the Mount and the Beatitudes. Grant turned to Socrates-Plato and Jesus as the well from which he let low his bucket. Needless to say, the politics of the *Gita* or the *Beatitudes* do not square well with the contemporary politics of the right, centre or left. It was this more profound and older textual, theological, philosophical and political tradition that Gandhi and Grant found more nourishing and consistent. The *Gita* and the Beatitudes take the attentive into the broader Indian and Christian epics: the Mahabharata and the *Bible*.

There is little doubt that both Grant and Gandhi were committed to a more contemplative and meditative way of knowing and being in opposition to an empirical and frantic activist life. The life of action and public responsibility had to emerge from a stance and state of listening, attentiveness and stillness. Both men, in their different ways, sought to challenge and reverse the dominance of the *vita activa* and call political activism, political theory, philosophy and theology back to the contemplative way, the *vita contemplativa*. This turn and reversal as a way of knowing and being was at the heart of much Classical Indian and Western thought, but it had been marginalized by many. Gandhi and Grant were committed to the fact that contemplation and action should not be separated, but the contemplative way had to be the grounding and foundation for all action. This is why Gandhi would spend hours and days in silence before hard personal and political decisions were made, and his life at the ashram and his spinning had profound meditative and contemplative dimensions to it. Unless the hard inner work was done, the outer work could dissipate and fragment in a variety of pointless directions. Gandhi knew that inner discipline was essential if substantive outer change was ever to bud, blossom and bear much fruit in both the personal, political and national life of India.

Grant fought his battles on different fronts than Gandhi, in some ways, but they had many of the same concerns. Grant was a professor at Dalhousie and McMaster universities all of his academic life, and in such a setting he encountered a way of doing philosophy that had little to do with the contemplative tradition of Plato and Aristotle, Augustine and Simone Weil, Heidegger and the Christian Orthodox way. He had to battle those who reduced philosophy to empirical hair splitting, and logical positivism. He thought many academics in the area of philosophy were merely errand boys for a narrow notion of science or museum archivists. Grant was convinced that good philosophy had to engage both soul and society and do so from deep and substantive places. This is why Grant turned to the contemplative traditions in the West, and why he had an affinity, like Thomas Merton, for the contemplative traditions of Gandhi and the East. In fact, Grant, in his foreward to Dr. Mukherji's *Neo-Vedanta and Modernity*, makes it clear why he thinks the deeper contemplative way of the East has much to teach the frantic and driven West. The foreword speaks much about Grant's interest in the Eastern meditative way of doing ontology, philosophy and theology. It is true that Grant and Gandhi tended to draw their contemplative vision from different sources, and the content of such a vision did differ, but both men did, for the most part, in thought and deed, hold the *vita contemplativa* higher than the *vita activa*. It was not a case of either-or, of course. Both men were fully engaged in the world of rigorous thought and action. It was more a case of what should be primary and what secondary in the ordering of desires and longings.

Conclusion

There is much more that could be said, of course, about the points of affinity between Mohandas Gandhi and George Grant, and this will be done for the longer paper that will be submitted after this seminar. But, in conclusion, Gandhi and Grant had three areas of convergence in their understanding on nationalism. First, the politics and nationhood should never become an end in itself. There had to be an eternal plumbline that was true to an ultimate order from which political decisions should be thought and made. Second, such ultimate sources had to be grounded in the sacredness of life and the Being that is and breaths life into all things. Third, the contemplative way had to trump the activist way as a means of knowing and being in the world.

It is in these three areas that the nationalisms of Gandhi and Grant converge, and it is in such a deeper and more integrated understanding of nationalism that both men remain towering peaks, lighthouses, prophets and sages in the nationalist issues of our day.

༄ ༅

5

GANDHI AND GRANT ON EMPIRE AND THE LONGINGS OF THE SOUL

Peter Emberley

There is something prepossessing about the experience of empire. Whether one is outraged by its audacity, envious of its success, or shares even modestly in the bounty it commands, empire's extravagance both mesmerizes and repels. The possibilities and limits of human life are projected on a vast canvas, allowing us to indulge, even if only vicariously, our deepest desires and face our greatest anxieties.

We are attracted because, aware of the fleetingness and perishability of all things, we understand why both individuals and nations want what they recognize as good to be imitated by others and to endure forever. Moreover, there is something in us that seeks escape from the routines of everyday life and politics as usual, by imagining a life of drama, portentous events and danger, which the adventure of imperial conquest assuredly provides.

We are repelled because study of the history of empire persistently demonstrates that those who defend denying the right of self-determination of others, do so by sententious claims of noblesse oblige ("the white man's burden," "planning for peace," "holy war," "the war to end all wars," "liberation"), or through questionable assertions that absolute knowledge of historical necessity, human nature, reality or salvation is known to them. In either case, parochial and venal interests - greed, love of dominion, moral indignation and self-righteousness, or sheer meddlesomeness - habitually parade as truth. And, in the absence of free consent, the imperialist makes his way of life universal by command and force.

Two thinkers who have given these matters great attention, both theoretically and in the example of their lives, are Mahatma Gandhi and George Grant. On the surface, merely a modest congruence between these men is obvious, though Grant did write that "in the long haul it may be the Vedanta which is most resistant to destruction by technology,"[1] which might explain his confession of being on "the Hindu wing of Christianity," the full meaning of which is regrettably unavailable[2]. Moreover, suggesting a deeper convergence of their thought, is highly problematic given how fraught with ambiguity cross-civilizational comparison often is. But if one resists taking the symbols ("God," "sat," "truth," "justice," "dharma," etc.) as primary phenomena, and truth as a set of objective propositions, and instead tries to uncover the constants of experiences, one may find equivalents which permit a truly comparative analysis. For example, Gandhi's "selflessness" and Grant's "I am not my own," have distinct pedigrees, and operate in different spiritual economies, but they are equivalent in the context of the soul's transparency to divine reality.

Both Gandhi and Grant experienced the subjection and deforming effect of empire, and the threat it posed not only to "autochthony," but equally to access to an adequate vocabulary through which to express alienation from sources of truth. Grant would speak of the "intimations of deprival" of the true, the good and the beautiful, in the "universal and homogenous state" represented by America, while Gandhi, by committing himself to ahimsa (non-violence) and tapasya (self-suffering), and eschewing direct defiance, exhibited to the Britishers an aide-de-memoire of a potentiality in human nature unaccounted for in "civilisation." Despite distinct approaches, both took as their task as reminding their contemporaries that the true human struggle was not on the plane where bodies were entangled in the dark mechanics of power and desire in the historical and political world, but on the plane revealing the human potentiality for transcendence. This potentiality was, in both cases, as yet insufficiently realized by the British and the Americans, or obscured by their enthralment with total power.

The visible sign of total power was evident to Grant in various guises. In his 1968 essay "In Defence of North America" Grant, in reference to the West's technical achievements, had already used the expression "enthralling fate," to denote the way in which we had been seized by a destiny, in whose frisson of continuous worldly self-overcoming, we paradoxically found a bewitching calm and release from the disruptive and uncertain, yet more existentially urgent human search for truth and meaning. Our faith in technical efficiency went beyond merely the universal use of the instruments and machines of technology in every sphere of human activity. It also detached us from autochthonous places which conferred a deep sense of belonging, (such as the Rockie mountains, the prairies, or Maritime coast), and from a European inheritance whose creative tension between its two civilizational primals - contemplation and charity - had generated prudent and successful institutions and political practices commanding belief and loyalty, and prudently accounting for the complex attributes of human nature. In short, technology, imperial in its effect, was usurping or colonizing all the sources of what had contributed to what is best in humans, and which supports their healthy plurality, and was gradually displacing all ways of being which could not be harnessed to "the pure will to technique," such as those goods and priorities that had emanated from religion, art, and philosophy.

How Grant expressed his understanding of how the limits had dissipated speaks to his debt to Leo Strauss, from whom he adopted his understanding of western history as a conversation begun in ancient Greece, which has accompanied our thoughts and actions to the present, so that when we speak, act and judge - and whether or not we are self-conscious of this conversation - we observe and validate our observations in its terms. Strauss is renowned for urging us to listen to that conversation, situate ourselves within it, and be particularly conscious of the transit points where the conversation shifted and developed new vectors. But the real hallmark of his thought, which he adopts from Hegel and Heidegger is that the story has come, or is about to come, to an irreversible end, driven there by its own ineluctable logic, the result of one philosopher after another, from Plato to Heidegger, experimenting with the radical potential of a prior philosopher's account (of nature, history, freedom, or power) and finally exhausting its theoretical utility, not to say its practical value in maintaining order. While Strauss was indebted to Hegel, in adopting this (by no means incontestable) idea of humankind in a lock-step process through history, he is more indebted to Nietzsche and Heidegger for the description of the end of history - an age of nihilism and tremulous anticipation, marked however by the substantial lowering of the bar on human possibility.

Strauss' dirge was, by far, not novel, and in some ways it harks back to the prophetic tradition, in its lament of the fallen ness of man, and the reminder of the covenant individuals and communities have with the order of reality. What makes the hopes for restoration nearly futile, however, is the overwhelming historical success in the 20th century of what Nietzsche calls the "Last Man" (or "herd man) or Heidegger the "inauthentic being" - one whose aspirations do not rise above animal contentment, the slavish follower of the herd, the bitter man whose resentment is turned against anything exhibiting vitality or greatness, the man even incapable of self-disgust. The Last Man is the final desultory result of a history of wars, sacrifices, and noble goals in the West, the being who is unable to live up to what was great in the action and though of the past, but instead takes comfort in the mere material prosperity and safety that historical actors who sacrificed themselves made possible. Sunk in the sempereternity of labour and consumption, the last man, confident that his life was the consummation of Western history's search for fulfillment, is even incapable of despising himself. And as Nietzsche says, the last man lives longest, not to say, he will also soon inhabit the entire globe if not universe.

Grant had arrived at this conclusion by two routes. the lectures of Alexandre Kojeve, under the title Introduction to the Reading of Hegel: Lectures on Phenomenology of Spirit, and Jacques Ellul's The Technological Society.[3] Kojeve supplied Grant with the insight that the dominant idea of modern society, supplying it with its agenda both for philosophical reflection and practice, was the "universal and homogeneous state."[4] This conclusion was supported by Kojeve's reading of Hegel's account of a universal or philosophical history, as the progress of Spirit as consciousness moving from the Far East (of which he writes that "China and India lie, as it were, still outside world's history") to modern Europe, depending on political tyrants to undertake the struggle and work to close down one era and open another. Impelled by an inherent necessity through a succession of concrete objective forms (the Greco-Roman world, the Germanic Christian world, the Protestant Reformation, the French Revolution) and accompanied and rationalized by systems of thought (eg. Platonism, Stoicism, Scepticism, Christianity, Romanticism etc.) which were merely way-stations along the way to the realization of wisdom of man's self-consciousness, history had reached its completion in the historical actions of Napoleon and in the wisdom of Hegel. Here, all the cultural, political and intellectual particularisms which had paraded as universals at different junctures in history, would be superceded in the universal world state, in which man's desire would be fulfilled, in that each would be recognized as a free and equal person under law. Having achieved this consummation of the objective of world history, there was no likelihood of reversion, though older ideas and moral standards might be recycled, perhaps as "life-style choices," even as occasional atavistic recorso, but unless they had been filtered through modern self-understanding, they had no public standing, even if they could be entertained privately.

As for the sociological aspect of the new universal, Grant found Jacques Ellul's The Technological Society, quintessentially captured the reality of the modern age. "Technique," Ellul wrote is "the totality of methods rationally arrived at and having absolute efficiency." This systematization of the technological ensemble means that all aspects of human activity are integrated and coordinated to conform to the "one best way," which is to say the most efficient. As it arrogates to itself all the activities of society - not merely industry and business, but equally education, politics and even religion, disregarding their separate ends of truth, plurality and salvation - technology instrumentalizes them, depriving them of their otherness. But technology's reach goes further, limiting itself not merely to external machines and procedures, but extending itself to our being. Technology becomes consciousness itself, when it arrogates all the other ways of being - such as thinking, loving, reverencing - to technological rationality.

Paradoxically, the more "autonomous" we believe ourselves to be, the more enmeshed we are with technology's rationality, in both cases seeing the world as object over against which we stand as free and autonomous beings, upon which - like masters - we legislate our designs and wants. This has undoubtedly brought us many useful and comfortable things of life, but it may also have obscured profounder ways of being, as might be given in reverencing, loving and thinking. To take just the example of love - Grant suggests that love is consent to otherness, but such consent does not exist when we see ourselves primarily in the mode of "challenging forth." Here, to use the Heideggerian terms Grant favoured, just as we had reduced nature to "standing reserve," merely there to be mastered, and thus permitted nature to appear only as it spoke to our needs and wants, we had also constricted ourselves to "subjects," who identify the distinctively "human" with the power to will the conditions under which reality will effect us. If this was harnessed at one time to the real needs of individuals and communities, in the fullest sense of what is good for humans, it could be justified, but as Neil Postman puts it so poignantly, today we are instead merely "amusing ourselves to death."

Grant used to refer to the casual manner in which we understand the technical devices with which we have surrounded ourselves by using the illustration of a natural scientist who had said "the computer does not impose on us the ways it should be used." But how, Grant asked, is the "should" to be understood when the coming to be of the computer (as a product of modern science, whose very possibility followed from Descartes' resolutive-compositive method, with its repudiation of formal or final causes in nature, and Bacon's re-orientation of science from a study of what is eternally to the historical project of ensuring the "relief of man's estate") had set aside the truth value of any statements on the good and justice. For, Descartes' and Bacon's displacement of pre-modern metaphysical science entailed the cancellation of classical metaphysic's apprehension of the substantive foundations which supplied a limit to the use of science. Hence, in the modern age, technology can only be its use for no rationally-known "shoulds" remain that would limits its use. We can make radioactive waste, and we can unmake the tiger without qualm, because any substantive account of the good which would restrain our action dissipated in the re-orientation modern science brought when it turned away from classical accounts of being, and abandoned the idea that there are formal and final causes in nature, an understanding of, in the form of natural law or natural right would serve to restrain human hubris. Henceforth we were to understand ourselves as subjects standing over the world, and representing it to ourselves as object. This "subjectivizing," especially as it came to reside within the project to control human and non-human nature, and was premised on the assumption that we can only know what we can make by control, meant that nothing, be it politics, education, science and even religion, can presence itself outside of the technological framework, for every human activity must absorb its instrumental rationality. It also meant that we ourselves are extracted forever from the natural and historical contexts which until Rousseau still compelled us to restrain our capacity to act.

In *Time as History*, Grant explored the nihilism of western civilization which followed necessarily once the fateful decision was made to turn away from nature as a limit, and instead to see history, or better, historicity as the context of human doings. To see ourselves as historical requires focusing our attention on genesis, not completeness, which is to say that we are an open-ended trajectory into the future, forever reconstituting ourselves, by reconfiguring our historical world, without limit until all are free and self-conscious. This is our new fate. It means we are released from any idea of human completeness or perfection, such as that of a philosopher, saint or citizen. Here, for Grant, lies the West's "dynamic" defining attribute, especially when tied exclusively to an orientation towards the future, and driven by the Hegelian spirit which experiments in successive cancellations of the particular in its march towards the universal. When nature was still a standard - in Plato's understanding of the erotic desire for the good, which subordinates self-overcoming to an objective good; or, in Aristotle's understanding of nature as teleologically ordered; or in Augustine's idea of creation as a rational order willed by God) - the full dynamism of the human power to order was subjected to rational limits. But when that was replaced by the dynamism of willing, the serious enterprise of legislating self-chosen purposes to ourselves *ad infinitum*, the collective result was a view of history as dynamic self-overcoming. To will is to command, not to suffer reality, and it entails bringing about whatever purposes we, from time to time, desire. Speaking truth to power involved understanding science (and, its inherent mode of actualization, technology) as the form of modern willing. It could not stop until it conquered the entire planet, and managed every aspect of human doing, and since such doing is without cessation, its empire was infinite, not only geographically, but also historically. Finally, as a consequence of the indefinite deferral of a conclusion of what it is to be "human," (reinforced by modern science's turn to genetic modification), there was no agreement on what a fulfilled state of human life might be, nor even what the necessary condition of a human life as such is, as the debates over abortion and euthanasia made clear. With no rational grounds to harness it, technology is, hence, autonomous and self-justifying. For Grant, the future - as a relentless celebration of dynamic willing - opened up as a "terrifying darkness," where no sense of justice as "owingness" or "reverencing" could limit technological assertion.

America was, for Grant the locus of technology's empire. America may have had roots in early-modern liberalism, with ideals of constitutional government and the inalienable rights of the person and property. These moderate principles and institutions, grounded on natural law, served to contain permanent dynamic change. But a second wave of modern thought, stemming from Rousseau, Kant and Hegel, and which was quickly adopted from continental Europe, emphasized less our natural limits, than our historicity and *perfectibilité*. Even America's originating religious tradition reinforced this perspective of dynamic mastery. Grant points to the vast impact that Puritanism had on American consciousness - the methodic, rational, solitary vocation of salvation, he writes, provided the political culture for efficient managers and administrators, engaged in the task of mastering human and non-human nature. If the task is not quite eternal, it is certainly infinite in scope, and politically such an expansive, conquering will can express itself only in the imperial conquest of the world. America was the engine of the universal and homogenous state, itself the dynamo of infinite perfectibility, efficiency, and universal empire. Under its appearance in the 20th century as "pragmatic liberalism" resided a will to power, which was still driven by the same protestant anxiety, and recourse to willing, of its origins. And even though rationality and freedom are believed to be the rationale of technological mastery and progress, 20th century philosophy had abandoned the task of justifying this belief. Knowing that its horizon was only a horizon, a projection of the will-to-power of the most dynamic players, left the West engaged in uncertain agitation for its own sake,

> *To say that man has a history and therefore cannot be defined is to say that we can know nothing about what we are fitted for. We make ourselves as we go along.... But what a burden falls upon the will when the horizons of definition are gone.*[5]

To know the horizon as horizons, is disturbing enough. To know that there is no answer to the question "who deserves to be master?" (nor for Grant should there be!) should be paralyzing, but perversely, it may also be a spur to unhampered resoluteness. Ideologies in the twentieth century mimicked the dilemma played out in the scientific laboratory. If modern science since Descartes had shown that our senses could not be trusted to reveal reality, then an alternative presented itself. Putting reality to the test under laboratory conditions could be shown to generate effects, which could be used to verify the truth of the hypothesis. The sophism of such circularity has not prevented its use, as was evident to Grant in the success of the propaganda in favour of the Vietnam War.

America's imperialism was transparent in the sorry mess that was the Vietnam War. Grant, as a pacifist, could not condone the claims made that Vietnam was the redoubt of the spread of Communism. He saw instead a clash of empires, the Chinese and the American, which while obviously different, shared more than what divided them, in their common destiny as 20th century ideologies, or, in other words, as technologies of power. Caught in-between was Vietnam which, like Canada, had to suffer the collateral damage which must be endured in the grand stakes of modernity. The most nettling matter for Canadians was the utter dependence of Canada on the United States without whose economy and military protection it could not survive, and with which is shared a common destiny on the North American continent, participating commonly in Western civilization, whose virtues it also enshrined and whose unfolding it contributed to. More prosaically, Canada also accrued gains from the demolition of Vietnam, in the "branch-plant" industry Canadians provided to the American war machine. The significance of this in broader terms was the reality that the survival of an independent Canada, and the luxury that independence represented, relied - in the Gordian knot that was the Vietnam war - on its dependence on the American economy. Canada had no choice. The price of the preservation of its form of life, paradoxically was to be co-opted into the designs of the American empire. The coercion it exercised was both blunt - economic and military dependence - and subtle - insinuated through culture, whose obvious effect, the erosion of Canadian independence, masked the equally bleak reality that the irreducibly different regional cultures of Canada were being homogenized, under the illusion that America threatened the "one true" "Canadian identity." In the poetry of Dennis Lee (Civil Elegies), whose threnodies of lost promise spoke to a generation of Vietnam War protesters, and in the haunting artistry of Alex Colville, whose landscapes attenuate human longing to its purest point, were at least "intimations of deprival" which, if only through absence, disclosed the gossamer imprint of what was lost.[6]

For Grant, the final wave of the west's fateful history was global conquest by technology. The coming to be of technique required the disencumbering of all vestiges of traditional, aristocratic, or pre-modern existence, which is to say, lives governed by the public affirmation of the beautiful or the noble, the charitable or the magnanimous, the contemplative or the holy. It also entailed extricating ourselves from "our own" - the "autochthonous" roots of our patrie, our native land, our nation and state (which speak to the unique of our historicity) - and conforming to the public form of justice as equal right under the law. Or, it implied seeing ourselves from some universal perspective, perhaps as masters of all destiny. The open-ended project to make the world over, by extricating it from its "autochthonous roots" was to be driven by the will to technique in every field of enterprise, homogeneously and universally. As Grant wrote, "technology is the ontology of our age." And that ontology is predicated on the "human absoluteness of choice."[7]

One indicator of the new orientation was the shift from "morality" - a language of the good, understood as natural, and inscribed eternally in the order of things, or implicit in the true ordering of the soul - to the language of "values. What we "value" arises from a subjective evaluation, not reference to an objective order of reality in which we participate and receive (from the authority of the gods, cosmic order, or tradition). Valuing emanates from an act of will, the assertion of our subjective being - whose wants are variable and limitless - on the meaninglessness and indifference of nature or cosmic order. But, "the will loves to will," and to be bound eternally (by God's commandment, or the authority of reason) is to negate the will, so value after value must be experimented with and discarded, in relentless willing. Yesterday's empowering values are today's repressions, and so values are discarded as quickly as they are acquired, and on it goes in infinite self-overcoming. Encrypted in the word "values" is the inherently nihilistic perspective that there is no order of reality which conditions or limits the will. True, we may "will" and "value" the good, thus imposing limits on ourselves, but to do so is already to have bought into the hypothesis that when we will, we will - and, indeed, will infinitely (the will, as St. Paul writes, wills to will) - into a boundless, hence meaningless universe. And while our political and judicial institutions may temporarily provide a bulwark against the instability of willing values, they too, by departing first from natural law, then natural right, leave only a right willed by the majority or by interest groups expressing the Zeitgeist, a genesis whose temporary holding pattern is forever threatened by the dynamism of its own historicist commitments. As Grant writes, "such destinies have a way of working themselves out - that is, of bringing forth from their principle everything which is implied in that principle."[8] Our destiny, that of nihilism, coincides in our time with access to nearly infinite power to recreate the conditions under which life was given to human beings (to make radioactive waste, to unmake the tiger). It was inevitable when first we abandoned natural law and then natural right, leaving the "right" to be positivistically defined, by the will. The West now stood at the giddy and reckless height impressed on us by Nietzsche, where we have turned our back on the prudent "grey-beards" of the tradition, and become again like a child:

The child is innocence and forgetting, a new beginning, a game, a self-propelled wheel, a first movement, a sacred 'yes.' For the game of creation, my brothers, a sacred 'yes' is needed; the spirit now wills his own will, and he had been lost of the world now conquers his own world."[9]

Grant, however, refused to compromise with the dark mechanics of matter, to be beguiled by the serpentine wisdom that counseled, as did Machiavelli, that since one must fall among those who are not good, it is necessary to learn to be not good, if only to prevent one's ruin. But he also learned that the defeat of an enemy often requires taking a leaf from their book. If no restoration of a community committed to virtue and the philosophical life could be entertained on Platonic or Christian grounds, it was still possible to disinter what had been buried in the historical rush to modernity, namely restorative possibilities which lingered like a remainder after the equation of modernity had been factored out, even if this meant not a recorso but a further radicalization of the present towards an unknown future. Grant found these in two sources: in the gnostic writings of Simone Weil and in Eastern Orthodoxy.

In his review of Jacques Ellul, Grant had already expressed misgivings about Western Christianity, hinting at its collusion with the fate played out in the modern world.

I am grateful for Ellul's common sense, but I am sad that his positivist Christianity prevents him... from asking the basic question: to what extent is modern technological society connected to, and a product of, the western interpretation of Christianity? This kind of questioning cannot be faced by a Christianity that envisages reason simply as a human instrument, and therefore cuts itself off from philosophy.[10]

The complicity of Western Christianity in the west's demise could be traced to two sources - St. Paul's strong emphasis on a decision of the will as the event which brought a new life (not the soul's longing for substantive truth or loving union with the divine), and Augustine's philosophy of history, which contributed to the Church's triumphalism, the bold assertion that imminent historical success is evidence of God's providence. From these momentous doctrinal formulations flowed many of the trajectories defining western civilization, including the dynamic impulse of technology, and the subjectivism which had derailed into nihilism. The attenuation of human nature to mere will was particularly the case in its severest form of Christianity, Calvinism, and especially in America where it reinforced the project of technological mastery of human and non-human nature, by supplying the idea of man's radical fallenness, and attenuating the "whole person" to the human subject who wills the embrace of God, and plies away at the vocation God has conferred, but who has no comprehensive vocation in His overall Creation.

Because these commitments had played a major role in spurring the Western malaise, Grant felt it necessary to find restorative sources elsewhere. Perhaps the most provocative was enlisting Simone Weil, who some called a "gnostic saint." What he acquired from her writings reinforced his understanding of what was historically sacrificed in the modern experiment of making the imminent world the substitute for the divine.[11] This dissatisfied remainder is the inspiration of Weil's stark antinomies: gravity and grace, divine love and affliction, void and compensation, the necessary and the good, attentions and will."[12]

"May God grant me to become nothing," she writes in her chapter on "decreation" in Gravity and Grace, compressing her theology into a pithy, but discerning insight, whose effect is to detach us from everything worldly that conditions us, and frees us from the hubris of our own judgement. A life worth living can no longer take everyday life as a living drama full of sacred presences and revelations about a divine drama within which individuals all play their proper parts. Her experiences of the divine mortgaged nothing to the necessity of the world, which she takes as ridden by affliction and the irrational conjunction of necessity and chance. Only a branch-and-root catharsis of traditional Christianity (eg. the traditional idea of man's comprehensive participation in reality) would suffice to restore what is properly human in us. Refusing any teleology which held out the promise of human perfectibility, or worldly projects attempting to fill the space of where "God was not" with projects of self-salvation, were doomed to failure. Weil saw an askesis and release which dissipated the dark materials of what she terms our "gravity" as man's sole redemptive possibility. "May that which is low in us go downwards," she writes, "so that what is high can go upwards. For we are wrong side upward. We are born thus. To re-establish order is to undo the creature in us."[13]

Such de-creation required rescuing the poles of human experience - divine love and affliction, necessity and the good, gravity and grace, void and compensation, necessity and obedience - from centuries of philosophers' efforts dialectically to synthesize them, or to discard the soul's capacities they represented as irrelevant. It also demanded the taming of our incessant busybody activity and interference in everything around us, to fill in the absence with projects and manifestos, impermanent objects and impressions, hoping for satiety, but in fact reinforcing the affliction, suffering, evil, and the brutish conjunction of chance and iron-clad necessity, comprising raw human experience.

Writing that "evil is the form which God's mercy takes in this world", Weil saw affliction as tearing down the worldly supports which inflate our rational confidence that we can surmount the brute force of necessity, and revealing what lies at the depth of affliction - the silence of God. Attention to this point of sheer rawness, in prayer for example, offered a release, and hence whisper of grace, allowing spiritual light to illuminate intelligence. For example it made loving affliction possible.

One can see in these formulations a way of being requiring a renunciation of all one desires on earth, and letting be to be seized. This God who loves more the absence than what is present, speaks to a love of great longing, and not possession. It is a God that withdraws behind all names and all bargaining, and yet does not condone a mysticism separated from clarifying reflection. Such a God still speaks to the beautiful - not perhaps the classical beauty of balance and proportion, but the kind of beauty that Edmund Burke had described as "sublime," a state of astonishment in the soul, in which all its motions are suspended, with some degree of horror. This God will take us on for our afflictions, nor our skill in conforming to Him. This God, to be sure, stretches almost to breaking the gossamer contact with us, but His withdrawal intrigues us enough to command our attention and clarity of mind. "God," Weil says, "can only be present in creation under the form of absence."[14] When Weil writes that "the greatness of Christianity lies in the fact that it does not seek a supernatural remedy for suffering, but a supernatural use for it," nowhere more profoundly exemplified than in Christ's anguished words from the Cross, "my God, my God, why has though forsaken me?" she attests to the purgative role of suffering in preserving our consciousness of reality.

What seems to have particularly attracted Grant to Weil was that in dis-uniting the reconciliations of western philosophy - especially positivistic knowledge and love - she was pointing to a profounder spiritual instinct, one with the potential of a sublime transcendence from the brutal mixture of chance and necessity. Her intent was not to emphasize our abasement, but to free us from the meanness and hubris of our own judgements, and to open up a possibility for strength which comes from dependence on the true wellspring of illumination and power. While agreeing with Plato that human societies always and everywhere contain the Great Beast of limitless desire and the inverted priorities of the Cave, neither Weil nor Grant, unlike other gnostic strands, allowed their aspiration for an unconditioned existence to derail into dreams of worldly perfection. A life well-lived would remain a compromise if only because, as Grant editorialized, "matter is our infallible judge."

Any desire which has not passed through the flesh by means of appropriate action remains a sentimental phantom, and in saying that, [Weil] affirms that our apprehension of the most important truths depends on the justice of our lives.[15]

If earthly sanctity was not a realizable aim, justice and a love of the beautiful were. As Weil wrote "the beautiful is the experimental proof that the incarnation is possible." Its pursuit, in contradistinction to technology, denoted a very light footprint on the earth - to be in but not of the world.

Grant had written his doctoral dissertation on John Oman, a theologian of the Cross. He was drawn to Oman's theology for reasons which he explains in the last sentence to his essay "Faith and the Multiversity":

The web of necessity which the modern paradigm of knowledge lays before us does not tell us that God is dead, but reminds us of what western Christianity seemed to forget in its moment of pride: how powerful is the necessity which love must cross. Christianity did not produce its own gravedigger, but the means to its own purification." [16]

In John Oman's theology of the Cross, Grant found an alternative to a strand of theology which, he felt, exhibited excess confidence that human reason can know divine purpose from knowledge of the purposiveness of nature, and which relied, for this conclusion, on the analogy of God as craftsman who makes the forms of living existence. In contrast to this "theology of glory," Oman had focused on the incompleteness of man, as represented by Christ's anguished cry from the Cross, "My God, my God, why hast thou forsaken me." In this "theology of the Cross" lay a religious way that could not be compromised by complicity with forms of control or domination, led by rational certainty as to what constitutes man's happiness and salvation.[17] Instead, it dwelled finest where there was humility, forbearance, and forgiveness. It required being open to the mystery which incomprehensibly withdraws on our approach. This deep piety led Grant to write

It seems true that western Christianity simplified the divine love by identifying it too closely with immanent power in the world. Both Protestants and Catholics became triumphalist, failing to recognize the distance between the necessary and the good. So they became exclusivist and imperialist, arrogant and dynamic. They now face the results of that failure.[18]

Grant had not seen his resistance as culturally specific. "Any man, whatever his beliefs may be," he wrote, "has his part in the Cross of Christ if he love truth to the point of facing affliction rather than escape into the depths of falsehood... Wherever there is affliction there is the cross".[19] Nowhere was this more evident than in the spectre of arrogant imperialism, and the roots of the malaise which drove it, as Western empires in the 19th century pursued an afflicting denial of self-determination on colonies in Africa, Asia and South America.

Nowhere was courageous and intelligent resistance more exemplified than in Mahatma Gandhi's satyagraha, which finally precipitated the British withdrawal from India. Gandhi's assessment of British imperialism was equally grim as Grant's. Despite his earlier training at the Inner Temple of the Inns of Court, where his study of common law would have exposed him to the sobriety of the rule of law, appeals to precedence and custom, stare decisis, judicial appeal, and limited jurisdiction, inter alia, and ought to have left him with admiration for this key plank in the British concept of civilisation, even begrudging respect for British rule, Gandhi - repeating Napoleon's remark that the British were a nation of shopkeepers, and adding dismissively that they "[took] their cue from the newspapers," - resolved that while England indeed represented "civilization," what this meant was an excessive devotion to the greedy desires of the body, to fractious disputation and, unthinking preoccupation with the mere succession of time. Later he would add railroads to the list of negatives, disparaging the British for having brought with it distinctions to India, or at least palpable experience of distinctions, and for having confounded the natural viz. immediate experiences of space and extension. Even their education, Gandhi averred, had corrupted India, speaking of "the hardness of the heart of the educated." Technology poses the same dilemma for Gandhi as it did for Grant - the loss of independence, and the loss of the need for human virtues, as harbingers of the loss of God.

God set a limit to man's locomotive ambition in the construction of his body. Man immediately proceeded to discover means of overriding the limit. God gifted man with intellect that he might know his Maker. Man abused it, so that he might forget his maker.[20]

The British empire, Gandhi would say, from its first claims on India through the British East India Company to its last demands of support in the Second World War, had pursued a policy founded on the meanest of wants. It was as if it had made a national choice of pursing the mechanization of spirit, rather than the spiritualization of matter, and by so doing confusing the absolute with world domination. This was evident in their idea of "Civilization," where individuals make bodily welfare the object of life, and fail to see that "Parliaments," for perpetuating the contention of wills, "are emblems of slavery."[21] Gandhi's animadversions against doctors and lawyers are supported similarly, in a manner reminiscent of Plato - by overextending a life focused on the hopes of pleasure, and thus becoming more acutely aware of pain, individuals had made themselves slaves of arts that were unnecessary, if instead they had kept on the path of dharma. The soul's finer capacities were numbed by being enmeshed in the dark mechanics of matter, a pathology which had the tendency to replicate itself. After all, empire was as evident in Indian's own tyranny over the untouchables. But Gandhi refused to be drawn into to the radical alternative of Hindutva, as advocated by Vinayak Damodar Savarkar, whose goals were to "hinduize all politics and militarize hinduism."

For Gandhi, the human task was not the radical transformation of the world as it now is, but the radical transformation of our understanding of its significance and insignificance. There was a limit to the perfection which could be achieved in the world, if in fact it should be attempted at all. It was better to know the world, and hence its limits, than to make the world the one best of all, a project efficiently advanced only by tyranny.

But Gandhi did not believe the British were tyrants, or at least not irremediably so. Explaining his 1932 "fast to the death," "You cannot fast against a tyrant," he wrote, "a tyrant is incapable of love, and fasting is a weapon of love."[22] Here, what in the West could only be explained as a monumental act of Stoic imperturbability, Gandhi showed that *satyagraha* was not limited to a mortification of the flesh for its own sake, but as a means of dissipating disorder in the world and restoring the human-divine tension of existence. British colonialism, violence, modernization, and untouchability were all emanations of an unrealized atman, in other words, they were what Eric Voegelin calls "pneumo-pathologies."

Much like Grant, Gandhi would write that technology was a false universal or, stated otherwise, a false transcendence:

> *Our difficulties are of our own creation. God set a limit to a man's locomotive ambition in the construction of his body. Man immediately proceeded to discover means of overriding the limit. God gifted man with intellect that he might know his Maker. Man abused it, so that he might forget his Maker. I am so constructed that I can only serve my immediate neighbours, but, in my conceit, I pretend to have discovered that I must with my body serve every individual in the Universe. In thus attempting the impossible, man comes in contact with different natures, different religions, and is utterly confounded. According to this reasoning, it must be apparent to you that railways are almost a dangerous institution. Man has there through gone further away from his Maker.*[23]

The over-extension of technique, when it passes beyond human need and scale, inflates desire and expectation, risking not only a dimming of the moral sentinels of the soul, but also seeding the hopes of a this-worldly salvation. While Gandhi also writes that "God never appears to you in person, but in action," implying that God may grace us with heightened agency in response to the contingencies of temporal life, he does not imply that such gifts as the god-given power to withstand great trials and endure mortifying *tapasya* such as *sanyasin* undergo, could be expected to free us from the structure of reality by overcoming all limits. The strength of which Gandhi writes is not the power of the will, but the power of affirming the truth. In the Gita, where war denotes spiritual war, within the dynamic of the *atman-brahman*, what must be struggled against and defeated is attachment and interest, which give a false sense of security and fulfilment. In never stooping to humiliate his enemy, and by enduring vicarious suffering, Gandhi took the route of mortifying himself instead of warring against the other. "Reducing himself to zero," or " trying to work from the bottom up," was Gandhi's mirror reverse of the power, greed, and vain-glory of empire.

Both Gandhi and Grant had experienced the sheer darkness of modernity and, as they both attest, that experience gave both a brief intimation of that quintessence of pure light that is symbolized by "God." It was sufficient to give both of them an understanding of the inner mechanic driving the love of empire. The reason was not merely the love of temporal goods. The classic locus for the analysis of empire, which brings to light its often hidden core, is Augustine's critical appraisal of the Roman empire. The Romans had wanted an *imperium sine fine*, an everlasting empire, the universal and homogenous society. The Romans believed that the continuous self-overcoming provided by conquest, and which allowed them to be infinitely sated with perishable things, would ensure their completeness. Instead, it inflated their desire, reminding them even more of the gap between desire and reality, and unleashing endless new rounds of conquest. Rome represented the choice of a world driven by the propensity to commit crimes and exercise an excess of passion just for the sake of it. Nonetheless, they claimed that what they were doing was just. Augustine's retort to this hubris was that while the Romans had received their due, God had not. The Romans, he argued, had come to love the eternal through the surrogates within their control. Theirs was a perverted imitation of the divine, which could only be interpreted as a bid to usurp God. Their greedy desire, manifest in the intense will-to-power and cruelty exhibited in their love of gladiator shows, was an attempt to sate their body with perishable things, and in their denial of a transcendent eternal, lay the hubris that believes that the power of the will is sufficient to re-create a world where only the will exists. The aspiration of an *imperium sine fine*, an everlasting empire, rests on the assumption that divine reality can be transposed into a this-worldly perfection, allowing complete satisfaction to both citizens longing for eternal peace, and to philosophers, the lovers of wisdom, for whom love would be consummated, and the search for wisdom completed - all without a remainder. A balanced consciousness realizes that there can be no immanent satisfaction of the desire for satiety.

Profound longing, as such, was not their error however. Augustine acknowledges that there is an authentic human desire "to be without change, relation, or need." This desire for the absolute could have been expressed by learning to enjoy God through their spiritual body but, instead, the Romans' desire to be "without change, relation and need" was channelled into a perverse desire to imitate God through earthly body - to be sated with perishable things - by pursuing rule of an empire. Not surprisingly, just as they had lived by the sword, they died by the sword.

The Romans' fundamental failure, an error repeated in American and British imperialism, was their idea that wilfulness alone is sufficient to recreate the world in which only will exists, which neither reason nor conscience can impede. The evil, he adds, was not that the Romans lived only by their body, but the lack of something in their souls that ought to have existed: the capacity for the love called charity. "I call charity," Augustine explains, "the movement of the soul towards the enjoyment of God." An act of charity, freely given, which expects no compensation of any kind, opens the soul up to an experience of the eternal. In cancelling out one's own desire, and emptying out the self, a wholeness is experienced, which no worldly possession - be it things or empires - can rival.[24] And, in its absence, greedy desire, stung by the vagaries of time which perpetually defer fulfilment, pursues a campaign of world conquest.

Augustine held out no hope that knowing the mechanics of empire would dissipate its allure. A history of empires has borne this out. The Byzantine Empire, the Frankish empire, the Norman empire, the Hungarian Empire, the British Empire, the Mongol Empire, and the German Reich, are merely the most illustrious of the over eighty empires attempted in world history, signaling the universality of the temptation to total power, even world domination, over transcendence. Indeed, the love of empire will never dissipate because the love of the absolute is a human universal. If benign, it is possible to comprehend such ambition as satisfying one's wish that the good one has experienced will be everlasting and universal. But, encountering resistance, as it inevitably must, it quickly transforms into domination and ceaseless mastery. To subvert total power masquerading as Pax Britannica or technological civilisation, Gandhi and Grant provided a rebuff which could not be colonized into another totalising whole. In appealing to intimations of deprival or "reducing oneself to zero" or discerning that "in the midst of death life persists, in the midst of untruth truth persists, in the midst of darkness light persists,"[25] both showed themselves to be thinkers of "absence." Gandhi's advice to Christians enamoured with Hinduism was to integrate, not the doctrines and rituals, which is too easy, but the spirituality of Hinduism into their faith. Grant opened up the canonical books of the west to interpretations drawn from the Vedanta. Disinterested action, where the craving "I" refuses to press its desire for satisfaction on otherness, and consent without attachment, were ways liberated from the desire to possess and control. They constituted a way of preventing the simplification of divine love by identifying it too closely with immanent power in the world. Here Grant and Gandhi spoke with one voice.

Yet there are also profound differences between Gandhi and Grant, whose meaning requires serious attention, though only a few suggestions can be entertained here. While Gandhi may write that "religions are different roads converging to the same point," he may be insufficiently acknowledging the very alterity whose recognition he pressed upon the British. For example, citing a couplet by Tulsidas, "Of dharma pity is the root as egotism is of sin," Gandhi substitutes the word "body" with "sin" - intimating that the hurdle to self-realization is not merely the impediment of sin, but the body itself. But embodiment in western thought enjoys a unique status because of the doctrine of the Incarnation. There is no correlate in

Hinduism to the specific meaning of Christ as God incarnate. Both *amsha* and *avatara* are theological concepts, the former connoting being a part of the whole, the latter, a corporeal manifestation of a divine being, which reveals the immortal essence of a living being.[26] What neither reveals is the concretely instantiated, historical individual (in the revelation of the mystery of the particularity of the human nature in the fullness of its dignity), nor the experience of a personal relationship with the person of the incarnate Logos, who weeps and suffers, and whose historical specificity is the key to the deliverance of the world. No avatar suffers the aches and longings of historical individuation. Hence there is no spiritual singularity correlating to historical singularity in our person, and no idea of a personal vocation distinct from the avatar's vocation. Tied up with this is the west's emphasis on time, not as merely the moving image of eternity, but of "time as history," with a beginning point, a defining historical event that structures the entire course of history, and a progressive movement towards a concrete resolution in truth and freedom. It cannot be homologized to a life focused on *dharma*, *bhakti* and and *moksha*, even with the manifestation of *avatara*. The Christian revelation, which has translated into the free world, and a world organized towards ameliorating the brokenness and despair in historical life announces a revelation of the particularity of human nature in the fullness of its dignity. It is how Grant came to his opposition to abortion and euthanasia. That revelation also underwrites the idea of the beautiful that makes us at home in the world, not exclusively as partaking in the divine.[27] And while *prasada* may be divine grace, it lacks the specificity incorporated in the idea of heightened agency in response to contingencies, the distinctive need which arises from thinking about existence in terms of time as history, and work in history as the human vocation. While non-Westerners and Westerners alike are all to painfully aware of how the implementation of these ideas has at times drastically fallen short, the failure to realize the full potential of these ideas is not a strike against them, but a sign that they must be re-energised.

As India, on its accelerated ingress into the current world configuration we are calling "globalization," goes through the equivalent of a "protestant reform," on a scale much larger than has until now occurred, it has the opportunity to adopt or re-craft some of these ideas, and find new syntheses which may ameliorate the conditions faced by scheduled castes, or women, or the handicapped, or adivasis. Such modifications may even be remedies to those Western ideas that have undergone historical sclerosis. It is unfortunate that Gandhi thought for a long while that the only way "to restore India to its pristine condition" was to return to it [and] "drive out Western civilization." [28] There was an alternative, though the chance was missed (yet it can be recovered), which was to teach the West to recover its own roots, especially those Eastern Christian and gnostic ways which resonate profoundly with the Vedanta, permitting precisely the "mutual benefit" of which Gandhi hoped "if the root of our relationship is sunk in religious soil."[29] Having missed that opportunity once, in the time of empire, one can hope that the recovery of the dialogue between Mahatma Gandhi and George Grant might teach us to think more about what we are doing, and to avoid making the error again of substituting world conquest or absolute power for spiritual openness to the whole and the charitable "consent to otherness" which is its dynamo.

Notes

1. "Faith and the Multiversity," p. 68.
2. Sheila Grant, "Grant and the Theology of the Cross," in Arthur Davis (ed.), *George Grant and the Subversion of Modernity* (Toronto: University of Toronto Press, 1996), p 256
3. Later he would explain that while Ellul had provided him with a sociological account of technology, Heidegger gave him his philosophical understanding. Cf. David Cayley, *George Grant In Conversation*" (Concord: Anansi, 1995)
4. George Grant, *Tyranny and Wisdom, Technology and Empire: Perspectives on North America* (Toronto: Anansi, 1969), p. 88

5. *Time as History*, p. 41.
6. A theme still evident in Denys Arcand's satiric film" The Decline of the American Empire."
7. George Grant, "Two Theological Languages," in Wayne Whillier (ed.) *Two Theological Languages by George Grant and other essays in honour of his work* (Queenston: Edwin Mellen Press, 1990)
8. George Grant, "Knowing and Making," *Transactions of the Royal Society of Canada*, 4th Series, 12:67.
9. Friedrich Nietzsche, *Thus Spoke Zarathustra*, First Part, in *The Portable Nietzsche*, translated by Walter Kaufmann (Harmondsworth: Penguin Books, 1968, p. 139)
10. George Grant, "Review of Jacque Ellul's *The Technological Society, Canadian Dimension*, 3, nos. 3-4, 1966, p.60.
11. Especially her works *Gravity and Grace* (Routledge, 1952) and *Waiting on God* (Perennial, 1950).
12. One may see here the long arm of William Ockham, especially his argument that reality is not a revelation of eternal wisdom, but a product of inscrutable divine choice, foreclosing man's extravagant hope that in discovering purposes in nature that could be taken as the signature of God, and as evidence of the reason we share with Him, we might bargain for our salvation.
13. *Gravity and Grace*, op. cit. supra, 39
14. Simon Weil, *Gravity and Grace*, op.cit.supra, p. 99
15. George Grant, "Petrement's Simone Weil," *Globe and Mail*, 12 February, 1977, p.43. Some of Grant's sobriety regarding the limits of perfecting the world came from his reading of Celine's fiction, especially In *Journey to the End of the Night* which supplies a surfeit of examples of the dark mechanics of necessity in which humans were enmeshed.
16. "Faith and the Multiversity," *Technology and Justice* (Toronto: Anansi, 1986), p.77)
17. As Grant writes, Western Christianity may have, through Augustine's account of the will, and the account of history to which it is attached, simplified divine love by identifying it too closely with immanent power in the world.

18. Appendix, "Faith and the Multiversity," p. 76. Grant found further supporting evidence of the west's triumphalism in the *filioque* clause debate between Western and Eastern Christianity, cf. *The Latin West and the Greek East* London: Oxford, 1959). Sherrard explained that the debate over the *filioque* clause was a festering controversy over three centuries, and was the precipitating factor in the final schism of the Church. Unlike the Latin western authority, which *ex cathedra* had added the phrase "and the Son" to the creedal statement "We believe in the Holy Spirit ... who proceeds from the Father," the Greek church opposed the amendment. The concern was that the Latin formulation elevated Christ as *Logos*, at the expense of the revelation of the interior presence of Christ at Pentecost, which speaks to the whole of man, not only his reason, and which does not subdue the profound, unfathomable mystery of Christ.
19. As cited in Sheila Grant, *op. cit. supra*, p. 256.
20. Mahatma Gandhi, *Hind Swaraj and Other Writings*, edited by Anthony J. Parel (Cambridge: Cambridge University Press, 1997), p.51
21. *Hind Swaraj*, 38
22. As cited in Louis Fischer, *Gandhi: His Life and Message for the World* (New York: Signet, 1954)
23. Gandhi, *op. cit. supra*, p. 51
24. It will seem strange to appeal to Augustine to compare Grant and Gandhi, the former who disliked Augustine, and the latter who shows no evidence of knowing him well. But the rationale is that Augustine is as much a "proof-stone" for measuring the completeness of a "lived life," as Plato is to the life of the intellect.
25. Mahatma Gandhi, *Yeravda Mandir*, http://www.mkgandhi.org/yeravda/yeravda.htm
26. I express my gratitude to Dr. Harsha Dehejia, Department of Religion, College of the Humanities, Carleton University, for guiding me through the debate on *avatara* and the Incarnation. Very useful commentaries can also be found in Noel Seth, "Hindu Avatar and Christian Incarnation: A

Comparison, Philosophy East and West," Volume 52, No.1, January 2002, pp. 98-125. See also Geoffrey Pinder, *A Comparison of Indian and Christian Beliefs* (Oxford: Oneworld, 1997)

27. *Cf.* Johann Huizinga, *Homo Ludens: A Study of the Play Element in Culture* (New York: Beacon, 1950) and Josef Pieper, *Leisure: The Basis of Culture* (New York: Omega, 1963)

28. *Hind Swaraj*, 106. One very promising exercise which may supply additional resources for engaging in substantive cross-cultural comparison, by focusing on experiential equivalents, may be found in the influence Henri Bergson and Eastern Orthodox theology had on the Canadian John Humphries as he wrote the first draft of the U.N Declaration of Human Rights, thus departing from mainstream Anglo-American rights literature, and the Thomist writings of Jacques Maritain. Bergson focused his attention on God's energies rather than his essence, and to the dynamic process whereby matter itself contributes to a full participation in eternal divine love. This distinguished him from the dominant Aristotlean tradition which understood *theosis* as the actualization of a being's final cause, and underwrote the rationalism which is the distinguishing hallmark of western philosophy. *Cf.* Clinton Timothy Curle, *Humanité: John Humphrey's Alternative Account of Human Rights* (Toronto: University of Toronto Press, 2007)

29. *Ibid.*, p. 115

ಲ ಐ

6

THE SAINT AND THE PROFESSOR: INTEGRATING NATIONALISM AND RELIGIOUS THOUGHT IN THE WRITINGS OF GANDHI AND GRANT

(George Melnyk)

In order to understand how two such distinct thinkers as Gandhi and Grant integrated nationalism and religion requires an understanding of how the two men both differed and were alike in their preoccupations. There are four fundamental differences between Gandhi, the consummate practitioner of non-violent civil disobedience, and George Grant, the Canadian philosopher of conservative nationalism. The first difference is in the arena of political action. Gandhi was an outstanding political practitioner, while Grant was a lifelong academic, who did not venture into the public arena except for his writings. The second is cultural. Gandhi's theory and practice rested on his interpretation of the Hindu religious tradition, while Grant's was rooted in his monotheistic Christian heritage. The third major difference is historical. Gandhi was a world-renown figure in the pre-World War Two period and an icon of non-violence thereafter, while Grant was a relatively obscure Canadian thinker from the 1960s and 1970s whose main political context was the Cold War that followed World War Two. The fourth and most important difference is their respective views on nationalism. Gandhi expressed an optimistic nationalism, which bore fruit with Indian independence in 1947 and coincided with the emergence of successful national liberation movements in the 1950s and 1960s that ended European colonialism. In contrast Grant espoused a pessimistic nationalism formed within the framework of a rising American cultural and political imperialism from which he felt there was no escape.

Gandhi's successes caused him to be viewed by many as a saint, while Grant was considered by Canadians as an eccentric professor at odds with modernity and the flow of North American history. In spite of these differences, there are an equal number of similarities that link the two men. First, they were both devout in their religious practice and fervent exponents of their respective religious and political traditions. Second, they were concerned about the impact of technological progress on their respective societies. Third, they were engaged specifically with questions concerning colonialism and national independence. Fourth, both men were pacifists of different sort.

Scholarly debate on the respective merits, sources, and vitality of their ideas continues, indicating that both thinkers remain vital to the intellectual community. Works on Gandhi in English alone fill long shelves in university libraries. Grant's commentators are significantly fewer, yet he continues to draw attention some twenty years after his death.[1] Because of their similarities and their differences there is sufficient ground to allow a comparison of the two men and how their political ideologies and religious beliefs were integrated in their writings, while leading to such divergent practices. What was it in their respective thinking that turned one into a world-renown exponent of non-violence and the other into an obscure thinker barely known outside his own country? While the answer may lie in the much broader field of what constitutes Indian versus Canadian political essentialism and how each man can be considered a symbol of their differing countries, but the pursuit of such a broad question is beyond the scope of this article.

Gandhi's Vision

Gandhi began his political practice in South Africa when he led the Indian community against widespread official discrimination. He had studied law in England and his derogatory treatment as an Indian in South Africa spurred him to work diligently for the emancipation of his community. It was in South Africa that he developed the fundamental integration of his life's work—that "thought came to have no meaning...unless it was lived out."[2] The techniques of non-violent resistance to discriminatory laws, which he developed and practiced, such as fasting, courting arrest through symbolic actions and peaceful marches, were all formed during his time in South Africa. He returned to India in 1914.

His views on Indian society and colonialism where voiced in *Hind Swarâj* (1910) his first book in which he called for a regeneration of a society that had lived under foreign rule. Only through social transformation would independence offer ordinary Indians some measure of equality was his argument. Because of his *satyâgrahas* or civil disobedience campaigns in India and the reputation he had garnered in South Africa, he became "an influential national leader."[3] In 1920 he launched a Non-cooperation Movement in India which included the burning of foreign cloth and the refusal to use government services. After his imprisonment he was elected President of the Indian National Congress. In 1930 he launched a new *satyâgraha* against the salt tax, which included a 24-day march. Eventually, his fame brought him back to London, where, dressed in his now iconic loincloth, he was followed religiously by the world media, both print and newsreels. Among the key issues at the conference was electoral representation for the untouchable caste and how the Muslim minority would fare in a state dominated by Hindus. The Muslim League, led by Jinnah, demanded a separate state for Muslims, which later on was realized as East and West Pakistan. Gandhi favoured a single, multi-religious Indian state. Eventually, Gandhi had to live through the tribulations of partition when independence came. He was assassinated by a co-religionist in 1948.

Gandhi's emphasis on individual and collective self-betterment, mutual respect and understanding among distinct communities, and the importance of building an egalitarian society was highly idealistic when applied to a mass society, but it was an ideal he himself practised fervently at his ashram. His religious faith was global in reach, attracting people from various countries. His thought encompassed the "truth" that he found in many religious faiths and out of which he formed his own religious ideals, including his famous dictum that "Truth is God." While the Hindu tradition formed the core of his thinking, he also drew on Christianity and Islam. The result was a religious eclecticism that invigorated his actions as a political leader and provided moral gravitas to his thought. He became famous for bringing vitality to concepts such as *satyâgraha* (truth-force as non-violent resistance), in which he elevated non-violent political action to a moral force based on a refusal to respond violently when violence was used on the protestor. He was highly critical of industrial society and its addiction to the technological imperative. He claimed industrial society created a secular, consumerist obsession that eschewed the spiritual side of humanity. In this he shared the views of thinkers like Ruskin and Tolstoy, and eventually George Grant.

George Grant's Vision

George Grant became well-known in intellectual circles in Canada when he published *Lament for a Nation* (1965).

The book is short, but it offered no practical proposals for Canada's survival as a nation based on Grant's belief that Canada as a nation was destined to disappear because historical progress was making small nations and their cultures redundant. The book went on to bemoan the impossibility of basing Canada on his own favoured conservative political philosophy because that was not the direction of the modern world. He argued that in the face of uncertainty about what is best "tradition is the best basis for the practical life."[4] He was saddened that it was tradition that was being erased by American power.

George Grant (1918-1988) was Ontario-born and bred. His grandfather, George Parkin, (later knighted) was a principal of Toronto's elite Upper Canada College in the late 19th century, as was his father William Grant. Grant himself was a student at this bastion of conservative upper-class privilege in the 1920s and 30s. Although his uncle, Vincent Masssey, was a prominent Liberal and a future Prime Minister of Canada, Grant came to espouse a communitarian Toryism or what is sometimes referred to as "Red Toryism" because of its emphasis on social responsibility. Like Gandhi he went to England to study though he did so courtesy of a Rhodes scholarship to Oxford, where he took his PhD in theology. He returned to Canada to teach philosophy, primarily at McMaster University in Hamilton, Ontario. His one major foray into activist politics was during the time of student protests against the Vietnam War in the mid-1960s, but even then he opposed civil disobedience as inappropriate to the circumstances of a liberal democratic society. He was very much an individualist of a conservative bend.

Differing Contexts/ Differing Histories: A Discussion of Four Differences

1. Activism versus Non-activism

Grant's anti-activism stands in stark contrast to Gandhi's campaigns of civil disobedience. While it can be said readily that this difference marks a disjuncture rooted in differing approaches to the state and nationalism, it would seem that the historical context in which each man operated was the determining factor. What Gandhi did in regard to independence was to create a middle ground between military action on the one hand and political rhetoric on the other. He astutely blended action with thought in non-violent mass protests that both empowered and mobilized millions. Terrorism was a secret, small-group activity waged by a minority of activists and so by definition sidelined the Indian masses. Likewise the political rhetoric of the tiny Indian middle and upper classes expressed normally in newspapers and books was equally limited in a society that was largely rural and illiterate. Gandhi positioned himself outside both groups in ways that hundreds of millions could understand and identify with.

Grant, on the other hand, lived in a political democracy that had already gained its independence from Great Britain. Public debate in the media and in Parliament was the normal expression of democracy. As an academic Grant was comfortable using word and text as his prime modus operandi. Living in the ivory tower he found it difficult to descend onto the street and there wage a campaign that reflected his ideas. Canada and India were at very different stages in their political evolution and this differing historical context was what each man responded to. The only political rhetoric over independence in the 1960s and 1970s in Canada was waged primarily by Quebecois politicians who were seeking an independent Quebec. For them the concept of Canadian colonialism and resistance to it through street-level activism was part of the national liberation tradition with which Gandhi is rightly associated.

2. Hinduism and Christianity

When George Grant wrote in the mid-sixties that "I speak as a Canadian nationalist and a conservative" he was avoiding an important underlying theme in his thought—religious faith.[5] Following the cultural model of the time in North America, he preferred to downplay religious associations when making political arguments.

In this model religion was a private matter and should be kept out of political discourse as much as possible. It was only in the 1980s with Ronald Reagan and then more fully in the era of the two Bush presidencies that the separation of church and state was severely whittled down in the U.S. But in Canada at this time and until the minority Conservative government of 2006 religion was effectively marginalized in public discussion. Gandhi was not so shy. His public writings are filled with references to God and to religious concepts as well as issues of morality and ethics. In the Indian context his personal faith and practice were totally integrated into his political work and this won public approval. Margaret Chatterjee in *Gandhi's Religious Thought* (1983) makes the point that the Hindu tradition encourages a "spiritual quest" in believers[6] and that the tradition itself is non-institutionalized in the way Christian churches.[7] This diversified and decentralized religion has a vast popular base so that its adherents could see in Gandhi's actions and ideas a reflection of the tradition they hold dear. It was precisely through his marriage of religion and politics that he was able to garner support at all levels of Indian society. If he had privatized his religious beliefs and separated them from his politics as Grant did, he would never have been recognised as a saint or holy man, which gave him such power in the Indian context. He would have stayed at the level of a mere politician vying among others for attention and power. It was his religious devotion that made him stand above the rest.

Grant would have risked even greater marginalization if he had presented a public persona similar to that of Gandhi. In an article titled "The Whole as Love" Canadian theologian Pam McCarroll states: "Though Grant did not write much about his faith; much has been written about how his faith, rooted in Christianity, shaped his thought in fundamental ways."[8] This divide between Grant, the political philosopher, and Grant, the believer, which is so different from the integration of faith and political action found in Gandhi can be explained in two ways. First, the Canadian context was not conducive to this kind of integration because of the strong tradition in the twentieth century toward a secular separation of church and state. In spite of the Anglican Church's position as the state religion in Britain, the division in Canada between Catholicism and mainstream Protestant churches meant that religious power was segregated and that religious issues were discretely kept out of the political domain in order to lessen sectarian sentiments.[9] Second, the Christian tradition itself, while powerful in terms of popular acceptance and social presence, was not homogeneous in viewpoint on many issues of public morality or practice. There was not a common tradition that the general public could associate with in terms of ideas and values. Unlike Hinduism with its polymorphous unity, Canadian Christianity was an entity that had wide adherence but in different ways. The institutionalization of Christianity in often opposing churches did not create a common field that could be appealed to by political thinkers like Grant. The difficulty that Gandhi had in winning support from the Muslim community is an indicator of how religious divisions can play out politically when attempting to reach a common goal.

3. Historical Periods and their Impact

Besides the differing cultural contexts that encouraged different approaches to social and political change, the differing historical periods in which the two men operated are an equally important causal factor in distinguishing them. Political philosophies and their practical manifestations are altered and generated as history unfolds. Gandhi operated in a period in which European imperialism was in decline, having reached its nadir in the 19th century. World War One ended German colonialism and brought the downfall of the Turkish Empire. The period between the two world wars saw the rise of national liberation movements in colonized countries, which found success after World War Two. Indian independence was one of the major hallmarks of this period. So Gandhi's efforts were part of a global movement to end European imperialism. In the 1920s and 1930s the world was interested in what was happening in

India and the progress of the independence struggle much more than it was in Gandhi's pre-World War One actions in South Africa. In the pre-WWII historical context the U.S. was not a significant factor in this issue. This was not the case after World War Two, which propelled both the U.S. and the Soviet Union to world power status. While Gandhi certainly wrote about capitalism and communism (condemning both) because they were two ideologies debated fiercely around the world after the Russian Revolution, they did not have the same established military power they came to have in Grant's time. In Gandhi's day India was a colonized Third World economy far from the eye of the ideological storm and a place where an alternative model could be developed, which was certainly Ghandi's view.

In Grant's day Canada was increasingly integrated into continental economic and military systems dominated by the United States using a system that was eventually described by some commentators as neo-colonialism. The Cold War defined world politics very differently from the preceding period. American imperialism, a concept that became popular during the Vietnam War period and garnered worldwide acceptance through the American invasion and occupation of Iraq in 2003 was something missing from Gandhi's universe. Grant saw the world as moving toward a homogenous tyranny of which the United States was the prime mover. Gandhi lived in a world in which British imperialism still meant something, operating as it did extensively in both Africa and Asia. In Grant's time British imperialism was almost non-existent because numerous African, Asian and Caribbean nations had independence. While it made sense for Grant to lament the decline of Canada's cultural roots in English Toryism in the historical context of American superpower status, it made sense for Gandhi to seek the end of British power and the establishment of indigenous power because British imperialism was still a powerful force.

If one were to look at historical process as a series of waves moving forward in a rhythm of rise and fall, ebb and flow, then we can see that Gandhi and Grant rose with different waves in twentieth century history. These different waves left a legacy, a distinct residue that the next wave incorporated into itself as it moved forward and crested before ebbing and becoming incorporated in a new wave. If we reflect on post-independence and post-partition India, on the one hand, and post-Grant Canada on the other, we can readily find this lingering residue. In Gandhi's case, India's statist approach to capitalism and its commitment to non-aligned politics under Nehru and his successors represented a much diluted form of Gandhianism, but it still spoke of a third way for developing nations, which Gandhi encouraged. For Grant the angst about the loss of Canadian sovereignty and identity under the juggernaut of American culture and politics survived as a minor but persistent feature of Canadian political life, mostly on the left, but occasionally in a wider context such as the Canadian government's opposition to joining the American invasion of Iraq. For example, intellectuals in post-Quiet Revolution and post-referendum Quebec[10] found in Grant's earlier thoughts on nationalism a worthy description of their own disappointing experience of secular freedom. The *nouvelle sensibilité* of these intellectuals is described as "opposition to the utopianism of the ideology of progress that triumphed with the Quiet Revolution and its aftermath."[11]

In both the case of India and Canada the fullness of thought was absorbed by each distinct historical moment, while the remnant of that thought later resurfaced in either a diluted or reworked form. The recent trajectory of the Indian economy toward Second World status and its concomitant transformation of the Indian class structure and rapid urbanization means that some of Gandhi's goals for social betterment are being met by other processes driven by the demands of global capitalism and American geopolitics.[12] The causes of the transformation are global rather than Indian in origin, which means that Gandhi's view of people pulling themselves up by their own bootstraps has been supplanted by the imperatives of capitalism expansion. Likewise, Canada's free trade status with the United States and Mexico has furthered continental integration since Grant's death in 1988 (40 years after Gandhi's death), but it has not resulted in any less independence for Canada than the country had 40 years ago, when Grant was creating his lament. The country remains sovereign and yet heavily tied to the U.S. economy as it was then. Curiously, neither Gandhi's vision for Indian society nor Grant's pessimism about Canadian independence have been realised in the half-century after their respective deaths. One might say that the radicalism of their respective visions have not become part of mainstream history, but they were important elements in the history of their day.

4. Polarities of Nationalism

The final difference between the two thinkers is their nationalism. Rabindaranath Tagore, the great Indian poet and intellectual, wrote the following about Indian nationalism, while speaking on the subject in Japan and the U.S. just as Gandhi was appearing on the Indian national stage:

> *Those of us in India who have come under the delusion that mere political freedom will make us free have accepted their lessons from the West as the gospel truth and lost their faith in humanity...Let our life be simple in its outer aspect and rich in its inner gain.*[13]

Tagore was suggesting, as Gandhi would as well, that there was an Indian way to national liberation that reflected the richness of Indian tradition. It was Gandhi who came to embody that distinctness. Through non-violent morality Gandhi hoped to not only have Indians achieve independence and national reconciliation, but to offer the world a model of national liberation that was not based on war. Since the subject of national self-determination was a central feature of the Versailles Conference of 1919 and a policy platform of the Woodrow Wilson American presidency, there was a momentum to the national question that captured the imagination of various colonized peoples at the time. Gandhi really believed that personal and collective transformation was possible and that non-violent political protest could achieve the goal of *swaraj* or independence for both individuals in their personal lives and in the life of the national body politic.[14]

Gandhi's view was perpetually hopeful about transformation and innovation, even in the face of horrendous obstacles such the partition crisis after independence and earlier traumas such as the Amristar Massacre of 1919. The whole of the Indian independence struggle from the late 19th century till the mid-twentieth century was an ongoing process of alternating advance and retreat, during which his spirituality did not allow him to lose hope. Perhaps, it was his successful blending of the complexity of Hindu tradition and the human rights tradition of Western thought that generated his sense of unwavering service to the cause.

Grant, meanwhile, was much less catholic in his philosophical roots and this may have been an important factor in his pessimism. His views on nationalism were formed strictly within the Western intellectual tradition and it was this tradition that gave rise to his concerns and doubts about success. As a conservative he valued tradition as a evolutionary process that held the excesses of progress at bay. It is not that he held to a steady-state, unchanging theory of political reality. Obviously, he did not because he was conscious of how tradition was being overthrown or made irrelevant by the march of history. Instead, he argued that the jettisoning of traditional beliefs and values that had played a vital role in the evolution of the Canadian polity created a threat to the survival of national difference, the same difference that Gandhi drew on for nationalist strength. Grant wanted that difference to remain so that a non-American identity could be fostered for Canada, but he saw that this was not happening. He saw a continentalist trajectory that was irreversible. It would seem that the straight line of historical progress that he decried as the Western tradition of liberalism was actually accepted by him as real enough but as a morally negative progress.[15]

Canadian Robert Wright in his *Economics, Enlightenment and Canadian Nationalism* (1993) offered insights into the criticism leveled against Grant's type of nationalism. "If the continentalist issue is approached from within the framework of orthodox economics, one is led inexorably to the conclusion...that Canada be subservient to the United States." he stated.[16] He went on to say that nationalism was perceived as defending the interests of a "parochial privileged class."[17] Wright goes on to reject these criticisms as equally self-serving for certain interests and posits his own model of nationalism, which, unlike Grant's, he believes will preserve Canadian nationalism in the face of pressures toward uniformity. In reviewing a book opposed to the impending of the Free Trade Agreement of 1988 between Canada and the U.S., Grant confirmed the continuing pessimism of his thought on Canada's future in this way:

> *It is surely a nobler stance to go down with all flags flying and all guns blazing than to be acquiescently led, whether sadly or gladly, into the even greater homogenizing of our country into the American mass.*[18]

Harmonies out of Disharmonies/ Similarities that Matter

1. On Being Devout

The most important similarity between Gandhi and Grant was in the arena of faith, which was also one of the differences between them. While Hinduism and Christianity are very distinct approaches to spirituality and arise from two different cultures, the fact that both Gandhi and Grant were deeply religious brings the two thinkers together in their approach to nationalism. Even though Gandhi was generous in his religious appreciation of other spiritual traditions, his religious viewpoint was deeply Hindu in its intellectual framework. His asceticism likewise was Hindu-based and his numerous commentaries and interpretations of sacred Hindu texts, including his own, unorthodox version of the *Bhagavad Gītā* published in 1930 are examples of how deeply immersed he was in the tradition. The very foundation of his political action was based on prayer and faith and a profound non-violent morality that taught respect and love for one's enemy. It would be fair to say that Gandhi's work on behalf of Indian national liberation would not have made the global impact that it did if he had not been the deeply religious man that he was. It was his moral superiority that was so attractive to a global audience.

George Grant was equally immersed in his religious faith and it can be argued that it was as fundamental to his nationalism as Gandhi's faith was to his nationalism. While a fundamental difference between Gandhi and Grant dealt with the fact that religion was often separated from politics in Canadian society, while being the opposite in India, the Canadian context meant that religious values often permeated political thought in oblique or covert ways. Grant's pessimistic nationalism could be aligned with various thinkers with a strong religious bent such St. Augustine and Simone Weil for whom salvation within history was extremely difficult. In an interview he gave on the topic of theology and history Grant made the comment that " I'm...nearest to the account of Christianity that is close to Hinduism in its philosophic expression."[19] It would seem that Grant believed that Hinduism carried a certain stream of immutability that he also found in Christianity. There is no doubt that Grant's reputation as a deeply religious person, who was constantly seeking philosophic analogies to his religious values, meant that his understanding of Canada's political status was rooted in these beliefs.

2. Resisting the Technological Imperative

An important unifying element in the religion-political spectrum was the resistance both men offered to the technological imperative. Arthur Kroker in his study, *Technology and the Canadian Mind* (1984) made the observation that for Grant technology created a dependency with negative consequences on human psychology and society.[20] Like other thinkers on the subject, including Jacques Ellul and Martin Heidegger, he found the U.S. a leading exponent of technological progress and therefore of universal homogeneity. For Grant progress was a myth.[21] Gandhi was also well-known for his opposition to a capitalist-valued technological imperative and he wanted to base his vision of a free India on one that emphasized social justice and equality above all else. Grant and Gandhi both found the liberalism that promoted the myth of progress to be immoral and nihilistic. It is empires that use, develop and depend on technological superiority for their overarching power. In the case of Britain it was its sense of industrial/technological superiority that Gandhi resisted because it gave India a backward image that he found unjustified on a number of grounds. Grant also linked technology and empire (the title of his 1969 book) and responded in an equally scathing critique of the technological imperative and how it leads to universal tyranny. American technological aggressiveness created a sense of inferiority in Canadian culture, which Grant, like Gandhi in India, sought to overcome by emphasizing the possibility of embracing moral superiority for the victims of empire. What both men were concerned about was technology's ability to frame the reality we live by and so inform our thinking and our values.[22] This thinking promoted sameness and rejected tradition and the past as irrelevant and a threat to progress and innovation. Gandhi's option was introspective innovation for everyone, while Grant argued for spaces both personal and social where a different way of life could be fostered.

3. From Colonialism to Neo-colonialism

The struggle for national independence under British colonialism (Gandhi) and under American neo-colonialism (Grant) both differentiated and associated the two thinkers. It is clear that Gandhi learned "the notions of political and economic freedoms from the West."[23] However, he enhanced and modified these notions with Indian philosophical and religious concepts such as *swaraj* and *satyagraha*. The idea of duty or responsibility was as important as the idea of a right to Gandhi and this fit well with Grant's orientation, which was based on a view of human nature that Gandhi may not have agreed with but would have understood. Both men opposed imperialism and their opposition had a strong basis in their understanding of the human condition and its limitations. Both men shared a sense of the common good that required restraint on personal or corporate power. Both men desired the continuation, if not flowering, of indigenous political culture or, at least, the valid and worthwhile aspects of that culture. They certainly were highly critical of their own societies and how those societies were structured in a way that was conducive for the continuation of communal and personal oppression. They saw that the trends in their societies needed to be reversed and that this required a moral mobilization. While Gandhi was able to speak to that mobilization, Grant was not.

Gandhi's process of mobilization linked personal self-rule with political liberation. He saw collective freedom as a spiritual exercise in which all could participate, including the colonizer. Regrettably, Grant did not go as far in his thinking on political freedom. He felt so overwhelmed by the power of American economic might and cultural aggressiveness that he considered its triumph inevitable. He saw no possibility for change in the imperial thinking of the U.S. and his thinking on this part of the subject has been confirmed by historical developments right into the 21st century. Gandhi, however, always held out hope. It is the lack in Grant's thought of a belief in human ability to change history that was problematic. Though Gandhi and Grant shared a powerful attraction to issues of personal and collective morality in their opposition to imperial power, Gandhi's opposition to colonialism had a very practical dimension and practice, while Grant's opposition did not. What was it in Grant's intellectuality that precluded his having any sense of possible revolutionary change that was good for mankind? It would seem that Grant realized that only by holding onto tradition, were secondary societies like Canada able to survive as distinct entities and defeat the imperial cause.[24] But holding onto tradition successfully placed a limitation on historical evolution as perceived by the majority of Canadians. It was because Gandhi was in tune with the aspirations of the vast majority of Indians for political freedom that his politics resonated with the masses. Grant never tapped into the reservoir of Canadian nationalist feeling because it felt that it was ultimately impotent.

4. Pacifism

Both Gandhi and Grant were pacifists of sorts. Of course, Gandhi's name became synonymous with non-violence and opposition to war. He had read Ruskin and Tolstoy on the issue but ended up supporting the British during the Boer War, where he organized an ambulance corps of Indians on the British side. He did likewise during World War One and upon arriving in India even helped recruitment of Indians for combat. So Gandhi's pacifism, if one can even call it that, was much tempered by his devotion to individual courage and moral fortitude. He did not want his opposition to violence to be seen as a kind of cowardice.[25] It would seem that the self-disciplinary and penitential aspects of his thought discouraged a total pacifism. While *ahimsa* (non-injury to others) was one of his core values, he did conceive that the path to finding truth could sometimes cross through violence.

Grant's pacifism was strengthened by his experiences in England during World War Two but it was never a major part of his public identity. Although pacifism has not a fundamental feature of institutionalized Christianity over the millenia, there were those Christians who felt that opposition to and non-participation in war was a key component of the faith. While Grant did not belong to pacifist Christian sects such as the Mennonites or Hutterites, he felt that his religious beliefs coincided with the pacifist tradition. And the fact that the U.S. was engaged in the Vietnam War in the 1960s and 1970s and he was opposed to U.S. foreign policy, gave his pacifism a strong political resonance with other aspects of his thought. However, he did not make it a cornerstone of his thinking, so pacifism had a peripheral status. Not being a practitioner of political protest, Grant did not have to face the obvious contradictions faced by Gandhi, who practised non-violence with passion, but who also saw his duty prior to independence as being one of support for the Empire when it was involved in war. Grant's opposition to American foreign policy was intense, but Gandhi's opposition to British foreign policy was much less so, except in the arena of Indian political freedom. One might conclude with reason that the pacifism that both men shared was compromised because of certain historical and political realities.

Conclusion

Comparing the similarities and the differences in the thought of Gandhi and Grant brings up the final issue of how both thinkers integrated their nationalism and their religious thought and why one form of integration led to renown and the other to obscurity. In Gandhi's case the nationalist project that he made central to his life in India after World War One was so deeply rooted in the language and the concepts of Indian religious culture, primarily Hindu, that it became the very basis of his success. The other pillar on which his success stood was the personification of non-violence and civil disobedience as the way to liberation that came from the way he lived his life. Gandhi without religion cannot be imagined. Gandhi without national causes also cannot be imagined. These two elements—one sacred and the other secular—were blended in both his thought and his persona. This did not, however, mean that his thought was always logical and perfectly applied. On the contrary, as he himself argued, the fact that religion and nationalism were integrated in a human being, meant that failure, contradiction, and error were normative. One only arrived at Truth as the Godhead through effort, through trial and error.

In Grant's case the integration of nationalism and religion was based on his view of human nature as needing salvation by a divine source. He did not believe that human innovation or progress necessarily led to a better world. History was always a failed experiment in which technology and empire became forces for tyranny. The secularism of science and technology and its every-increasing influence on human existence was anathema to him. He felt that only an existential belief in God as the source of goodness, rather than human effort, would work to improve humanity. And this view supported his pessimistic nationalism—a belief that certain historical forces carried a powerful inevitability. In the struggle between History and the Divine, only the sacred offered relief. Grant's conservatism in this regard was not possible without his living Christian faith, but that conservatism was rather narrow in its articulation.

Both Grant and Gandhi owed a great deal to their respective religious traditions and their nationalism reflected those traditions. While both their nationalism and their religious beliefs were different, they still shared sufficient elements to make a comparison between the two men a worthwhile exercise in how cultures can speak to each other and respond to each other. By comparing the differences and similarities in their thought, one can see the outlines of why Gandhi has come to be viewed as a successful model and Grant as a failed model of nationalism. It was Gandhi's openness to the world's religions and morality and his exemplary personal lifestyle that appealed across nations and cultures. In contrast, it was Grant's narrowness in the Tory tradition and his pessimistic Christianity that made him much less appealing to a wide audience. Besides there was nothing heroic or exemplary in his career as an academic. He simply wasn't much an exciting role model like Gandhi. It is clear that effective emulation and praise belong to those that engage the world directly, while those who view it from the sidelines, no matter how perceptive their analysis, are generally ignored.

It is not possible to integrate Gandhi and Grant as thinkers because of these two fundamental features, just as it is not possible metaphorically to integrate Canada with India. While the saint and the professor shared a common commitment to humanity's quest for a moral and just life, the element of hope that one offered and the other did not was the deciding factor in how each man was received in their societies.

Notes

1. The latest work published in Canada is *Athens and Jerusalem: George Grant's Theology, Philosophy, and Politics* ed. by Ian Angus, Ron Dart, and Randy Peg Peters (University of Toronto Press, 2006).
2. Bhiku Parekh, *Gandhi: A Very Short Introduction* (Oxford: Oxford University Press, 1997) 6.
3. Ibid., 15.
4. William Christian and Sheila Grant, *The George Grant Reader* (Toronto: University of Toronto Press, 1998) 82.
5. Ibid., 84.
6. Margaret Chatterjee, *Gandhi's Religious Thought* (Notre Dame: University of Notre Dame Press, 1983) 5.
7. Ibid. 185.
8. Pam McCarroll, "The Whole as Love" in Angus et al., *Athens in Jerusalem*, 270.
9. This was not the case in the nineteenth century when religious differences caused serious civil turmoil such as over the hanging of Louis Riel or the Manitoba Schools Question, in which religious divisions became politicized and confrontational.
10. After the election of the Parti Québécois in the 1970s and 1990s, the province held two independence referendi, both of which were defeated, the latter by a very small margin.
11. Christian Roy, "Echoes of George Grant in 'Late Boomer' Critiques of Post-Quiet Revolution Quebec" in Angus et al. *Athens and Jerusalem*, 197.
12. In the 21st century the U.S. has worked hard to accelerate the industrialization of India to balance the amazing success of reformist China in the world marketplace.
13. Rabindranath Tagore, *Nationalism* (New Delhi: Rupa & Co., 1992) orig. published 1917. 94 &99.

14. For a contemporary discussion of Gandhian nationalism see Manfred B. Steger, *Gandhi's Dilemma: Nonviolent Principles and Nationalist Power* (New York: St. Martin's Press, 2000). In particular the introduction (1-14), especially p. 5.
15. One of the most notable of Canadian nationalists, who in the 1980s and 1990s warned of American domination of Canada, was the publisher Mel Hurtig, Among his books on the subject are: The betrayal of Canada (1991), The Vanishing Country (2003) and The Truth about Canada (2008).
16. Robert W. Wright, *Economics, Enlightenment, and Canadian Nationalism* (Kingston and Montreal: Mc-Gill Queens University Press, 1993) 108.
17. Ibid.
18. Christian and Grant, *The George Grant Reader*, 153.
19. Larry Schmidt ed. *George Grant in Process: Essays and Conversations* (Toronto: Anansi, 1978) 102.
20. Arthur Kroker, *Technology and the Canadian Mind: Innis/ McLuhan/Grant* (Montreal: New World Perspectives, 1984) 48.
21. Christian and Grant, *The George Grant Reader*, 389.
22. Graeme Nicholson, "Freedom and the Good" in Angus et al. *Athens and Jerusalem,* 333.
23. Anthony J. Parel, "Gandhian Freedoms and Self-Rule" in Anthony J. Parel, ed. *Gandhi, Freedom, and Self-Rule* (Lanham, Maryland: Lexington Books, 2000) 2.
24. For a general discussion of Grant's conservatism versus imperialism ideas see Robert C. Sibley, "Grant, Hegel, and the 'Impossibility of Canada" in Angus et al. *Athens and Jerusalem,* pp. 93-107.
25. An excellent discussion of the contradictions in Gandhi on the issue of pacifism, see Steger, *Gandhi's Dilemma*, pp. 141-179.

৪০ ଓଷ

7

RETHINKING DEMOCRACY AND BEYOND
(IN THE BACK DROP OF GANDHIJI'S VIEWS)

S R Bhatt

I

One of the most striking features of contemporary political scenario is widespread popularity of democracy so much so that many people think that there can be no other desirable alternative. They may argue that there is end of history/ideology and with democracy saturation point has reached in political thought. They may assume democracy to be the best form of government that can be conceived by human mind and think that no alternative to democracy is conceivable. There is an end to human rational capacity and there can be no advancement beyond. 'Thus far and no further' position seems to be the point of culmination of thought to them.

It may also mean that other forms of governance practiced so far, or being practiced, are either outdated or not good. In the past monarchy, oligarchy, aristocracy and several other forms were prevalent as different modes of political organizations and people were not satisfied with their functioning. Though monarchy still continues in some countries it is mostly nominal and on the way out in favor of democracy which is the latest trend. Because it is most modern and has acquired some prestige and putative position it is to be accepted without question.

Both the positions seem to be logically untenable. To take the second viewpoint first, one need not be dogmatic or biased against the past. There may be some merits in other forms of governance practiced in the past and this fact cannot be denied or overlooked. There may be some positive aspects of history. They need to be revisited for possible service as history has its own lessons to teach. It is not good to regard the past as dead and useless. History is embodiment and carrier of experiences of our ancestors and it is possible that we may be benefitted by them.

As regards the first position, to a rational and creative human mind it is irrational to think and talk of end of history or saturation in thinking. To ask reason not to think further is to ask it to commit suicide. Innovative thinking, transformative thinking and radical thinking should be regarded as natural to human mind.

Therefore, with regard to political thinking also there must be rethinking about democracy leading to search for an alternative. To safeguard freedom and justice we shall have to reexamine tenets of modern political thinking, premises upon which it is built and policies upon which it acts. The alternative may or may not be radically different but it must surely be essentially different in the sense that it should transcend all the deformities, drawbacks and demerits of democracy, particularly the ones of the manifold forms of democracy practiced in modern times. It is not a plea to distrust or reject but to reexamine it, to transform it, to cleanse it and if needed to go beyond it and look for an alternative. It is too well known to argue that all is not well with democracy. The search for an alternative requires newer intuitions, fresh insights and innovative thinking. If necessary, it may call for paradigm shift in end, means and modalities, and consequent structuring of new vocabulary and phraseology. It may involve drawing out new ideas and ideals and practices and disowning the prevalent ones that may not be useful or that may be obstructive. There has been pervasive confusion over the nature of political governance and freedom. James Boward in his book "Freedom in Chains (Introduction, p. 2) writes, "The effort to find a political mechanism to force government to serve the people is modern search for the Holy Grail. Though no such mechanism has been found, government power has been relentlessly expanded anyhow." One may not fully agree with this pessimistic view, but one cannot also ignore the atrocities committed in the name of democracy. To some extent he is justified in writing that "Nowadays "democracy" serves mainly as a sheepskin for leviathan, as a label to delude people into thinking that government's 'big teeth' will never bite them." (p.3)

II

It must be admitted that democracy is the best form of governance evolved so far but it cannot be said to be the best or that there can be or should be no scope for modification or improvement in its theoretical foundations and actual functioning. As Winston Churchill once remarked, "No one pretends that democracy is perfect or all-wise. Indeed it has been said that democracy is the worst form of government except all those other forms that have been tried from time to time." (Hansard, November 11, 1947) There is lot of truth in what Churchill opined. Plato's well known objections to democracy that it puts power in the hands of ignorant and unwise people also cannot be overlooked. Mahatma Gandhi in his seminal work "Hind Swaraj" referring to British Parliamentary system of democracy writes as follows,

> "That which you consider to be the Mother of Parliaments is like a sterile woman and a prostitute. Both these are harsh terms, but exactly fit the

case. *That Parliament has not yet, of its own accord, done a single good thing. Hence I have compared it to a sterile woman. The natural condition of that Parliament is such that, without outside pressure, it can do nothing. It is like a prostitute because it is under the control of ministers who change from time to time. Today it is under Mr. Asquith, tomorrow it may be under Mr. Balfour.*

Reader: You have said this sarcastically. The term, "sterile woman" is not applicable. The Parliament, being elected by the people, must work under public pressure. This is its quality.

Editor: You are mistaken. Let us examine it a little more closely. The best men are supposed to be elected by the people. The members serve without pay and therefore, it must be assumed, only for the public weal. The electors are considered to be educated and therefore we should assume that they would not generally make mistakes in their choice. Such a Parliament should not need spur of petitions or any other pressure. Its work should be so smooth that its effects would be more apparent day by day. But, as a matter of fact, it is generally acknowledged that the members are hypocritical and selfish. Each thinks of his own little interest. It is fear that is the guiding motive. What is done today may be undone tomorrow. It is not possible to recall a single instance in which finality can be predicted for its work. When the greatest questions are debated, its members have been seen to stretch themselves and to doze. Sometimes the members talk away until the listeners are disgusted. Carlyle has called it the "talking shop of the world". Members vote for their party without a thought. Their so-called discipline binds them to this. If any member, by way of exception, gives an independent vote, he is considered a renegade. If the money and the time wasted by the Parliament were entrusted to a few good men, the English nation would be occupying today much higher position. Parliament is simply a costly toy of the nation. These views are by no means peculiar to me. Some great English thinkers have expressed them. One of the members of that Parliament recently said that a true Christian could not become a member of it. Another said that it was a baby.

And if it has remained a baby even after an existence of seven hundred years, when will it outgrow its babyhood?

Reader: You have set me thinking; you do not expect me to accept at once all you say. You give me entirely novel views. I shall have to digest them. Will you now explain the epithet "prostitute"?

Editor: That you cannot accept my views at once is only right. If you will read the literature on this subject, you will have some idea about it. Parliament is without a real master. Under the Prime Minister, its movement is not steady but it is buffeted about like a prostitute. The Prime Minister is more concerned about his power than about welfare of Parliament. His energy is concentrated upon securing the success of his party. His care is not always that Parliament should do right. Prime Ministers are known to have made Parliament do things merely for party advantage. All this is worth thinking over.

Reader: Then you are really attacking the very men whom we have hitherto considered to be patriotic and honest?

Editor: Yes, that is true; I can have nothing against Prime Ministers, but what I have seen leads me to think that they cannot be considered really patriotic. If they are to be considered honest because they do not take what are generally known as bribes, let them be so considered, but they are open to subtler influences. In order to gain their ends, they certainly bribe people with honours. I do not hesitate to say that they have neither real honesty nor a living conscience." (Pp. 27-29, Fourteenth Reprint, October, 2001.)

About the English voters Mahatma Gandhi wrote as follows:

> "To the English voters their newspaper is their bible. They take their cue from their newspapers which are often dishonest. The same fact is differently interpreted by different newspapers, according to the party in whose interests they are edited...." He further writes, "These views swing like a pendulum of a clock and are never steadfast. The people

would follow a powerful orator or a man who gives them parties, receptions etc. As are the people, so is their Parliament. "(Ibid, Pp. 29-30)

III

What Mahatma Gandhi held in 1908 when this booklet was written in Gujarati, that still holds good even in 2009, and it may continue to be so unless there is radical review of functioning of democracy all over the globe.

Pandit Deendayal Upadhyaya in his booklet "Integral Humanism" very correctly opines about the functioning of democracy in India. He writes, "Consequently, opportunists with no principles reign in the politics of our country. Parties and politicians have neither principles nor aims nor a standard code of conduct. A person feels there is nothing wrong in leaving party and joining another. Even alliances and mergers of parties or their bifurcations are dictated not by agreements or differences in principles, but purely by gains in elections or in positions of power....Now there is complete license in politics. As a result, in public mind there is distrust for everyone. There is hardly any person whose integrity is beyond doubt in the public mind. This situation must be changed. Otherwise unity and discipline cannot be established in society. (P.4) Whatever is described above regarding England and India holds good about all other countries which practice democracy.

IV

History of political thought has witnessed several forms of political organizations ranging from autocracy to democracy. These various forms need not be enumerated. Some of them continue even now along with democracy. Of democracy also we find various brands. There are most liberal as well as most dictatorial forms and both call themselves democratic. Democracy is thus the most contested concept. Different people mean different things by democracy with the result that the word democracy has lost its meaning. We have people's democracy in which people are hardly involved in governance. We have liberal democracies that are most conservative and despotic. We have socialist democracies in which freedom, equality and justice are trampled with. In the name of democracy the powers that be can do anything and everything for self-interest and self- aggrandizement. Opponents and dissenters can be crushed and wiped out. It is quite evident from history that the democratic England promoted colonialism and democratically elected heads of states or prime ministers have become dictators. We have deliberative democracy in which people hardly deliberate. We have guided democracy in which only one or a few persons assume powers.

V

Theoretically, the essence of democracy consists in people's participation in self-governance. That is why Abraham Lincoln's most popular definition is universally accepted as, "government of the people, by the people and for the people." But this is all in theory only. It has only remained as delusory ideal. James Boward, in his book "Freedom in Chains", describes its functioning as "largely an over glorified choice of caretakers and cage keepers" (p.4). Sometimes democratic governments have behaved like 'lumbering giant bulldozer'. "We the People" has been a vacuous phrase. In actual practice no government, even in direct democracies, has truly been representative of people's will in toto. No form of democracy has been able to ensure all people's participation genuinely. In thought only in direct democracy it is conceivable but in practice it has never been so. In modern times with large population it is not feasible at all. What we have is not people's participation by themselves but through their representatives. But it is well known what sort of representatives they are, and how they manage to become representatives. For effecting representation generally adult franchise is used as a mechanism but how it operates is also too well known. Boward reports (ibid p.112) that Georgia legislature meets only 4o days each year. Most representatives say that they have only weak familiarity with the policies they put into law. He cites observation of California State Senator H.L.Richardson who writes, "Legislators consistently vote on legislation without understanding what is in it, especially when final vote is taken. Every legislature has his own system of judging how he will vote, but reading the bill usually is not part of the procedure". (What Makes You Think We Read the Bills?, Ottawa, 12, Carolina House, 1978, pp. 38-39). On page 97 Boward compares the functioning of representatives with "two wolves and one lamb voting on what to eat for dinner" (p.97) He quotes on page 100 the opinion of John Cartwright as "that poor consolatory word, 'representation' with the mere sound of which we have so long contended ourselves.". The common opinion is that the pretensions of representative democracy are as hollow as that of bygone monarchs to 'serve the people'.

Democracy is considered as rule of majority, but how much is the percentage to form the majority is something to be pondered over. Less than half of the people are the voters, less than half of the voters show up for voting at the polls, less than half of the voters who show up understand the issues, and politicians themselves are often unaware of what lurks in the bills they vote for. It is difficult to ascertain majority and that apart majority is not always right. Not only there is 'illusion of majority rule' measures are more often decided not according to the rules of justice or public well being but by the superior force of interested and overbearing majority, silencing the minority even though it may be enlightened and right.

Another feature of democracy is rule of law, but a distinction must be drawn between supremacy of "an authority" and supremacy of a person or group of persons "in authority", between "law as sovereign'" and "law emanating from sovereign." "Rule of law" has been really a very attractive proposition but it has proved to be utopian in democratic framework. Sometimes freedom under law becomes freedom under leashes. The constitution can be said to be 'an authority' but it is quite often relegated to the background by the persons 'in authority' who become dictatorial. Imposition of 'emergency' in India by Mrs. Indira Gandhi can be cited as an example. Constitutions have been mutilated, suspended and overthrown and laws have been misinterpreted mercilessly. It needs to be seriously thought over as to how to preserve and safeguard the supremacy of 'an authority' so that sanctity and functioning of constitution is not suspended or abrogated by powers that be who manage to be in authority.

The hallmark of social progress and of civil society is respect for human dignity and human freedom within an ordered cosmos. This involves cultivation of values like liberty, equality, justice and fairness. It should be realized that each individual has immense potentialities and capabilities and should be given freedom and opportunities to manifest them. In different individuals there are diverse capabilities and all are useful for social progress. Every human individual is a potential person and should be given scope to cultivate personhood. Personhood is an achievement concept. A person is one who is knowledgeable, ratiocinative, free and responsible being. He has to be an integrated, creative and freely acting social and moral being. He must know and realize the meaning of life, justify his existence and make it valuable and worthwhile for himself and the society.

The criterion of social progress is realization of the spirit of fellowship, democratic mode of thinking and living and not just democratic form of state or political governance. Genuine democratic spirit prevails only when diversity is fully recognized and well accommodated in an overall unity. In the unity differences are to be protected, preserved and enriched. They should receive natural and reasonable place and respect within the unity. Diversity is an outer expression of inner unity, like seed and tree. The unity in seed finds expression in various forms – the roots, trunk, branches, leaves, flowers and fruits and multiple seeds. All have different forms, colors, and properties. Genuine democratic process should not be suppression of thoughts, feelings and aspirations of any section of people but their enfoldment and reinforcement. In other words social progress has to be in the form of inclusive pluralism, having multiplicity well situated in unity like the organs surviving and thriving in an organism. In the ultimate analysis there should be no difference between 'I' and the 'other'. On the front gate of Parliament House of the Republic of India in New Delhi a verse from the traditional Indian culture is inscribed which states that the notions like "This is mine or this is that of others" is nurtured only by persons of mean mentality and narrow mind. For broad minded persons entire universe is a family. The implication is that instead of viewing differences as "I and the other" they should be viewed as "I and mine". The other is not to be regarded as an alien, an adversary, a competitor, or a threat to one's existence but a partner, a companion, a fellow, an aid or help.

Democracy in all its present forms does not ensure any of the above stated aspirations and requirements. In actual functioning democracy in all its three wings of legislature, executive and judiciary is vitiated with multiple and incurable drawbacks, deficiencies and deformities. Though theoretically there is separation of powers among these three, often there are confrontations. Most deplorable has been the functioning of legislature, to which Gandhiji and Deendayalji have referred. To use Indian vocabulary, though Indian democracy is called svarajya (self-rule) it has never been surajya (good government). It is debatable whether democracy failed or people failed democracy. Even if it is granted that democracy in itself is good but we could not evolve suitable mechanism to practice it, this also calls for rethinking about democracy. We have also to think going beyond democracy, if need be. Going beyond does not mean rejecting the basic spirit or merits of democracy. It only means rejecting all that is not good and beneficial, that which is detrimental to well-being, and that which is harmful. It is only rejecting the darker side of it. At any cost people's participation in self-rule, freedom of expression and rule of law are to be ensured. Important point is that we should at this juncture be willing to rethink the notion of political organization.

VI

Out of several possible alternatives, it is proposed for considerations of scholars that a good alternative can be sought and worked out from the age-old organic approach to understand the Reality and its manifestations in myriad social and political and other forms. The analogy of organism may be helpful in drawing out an outline of such an endeavor. It will be natural also as the order and harmonious functioning in an organism is built in it by nature itself. It has a sort of pre-established harmony, to use Leibnitzian phrase. The whole organism, along with its multiple organs, functions smoothly in perfect coordination. It presents a model of peaceful coexistence, of harmonious functioning, of mutual care and share, and of multiplicity co-inhering in unity both at macro and micro levels. It is an apt and rich analogy that may profitably be harped upon.

In an organism there is a built in organization but no outside control and imposition, though there are external influences, some good and some bad. The good ones are to be assimilated and bad ones are to be thwarted. There is no ruler-ruled relationship, no hierarchical order or authoritarianism in the functioning of organism. It is incorrect to understand that the cerebral system controls the nervous system unilaterally. There is supportive mutualism. Every organ in an organism functions in a natural way and contributes to the functioning of the total organism. The organism nourishes all its organs and is in turn nourished by each one of them. The functioning of organs and the organism is not rights-based. No one organ has any special privilege or position. The organs do not function in isolation or in collision. This is how the whole macrocosmic and microcosmic cosmos functions. In the cosmic process every one performs its assigned role dutifully and naturally.

This analogy has very interesting and promising implications for political thought. Some of the seminal ideas which can be attended in this regard are (a) corporate living with peace and harmony, (b) co-existence and cooperation, (c) mutual caring and sharing, (d) collective functioning, (e) self-regulation and self-control (f) no demands for rights and privileges but only proper discharge of duties and obligations etc.. In organic form of political organization there is no governance but regulation. Every one is equal and every one serves the other with mutual care and respect. Every one acts in cooperation performing the role assigned in the social setup. Though there will be no external authority, there will be a regulatory force and that will be a body of rules and regulations, checks and balances. There will be a set of rules and regulations "in authority" but there will be no person or a group of persons as "an authority" imposing their will from outside, a situation contrary to the present one. It will be rule of law and not of individuals. Equality, fraternity and intra and inter generational justice will be the guiding principles. This form of political organization can be termed as DHARMOCRACY. This was the ideal of ancient Indian polity where the king at the time of enthronement was required to take an oath that he would abide by dharma and serve as a servant of the people and not as a master. The concepts of 'raja', 'nrpa' etc. etymologically imply that even if it is rule by an individual he/she has to look after the happiness and well-being of the public who is under his/her protection and not to bother for self-interest. The goal of any human organization, political or otherwise, should be 'p'alana' which stands for maintenance, protection and promotion. This is the rule of dharma. In this context the analogy of pregnant woman is put forth who protects and nourishes the fetus in the embryo even at the cost of self-sacrifice. We find many statements in the Mahabharata, the Artha Shastra, Tripitakas and other texts to this effect. Adherence to rules and regulations will be spontaneous and natural and not forced or imposed. Life has to be natural and spontaneous. It has to be in harmony with other existences. Coexistence, cooperation, reciprocity in help, mutual caring and sharing etc. are hallmarks of a civil society. To talk of conflicts and clashes or to indulge in them is uncivilized, a decadence, a regression and a perversion. There has to be coexistence or confluence of cultures and civilizations. All regulations should be in the form of self-regulation. It means each one minding one's own business, each one taking responsibility for one's own actions, each one respecting the person of others and refraining from intruding into the lives of others. All this is possible through proper education of body, mind and will. This is what ethical teachings of seers and saints, particularly of the East, stand for. If there can be self-regulation there will be no need of government. To govern is to control and to control is to coerce or to use force. It is said that if men were angels no government would be necessary. And why can we not make humans angels. Why can there be no moral and spiritual progress? Why should education not be human-making? Boward reports (p.26) that the Montgomery County, Maryland, government sought to soften its image in 1985 by dropping the word "government" from the County Seal, from government workers' business cards, and even from the sides of County government automobiles. County Executive Douglas Duncan justified the change by saying that the word 'government' was "arrogant" and "off-putting" and "did not present the image of public service". This was the situation in ancient India, as has been reported, when social and political organizations were in the form of " Panchayata". In the booklet "Hind Swaraj" cited earlier there is citation of the views of Sir William Wedderburn Bart in the Appendices and it may be reproduced here for our perusal. It runs like this,

"The Indian village has thus for centuries remained a bulwark against political disorder, and home of the simple domestic and social virtues. No wonder, therefore, that philosophers and historians have always dwelt lovingly on this ancient institution which is the natural social unit and the best type of rural life: self-contained, industrious, peace-loving,

conservative in the best sense of the word.... I think you will agree with me that there is much that is both picturesque and attractive in this glimpse of social and domestic life in an Indian village. It is a harmless and happy form of human existence. Moreover, it is not without good practical outcome."

It is not that we have to imitate the past blindly but, as Pt. Jawaharlal Nehru once opined, it is good to be benefitted by revisiting the past. Of course it is desirable that governance or political organization should be by the people but more basic is that it should be for the people. It must be kept in mind that any organization, political or any other, is for what or for whom. Peace within and peace outside should be the ultimate goal of all human endeavors. Peace and prosperity go together. Prosperity has to be a shareable good and genuine prosperity is holistic and universal based on inter and intra generational justice. State and government are human institutions which can be made and unmade. They are for humans and humans are not for them. H.L.Mencken in "Treatise on Right and Wrong" (1934) (quoted by Boward on page 213) writes, "The great failure of civilized man is his failure to fashion a competent and tolerable form of government". There has been a saying," That government is the best which governs the least". If this is the case then why crave for 'statism' and why not to seek alternative. There can be alternative in allowing people to lead their own lives provided people are properly educated from very childhood in the ethics of self-regulation.

In fact this organic model calls for a paradigm shift of values and structuring of a new set of suitable vocabulary. Some vocabulary like that of 'public servant' can be retained, if it helps. It further requires a suitable system of education, as the new value system is to be cultivated right from childhood. Education is the best and surest means available to humankind. How education can effectively mould the minds in right or wrong direction can be learnt from the experiments of communist countries like China and North Korea. The way pet animals are trained and their mindset conditioned the same can be applicable to rational human beings who are more amenable to education and transformation. In the history we have experimented with many forms of governance, and even now we are experimenting with democracy and communism, and it is hoped that this model can also be given fair trial. But care is to be taken that the basic spirit and good features of democracy are not bartered. Only the deficiencies, drawbacks and pitfalls painfully experienced every where are rectified and removed. As the society progresses human mind also develops the capacity of innovative thinking and therefore the question is can we not think of a system better than democracy, a system in which all the merits of democracy are well preserved and demerits negated. Though we have come to stay with democracy as the best so far available form of political governance, this cannot be treated as the end of history. The rational and ingenious human mind should not entertain the idea of end of human reason or thinking capacity. It should be possible for the creative mind to grow, to move ahead and to evolve to think of a state higher and better than democracy, a state which encapsulates all the virtues of democracy and discards its vices and defects.

Notes

1. It may be mentioned here that though a distinction is drawn between state and government in political thought, in actual practice the distinction gets obliterated. Functionally state and government coalesce into one reality.
2. In the state of nature, it is believed, there was no state or government. People lived together either in harmony or in conflict. (Opinions differ) State and government have come into existence much later in human history and they have not really served the intended purpose though there might be some exceptions. In the organic model also there will ultimately be nominal state or government but only regulated organizations.
3. This model approximates the anarchist views of William Godwin, Mikhail Bakumin, Ruskin, Leo Tolstoy etc. All anarchists agree that state is an unnecessary evil to be

abolished in favor of a system of voluntary organizations. But the basic premises of this model are different

4. Some of the ideas, concepts and sayings of ancient classical literature and views of Mahatma Gandhi, Deendayal Upadhyaya, Jaiprakash Narayana may be helpful to develop the alternative suggested here.

ೲ ಚ

8

GANDHI, HEIDEGGER AND TECHNOLOGICAL TIMES

(R. Raj Singh)

The phenomenon of technology was already visible to Gandhi as the spirit of the twentieth century. He had begun to comment on the relation between man and machine and on the problems associated with the impacts of technology were taken up in his later writings. His probes into the spirit of the times in terms of technology as a phenomenon are largely misunderstood in the secondary literature. Gandhi is often dismissed by many as an orthodox thinker who advised the eastern peoples against the aping of the West and is described as an enemy of technology whose economic thought was based on a rejection of modern civilization. The relation between Gandhi's thought on man and machine and his central concepts of satya and ahimsa is seldom traced. It is true that in his South Africa years Gandhi spoke against modern civilization in rather radical terms, and he called modern material progress both evil and satanic. However, consistent with his ongoing experiments with Truth, and being always willing to revise his relative truths, he sought in his later years to deal with the problems of modernity as an insider.

Some of the most original analyses of the technological times are to be found in the writings of Heidegger and Gandhi, two of the leading thinkers of Western and Eastern streams of philosophy in the twentieth century. Their philosophies concerning the phenomenon of technology are rooted in their respective fundamental ontological standpoints reflectively pursued and elucidated in their prolific writings. To claim that their analyses of technology as well as their inquiries into the meaning of Being have something in common will immediately raise some eyebrows. How can the work of an eastern mystical political activist be compared with the philosophical achievement of a western academic philosopher? How can an armchair philosopher and political novice who might have shied away from his political responsibilities be compared to a servant of the people and a philosopher king like Gandhi? All these glaring contrasts notwithstanding, these two representative thinkers of our age openly declare that their chief thought-quest is nothing but the meaning of Being and both strive to outline the subtle but far-reaching impacts of technology based on remarkably similar concerns. Both seem to longingly envision and outline the features of what could have been and can be a truly non-violent and poetic human life, without having to wish technology away.

The first prejudice that needs to be overcome is concerning the widespread impression that Gandhi was merely a political crusader who advocated and put in practice the methods of non-violence. While all this is well known and true about Gandhi, what is not well known is that Gandhi was also an original thinker who made an outstanding contribution not only toward a reinterpretation of some important concepts of eastern philosophy, but also to ontology as such. At the same time, it is also not wise to dismiss Heidegger's thought as entirely academic, to be kept clear of practical applications. Although Heidegger expresses reservations concerning hasty applications of philosophy under the umbrella of recently mushroomed applied philosophies,[1] his thought goes a long way toward providing the conceptual framework for the self-understanding of the contemporary human entity consumed and overawed by the supremacy of the technical. While Heidegger does not pretend to be a saviour and leaves that task metaphorically to a god to come, he is open to a possibility of us being saved in our humanity. However, he does not believe that it is up to a philosopher to change the world on a piecemeal basis.

Ontological Grounds of the Philosophies of Heidegger and Gandhi

A thinker needs to have a single and fundamental object of thought. This object is both the inspiration and final aim of all his or her thoughtful pursuits. "To think is to confine yourself to a single thought,"[2] says Heidegger who is convinced that "thought's courage stems from the bidding of Being."[3] According to Heidegger, this single point of departure, this rootedness in Being is the innermost energy of the craft of philosophizing, which begins from a wonder about Being and turns into a preoccupation with and investigation of the meaning of Being.

A philosophical study of Gandhi's writings shows us that his thoughtful understanding of the meaning of Being as non-violence or ahimsa is a major contribution to ontology and as a thinker he not only confined himself to a single thought but also endeavored to carry out the bidding of Being. Gandhi's name for Being is especially chosen simple expression satya or truth. What Heidegger calls Being and the temporal and existential implications of which he traces in his writings is not essentially different from what Gandhi calls satya and regards it as a coin the other side of which is ahimsa.

Heidegger's remarkable contribution lies in his valuable reminders to contemporary western philosophy that thinking about Being must remain part and parcel of the activity called philosophizing or more appropriately, thinking. Even though Heidegger clearly states his openness to other possible means of Being,[4] he confined himself to an exposition of the temporal meaning of Being in accordance with the traditional Greek understanding of Being lodged in a temporal span. Gandhi, however, offers an entirely new basis for a fundamental understanding of Being to contemporary ontology. This new point of departure for ontological contemplation is what he calls ahimsa (non-violence), the other aspect of satya (truth) that is sat (Being). Gandhi's originality lies in proposing an alternative framework for an understanding of the concept of Being to its age-old temporal meaning. Thus, he proposes a new challenge to "thinking about Being" with its infinite possibilities and prospects for "thought". Furthermore, although Gandhi borrows the concepts of satya and ahimsa from his own tradition of Indian philosophy, acknowledging these as "as old as the hills,"[5] what remains his original contribution is as follows: (i) uplifting of ahimsa in its traditional characterization as an ethical virtue to its new exposition as the ontological ground, (ii) the application of ahimsa as fundamental ideal to the practical problems of human existence as well as to the contemporary social and political problems. Thus, satya to Gandhi is what Being is to Heidegger. Gandhi's contribution to human thought lies in his exposition of ahimsa as an ontological ground in which human being by nature participates in order to be essentially human. In his own words, "ahimsa is the law of our Being". He explains that ahimsa is not a mere ethical value, and violence and non-violence are not two equally open alternatives of conduct. Violence is but a violation for it violates the core of Being. It is inhuman because it is a violation of what is, as a matter of course, our basic Being.

Gandhi uses the term satya or truth for the ultimate reality, and calls it "his pole star all along during life's journey."[6] Satya is "one absolute truth which is total and all embracing...indescribable because it is God."[7] Gandhi's choice of the term satya or truth for what essentially is Being of beings is based on several considerations: firstly, truth is a concept well known to all, even to the most innocent villager, i.e., it is not a term merely for scholars and intellectuals. Secondly, it is not a sectarian or even religious term confined to a particular religious or cultural tradition. It makes sense even to atheists. However, there is no doubt that what Gandhi means by satya is sat which is the first attribute of what Vedanta calls Brahman:

> *The word satya comes from sat which means "to be" "to exist". Only God is ever the same through all time...I have been striving to serve that truth.[8]*

The word satya is derived from sat, which means that which "is". Satya means a state of Being. Nothing is or exists in reality except truth. That is why sat or satya is the right name for God. In fact, it is more correct to say that truth is God than to say God is truth.[9]

The equation of truth with God is not only indicative of Gandhi's bhakti, an affirmation of a devotional pursuit of truth, the other side of which is non-violence, but also an attempt to desectarianize God. Gandhi's elevation of ahimsa to the level of Being makes it much more than mere "non-injury". It is given a positive meaning, which is posed as a challenge to human thought. Thus, it is not easy for anyone to tell himsa and ahimsa apart:

> *Non-violence is not an easy thing to understand, still less to practise, weak as we are.[10]*

> *I have never claimed to present the complete science of non-violence. It does not lend itself to such treatment.[11]*

Violence is not just bloodshed and killing, but also inhumanity and slow killing all around. To recognize violence and the causes of violence is the first task of citizens and policy-makers. All cases of injustice and inequality are cases of violence. Violence is the result of systemic inequalities prevalent in the world today.

> *The first condition of non-violence is justice all round in every department of life. Perhaps it is too much to expect of human nature. I do not,*

however, think so. No one should dogmatize about the capacity of human nature for degradation or exaltation.[12]

Gandhi recognizes that perfect non-violence is impossible. Our breathing, eating, moving about necessarily involves some violence. He admits that even taking life sometimes may be a duty. But to actively seek to reduce the cycle of violence, as far as possible, is part and parcel of the creativity and self-advancement of the human entity.

An Analysis of the Technological Times by Heidegger

Heidegger's analysis of the phenomenon of technology is explicitly discussed in his famous lecture-essay, The Question Concerning Technology, composed in 1949 and published in 1954. But his insights on the basic features of our technological times appear in several of his later works, most notably in An Introduction to Metaphysics (1953), "The age of the World Picture" (1954), "Building, Dwelling, Thinking" (1956), "Poetically Man Dwells" (1954) etc.

Heidegger confronts the issue of the essence of technology in his celebrated essay, The Question Concerning Technology, and maintains that "Everywhere we remain unfree and chained to technology whether we passionately affirm or deny it. But we are delivered over to it in the worst way when we regard it as something neutral."[13] Technology is not a mere means at the disposal of man nor a merely human activity but "a way of revealing" a peculiar disclosedness of truth.[14]

Therefore we must take that challenging that sets upon man to order the real as standing reserve... We now name that challenging claim.. Gestell (Enframing).[15]

That revealing concerns nature, above all as the chief storehouse of the standing energy reserve.[16]

The rule of Enframing threatens man with the possibility that it could be denied to him to enter into a more original revealing.[17]

According to Heidegger, technology is a kind of disclosedness that has enframed our age in an overwhelming way and rendered other ways of knowing as inferior. So that "everything will present itself only in the unconcealment of the standing-reserve". Technology as a dominant way of knowing has the nature of displacing all other ways of knowing and constitutes the destiny of our planet. It is obvious from Heidegger's analysis that alternative world-views don't stand a chance against the steamroller of technology which is bound to crush and flatten all rival ways of knowing. And all this is happening while technology is still being taken as a mere means at the disposal of man.

Gandhi's exhortations to his people not to ape the west and to be wary of the blind applications of the machine-technology assume a new meaning in the light of Heidegger's analysis. Gandhi warned that "if the village perishes, India will perish too. India will be no more India. Her own mission in the world will get lost."[18] This indicates that Gandhi understood and foresaw the impending selfsameness of technology and its threat to the eastern ways of knowing and living.

However, both Heidegger and Gandhi remain optimistic. Heidegger quotes Hölderlin: "But where danger is, grows the saving power also"[19] and expresses a deep conviction about the basic human being-in-the world having something poetic about it. Heidegger expands on the Hölderlin's words "poetically dwells man on this earth" in an essay about the same title and profoundly states:

> Dwelling can be unpoetic only because it is in essence poetic. For a man to be blind, he must remain a being by nature endowed with sight... That we dwell unpoetically, and in what way, we can in any case learn only if we know the poetic... How and to what extent our doings can share in this turn, we alone can prove, if we take the poetic seriously.[20]

An Examination of the Technological Times by Gandhi

Gandhi may be one of the first eastern philosophers who have analyzed the essence of technological times and who have emphasized that since technology is here to stay, we must study its human and international impacts. The purposes of such a study according to him are as follows. Since the return to a machineless state is neither possible nor desirable, the violence embedded in technology and industrialism can be and should be reduced through a non-violent restructuring of human society. In the midst of our craze for machines, the basic, innocent and spiritual aspects of human life, which has nothing to do with technology, ought not be dismissed.

Gandhi understood quite well that the overwhelming advance of technology will not only complete the process of the Europeanization of all standards and standardization of all measure of reality. The world will be a poorer place if the steamroller of westernization in the form of technology transfers, levels off and crushes the heads of eastern alternatives to living. Gandhi's concerns about the east-west meltdown and most especially the impending demise of the Indian village republics are captured in his very simple warning: "If the village dies, India will die too." Gandhi's originality as an analyst of our times is acknowledged in the following words of Chester Bowles, the former U.S. ambassador to India:

> It has been said that there is scarcely an individual on this earth whose life has not been affected in some essential way by Gandhi. This is so because no other public figure of our era so clearly understood or so confidently welcomed the implications of the revolutionary age in which we live.[21]

Along with thinkers like Ortega y Gassett, Karl Jaspers and Heidegger, Gandhi strove to calm the unbridled passion for technology, which was already underway in his lifetime. In his early South African days, Gandhi in his pursuit of the simple life as well as moksha (salvation) from materialism or mammon-worship, opposed machine-technology's part in what he thought were the ills of modern civilization. In an article written in response to a disastrous fire in a Metro train in Paris, Gandhi said:

> Nothing that the modern civilization can offer in the way of stability can ever make any more certain that which is inherently uncertain; that,

> *when we come to think of it, the boast about the wonderful discoveries and the marvelous inventions of science, good as they undoubtedly are in themselves, is, after all, an empty boast. They offer nothing substantial to the struggling humanity.*[22]

While retaining his fascination for the splendour of the simple, Gandhi revised his attitude toward machine-technology during the course of his life of experiments with truth. He came to realize and accept that machinery is here to stay and technology is bound to penetrate the remotest corners of the earth. His main concern with it was the displacement of human labour. As he wrote in 1924 and 1925:

> *Machinery has its place; it has come to stay. But it must not be allowed to displace necessary human labour... What I object to is the craze for machinery, not machinery as such. The craze is for what they call labour-saving machinery... Today machinery merely helps a few to ride on the backs of millions. The impetus behind it all is not the philanthropy to save labour, but greed.*[23]

But Gandhi's real concern with technology was twofold: (I) that technology was a threat to East-West diversity. That is, its blind introduction will lead to a super cession of the eastern way of life as well as the eastern world-views. (ii) Too much fascination with technology will result in obstructing from our view the simple graces of human life. The a technical life will be dismissed as inferior to the technological conveniences and distractions. This second consequence or what he calls "superstition" is explained by Gandhi as follows:

> *It has still to be proven that the displacement of the hand by the machine is a blessing in every case. Nor is it true that that which is easy is better than that which is hard. It is still less proved that every change is a blessing or that everything old is fit only to be discarded.*[24]

The first consequence of technology, the selfsameness as well as exploitation and promotion of inequities, which necessarily lead to violence, is exposed by Gandhi as follows:

> *What is the cause of present chaos? It is exploitation, I will not say, of the weaker nations by the stronger, but of sister nations by sister nations. My fundamental objection to machinery rests on the fact that it is machinery that has enabled these nations to exploit others.*[25]

Concluding Remarks

Gandhi realized, just as Heidegger did, that technology has the nature of being all encompassing. It trivializes alternative world-views, centralizes power structures that depend on violence to protect themselves and standardizes all measures of reality. Heidegger defines technology "as a singular way of revealing entities, overwhelming man and entities and all other ways of revealing."[26] This is exactly what Gandhi finds alarming in the advance of technology, for "the other ways of revealing" which includes eastern world-views must not be allowed to disappear. Gandhi exhorted India to remain being India and not to lose its soul in aping the west, not because he loved only India as his own, but because the world must continue to be diverse and have equally strong alternative world-views. Otherwise, we will have nowhere to come from and nowhere to go.

Non-violent reform can never mean to alter the world into a technological selfsameness. Diversity is the cornerstone of a non-violent society. Blind transfers of technology, widespread greed for money, dismissal of the religious sentiment as being outmoded, religious and political conversions will not form a better world, but morally and culturally a poorer world. All cultures, religious and world-views should be allowed to exist and grow. That the East must not imitate the West was one of Gandhi's personal goals. It is better even for the West that the world retains its diversity, so that the questions are asked and answers are found based on thoughtfully diverse concepts and several possible standpoints. Gandhi certainly introduced a new dimension in the philosophy of Being. "To be is to be in non-violence" is an insight, which will challenge philosophical thought for centuries to come.

Notes

1. Martin Heidegger, "Letter on Humanism" trans. Edgar Lohner in William Barrett and Henry D. Aikin, ed. Philosophy in the Twentieth Century, Vol. 3 (New York: Random House, 1962.

2. Heidegger, "The Thinker as Poet" in Poetry, Language, Thought, trans. Albert Hofstadter (New York: Harper Colophon Books, 1975), p. 4.
3. Ibid., p. 5.
4. Heidegger, What is Called Thinking, trans. F.E. Wrick and G.G. Gray (New York: Harper and Row, 1968).
5. M.K. Gandhi, Harijan, March 28, 1936, from All Men are Brothers, ed. Krishna Kriplani (New York: Continuum, 1987, p. 1. Henceforth abbreviated as AMAB.
6. M.K. Gandhi, The Essential Writings of Mahatama Gandhi, ed. Raghavan Iyer (Delhi: Oxford University Press, 1993), p. 229 (Young India, Dec. 10, 1925). Henceforth abbreviated as EWMG.
7. EWMG, p. 224 (Navjivan, Nov. 20, 1921).
8. EWMG, p. 225 (Navjivan, Nov. 20, 1921).
9. EWMG, p. 231 (Letter to Narandas Gandhi, July 22, 1932).
10. AMAB, p. 89 (Young India, Feb. 7, 1929).
11. AMAB, p. 79 (Harijan, Feb. 22, 1942.)
12. AMAB, p. 77 (Mahatama, V, Apr., 1940.)
13. Heidegger, "The Question Concerning Technology" in The Question Concerning Technology, trans. William Lovitt (New York: Harper and Row, 1977), p. 4. Subsequently abbreviated as QCT.
14. QCT, p. 12.
15. QCT, p. 19.
16. QCT, p. 21.
17. OCT, p. 28.
18. AMAB, p. 116 (Harijan, Aug. 29, 1936).
19. QCT, p. 34.
20. Heidegger, "Poetically Man Dwells" in Albert Holfstadter, ed. Poetry, Language, Thought, p. 228.
21. Chester Bowles, "Gandhi As I Understood Him" in J.S. Mathur, ed. Gandhian Thought and Contemporary Society (Bombay: Bhartiya Vidya Bhavan, 1974).
22. EWMG, p. 86, (Indian Opinion, Aug. 20, 1903).

23. AMAB, pp. 114-115, (Young India, Nov. 5 and 13, 1924).
24. EWMG, p. 398, (Young India, Jul. 2, 1931).
25. AMAB, p. 114, (Young India, Oct. 22, 1931).
26. QCT, pp. 3-35.

9

GEORGE GRANT AND HINDUISM: CONTEMPLATIVE PROBES

Ron Dart

Christianity seems in a certain way closer to Hinduism than it does to its fellow religions that arose in the Middle East.

George Grant
George Grant in Conversation (1995) p. 176

In talking about a philosophical response, are we not supposed to have agreed upon understanding as to what philosophy is? And certainly one should not try to take advantage of the fact that there is no definition of philosophy on which all are agreed.

John Arapura
Modernity and Responsibility:
Essays for George Grant (1983) p.52

The recent book, *Athens and Jerusalem: George Grant's Theology, Philosophy, and Politics* (2006), probed Grant's deeper theological roots, but in the doing of this, Grant's interest and affinity with the Orient and Hinduism was missed and ignored. This is a serious lack and weakness in an otherwise needed and necessary commentary on Grant.

Grant saw himself as standing within the 'Hindu wing of Christianity', and, as mentioned above, he thought the contemplative and mystical core of Christianity made it 'closer to Hinduism' than to either the Jewish or Islamic traditions.

What did Grant mean by the statements mentioned above, and why was he, as a Canadian, at the forefront of probing greater contemplative depths in the Christian Tradition, and, by doing so, opening up new trails for interfaith dialogue?

If Grant's interest in the East is ever to be properly understood, it is essential that the state of Western philosophy he encountered, opposed and resisted be brought into focus. Grant confronted the philosophic Brahman class in Canada as a young man. Fulton Anderson was one of the most important philosophers in Canada in the 1940s (he taught at University of Toronto), and in 1949, Anderson's *The Philosophy of Francis Bacon* was published.

Anderson did not raise serious criticisms of either Bacon's empirical method and some of the conclusions Bacon reached and Anderson accepted. Grant just thought this was a case of philosophy being co-opted, assimilated and uncritically genuflecting to a form of scientific rationalism. Such an approach to knowing and being, Grant thought, was reductionistic and undermined the classical contemplative approach to philosophy. Grant did a review in *Dalhousie Review* (Volume 28:1948-1949) of *The Philosophy of Francis Bacon*, and Anderson was not pleased. Anderson was a senior scholar and elder in the philosophic clan in Canada, and Grant a younger apprentice. Grant had dared to challenge the master. Anderson would not forget nor forgive such impertinence, but Grant's criticism of Anderson-Bacon did speak much about his emerging way of understanding and doing philosophy. Grant objected, in short, about the increasingly limited way that philosophy was being defined and defended.

George Grant's uncle, Vincent Massey, became the first Canadian born Governor General in Canada, and in the early 1950s, Vincent Massey launched the Massey Commission. The purpose of the Massey Commission was to examine the state of arts and culture in Canada and make recommendations to the government about a post-WW II way forward for Canadians. Vincent Massey asked George Grant to do the article in the Commission on philosophy. The article was published in 1951 as 'Philosophy'. Grant makes it quite clear in 'Philosophy' that he thinks most Canadian philosophy and philosophers had lost their way. They had given themselves to an empirical and narrow scientific rationalism, and this simplistic form of the 'vita activa' had banished the classical notion of the 'vita contemplativa'. Grant urged and argued, insisted and pleaded, made it clear and obvious that if philosophy was merely going to be an errand boy to science, the death knell of philosophy was already ringing. Grant's straight on criticisms of the state of Canadian philosophy in 'Philosophy' drew forth the ire of Anderson and tribe. They would and could not accept Grant's approach to philosophy and his criticism of them. The Brahmin class gathered to protect their commitments.

'Philosophy' was published in 1951, and in 1952, a symposium was held, PHILOSOPHY IN CANADA, in which Grant was brought to the dock. *Philosophy in Canada: A Symposium* (1952) makes it more than clear that Grant's contemplative approach to doing philosophy would not be accepted, and, predictably so, Fulton Anderson led the intellectual armada against Grant. Needless to say, Grant learned quite early in his academic career that the classical contemplative way would not be welcomed in a serious approach to philosophy or, by extension, in theology. Theology, to a greater or lesser extent, had also been co-opted by an empirical, confessional and rationalist method that had little to do with the classical contemplative way of knowing.

Western philosophy had become, for the most part, a plaything of rationalism and empiricism, and the study of religion and theology followed the same path. Grant began the task in the 1950s of casting about in different directions for traditions that embodied an older and more contemplative way of knowing. This is what, of course, walked Grant to Plato and Aristotle and to the East.

The tale and drama was to heat up further, though, for Grant. Grant decided to leave the philosophy department of Dalhousie in 1959. He had been offered a position in philosophy at a new university in Toronto (York). The founding of York University was part of the birth of many new universities in Canada in the 1960s. The older universities could not accommodate all the new students. York was formed as a companion university to University of Toronto, and, in many ways, it became a counter cultural opposition to it.

Grant, as I mentioned above, was hired to provide leadership to the fledgling Philosophy department at York. It was just a few months before problems emerged. York University was to be under the watchful eye of University of Toronto for the first few years, and this meant that George Grant was to be responsible to Fulton Anderson for how he taught courses and the text he used. Anderson strongly recommended Grant use a text written by Marcus Long (a friend and colleague of Anderson's). *The Spirit of Philosophy*, by Long, had little to do with Grant's approach to philosophy. Philosophy, for Long, was about critical reflection on arguments and issues, and Long's notion of the philosophic spirit was more about skepticism and cynicism than anything else. Grant refused to view philosophy in such a way, he insisted such a text would not be used, and he would not bow the knee to Anderson and the University of Toronto. Grant wrote a letter to the president of York in April 1960, clearly explaining why he had to resign from York.

Grant was committed to teaching philosophy, but, throughout the late 1940s and 1950s, it became clear to him that his understanding of philosophy stood in stark opposition to the reigning paradigm of the time and the Brahmin class that protected such a worldview.

The Great Ideas Today series published in 1961 a long article by Grant. 'The Year's Developments in the Arts and Sciences: Philosophy and Religion' takes a long and hard look at the failings, limitations and possibilities of both philosophy and religion. Most of the article is on the state of philosophy, but there is a significant aspect in the article on religion. It is in this article that Grant began to unpack, in a deeper and broader way, some of his thoughts on Eastern religions. These reflections on the Orient are important for two reasons; first, this signals a conscious turn by Grant to a formal interest in the East: second, Grant became the chair of the religious studies department at McMaster, and McMaster's religious studies department became a centre in Canada at both an undergraduate and graduate levels for studies in the East and Orient. Grant was front and centre in all this work at McMaster.

Grant saw, most clearly, three trends emerging on the cultural scene in Canada and beyond in the 1960s. First, the age of Christendom and Christianity was on the wane. Second, there was a growing interest in the East (some of it naïve and shallow, some of it substantive). The interest in the East was heralded by an interest in the East as a more meditative and contemplative way of knowing. Third, the rational and empirical way of knowing that seemed to produce such objective facts and information had to be challenged at the university level. There were deeper ways of knowing and being, and Grant was doing serious sleuth work on the places and sites of such wisdom.

There were two prominent Indian thinkers that held Grant at this period of time: Gandhi and Tagore. Grant, in 1966, addressed many students that were opposed to the Vietnam War, and his article, 'A Critique of the New Left', holds high Gandhi as a model to heed and hear rather than naïve and idealistic protest politics that wither when the hard times come. Grant offered a solid and penetrating critique of the New Left, and handed out many accolades to Gandhi. He said, and much was said in some a compact way: 'The central Christian platitude still holds good. The truth shall make you free. I use freedom here quite differently from those who believe that we are free when we have gained mastery over man and over nature. It is different even from the simple cry for political liberty: Freedom now. For in the long haul freedom without the knowledge of reality is empty and vacuous. The greatest figure of our era, Gandhi, was interested in public actions and in political liberty, but he knew that the right direction of that action had to be based on knowledge of reality—with all the discipline and order and study that that entailed'.

I should also mention that for Gandhi the *Bhagavad Gita* and the *Sermon on the Mount-Beatitudes* (taught by Jesus) were basic to understanding the discipline, order and study that birthed genuine freedom. Gandhi's commitment to the *Beatitudes* is central to understanding his core ethical vision. George Grant's ethical centre was also thoroughly rooted and grounded in the *Beatitudes*. Grant stated this quite clearly in his 'Five Lectures on Christianity'. He had this to say in the second lecture: 'Let's start with the teaching from the Sermon on the Mount. Matthew chapter(s) 5 to 7 reveal a perfect account of justice or righteousness.... What is breathtaking also in the teaching is its immediate clarity and comprehensibility'. Grant and Gandhi both shared a commitment to the Beatitudes as the foundation of the inner-outer life and the pathfinder for a healthy soul and civilization.

Grant saw in Gandhi an Indian thinker and activist that had integrated, in thought, word and deed, the real meaning of philosophy and politics. This is why, for Grant, Gandhi was the 'greatest figure of our era'. This was philosophy that had not retreated from the fray or bowed to the scientific way and modern industry. This was truly classical philosophy embodied in the modern era, and just as Gandhi felt the opposition for challenging the juggernaut of modern technology, so did Grant.

Grant was also quite fond of Rabindranath Tagore. Sheila Grant, in 'George Grant and the Theology of the Cross' in *George Grant and the Subversion of Modernity: Art, Philosophy,*

Politics, Religion, and Education (1996) makes this quite clear. Sheila Grant had this to say about Grant's interest in Tagore. Sheila mentioned that Grant often used this prayer by Tagore 'when taking a service for students':

> *Give me the supreme faith of love, this is my prayer; the faith of the life in death, of the victory in defeat, of the power hidden in the frailness of beauty, of the dignity of pain that accepts hurt but disdains to return it.* P. 225

There is little doubt that Grant found in Gandhi and Tagore a merging and meeting of contemplation, poetry, politics and action. This was a different approach to philosophy than Grant had encountered at universities in the west. There was something life giving and authentic about such an approach.

There was more than this, though, to Grant's interest in Hinduism.

George Grant left McMaster in 1980, and in his letter of leaving, 'The Battle between Teaching and Research' (1980), he makes plain, simple and clear why and how Universities have lost their way. The older way of knowing has been abandoned for modern empirical and technical ways of knowing, and our souls have been lost in the process. Grant turned again to the Maritimes and Dalhousie to spend his last few years.

William Christian/Sheila Grant mention in *The George Grant Reader* (1998) that 'Of all his colleagues at McMaster, Grant felt closest to those who studied Hinduism. His understanding of the meaning of the Gospels was informed not just by Plato but also by what he had learned from Indian religion' p.459. Bithika Mukerji had published a book, *Neo-Vedanta and Modernity* in 1983. Grant wrote an appreciative Foreward for Mukerji's book. Grant makes it more than clear in the Foreward that modernity-westernization has done much to 'obscure' the meaning of 'bliss' in the older Vedantic tradition. Grant is more than drawn to Mukerji's notion of 'ananda'. The deeper Indian notion of Being that the West has lost means that the West has sought joy and bliss in areas in which such gifts cannot be offered. The Neo-Vedantic understanding of Being takes the honest pilgrim to places the West cannot go for the simple reason it has lost its way.

George Grant turned 65 years of age in 1983. He had challenged the reigning educational, political, economic and philosophic Brahmins in Canada most of his life. A *festschrift* was written and given to him to celebrate many years of hard service and much turmoil. *Modernity and*

Responsibility: Essays for George Grant (1983) has a fine essay in it by one of Grant's dearest Indian friends from McMaster days: John G. Arapura.

Arapura's essay, 'Modern thought and the transcendent: Some observations based on an Eastern view' goes straight to the heart of Sankara and Vedantic thought. Arapura makes it clear that with the rise of an empirical method, the issue of the transcendent has become a problem. How can the reality of the transcendent be verified or falsified within a rationalist and empirical method? Arapura's article is short but to the poignant point. Arapura, like Grant, turned to Heidegger to highlight the problems with the modern understanding of thinking and reason. Heidegger, more than any other modern western philosopher, undermined and undercut the foundation of modern reason and opened older paths to knowing. These older markings and signposts pointed the way to a deeper way of knowing and understanding the meaning of thought and thinking. Kant and reason are left behind. Heidegger leads the way to Sankara and his understanding. The path is opened to the transcendent once again once the single vision and one dimensional view of empirical reason is doubted and questioned as the only way of knowing. Arapura's use of the *Upanisads* and Sankara's interpretation of them also points the way to a dialogue between Sankara and Plato. This meeting much interested Grant and Arapura. 'Modern thought and the transcendent: Some observations based on an Eastern view' brought Grant and Arapura together yet closer in their desire to understand how an older contemplative Hinduism and an older contemplative form of Christianity might have some important points of affinity. This is why Grant thought he had much in common with the 'Hindu wing of Christianity'. Both Arapura and Mukerji taught Grant much about a deeper and older Indian and Hindu way, and Grant was more than eager to hear, heed and learn.

John Arapura's book, *Gnosis and the Question of Thought in Vedanta* was published in 1986. Arapura sent Grant a copy of the book, and Grant replied to Arapura in a letter (12 November 1987). Grant says. 'Your book is wonderfully illuminating'. The rest of the short letter goes on to explain how and why *Gnosis and the Question of Thought in Vedanta* is illuminating. Grant had less than a year to live, but he was always willing to be led and taught about the depths of Sankara and Neo-Vedantic thought, and how such an ancient line and lineage might assist Christians in both going deeper in their own journey and, equally important, challenging the narrow approach to knowing of modernity.

There is one more thinker we need to ponder as Grant engaged Hinduism. This is Nietzsche. Both John Arapura in 'Modern thought and the transcendent: Some observations based on an Eastern view' and, interestingly enough, Ronald Beiner in 'George Grant, Nietzsche, and the Problem of a Post-Christian Theism' in *George Grant and the Subversion of Modernity* (1996) deal with Grant, Nietzsche and Hinduism.

The 19th century witnessed two important events; Science replaced Christianity as the new religion and source of authority; this is an aspect of modernity. As Christianity was marginalized and science rose to the throne,

> *a spiritual thirst still existed that science could not slake. There was a turn to the East to make sense of such a thirst and hunger. Western modernity had marginalized Christianity, but the spiritual void was filled by an increasing interest by westerners in the Orient. Germany was front and centre in this turn to the East, and Nietzsche had a part to play in the drama.*

Nietzsche's oft quoted 'God is dead' obscures his deeper ponderings on the meaning and significance of Christianity, religion, spirituality and the Orient and Ancient Near East. Nietzsche, like Grant, had serious doubts about the spirit and forms of modernity, and he looked to the Classical past for insight and guidance. Nietzsche makes it quite clear in books such as *Will to Power, Genealogy of Morals, The Antichrist, Thus Spoke Zarathustra* and *Twilight of the Idols* where his commitments were and why. Nietzsche preferred Roman Catholic Christianity to Protestant Christianity, he preferred Hinduism to Buddhism, the warrior gods of Homer and the Jewish warrior God to Christianity and Buddhism. He was quite drawn to the Hindu caste system, but his view of hierarchy and caste was based on nobility, risk, energy, courage and effort rather than an inherited Brahmin class. Nietzsche countered the leveling of values that modernity brought, and he thought Christianity and the Enlightenment were to blame for the problem. Christianity was as much part of modernity as was the Enlightenment for

Nietzsche, and Nietzsche wanted little of either. Grant and Nietzsche both shared deep suspicions of the modern project, and both turned to the wisdom of the past to counter the modern ethos and mood. Both had an interest in Hinduism, although they were interested in different parts of Hinduism. The lawbook of Manu spoke to him of aristocracy and heroism, of those who overcome for a higher ideal. Beiner's 'Grant, Nietzsche, and Post-Christian Theism' highlights how both Grant and Nietzsche turned to the Classics in opposition to modernity, but their interpretation of the Greek and Indian Classics went in different directions. It is essential, though, that most thinkers that opposed modernity (like Grant and Nietzsche) turned to both the Occidental and Oriental past as a means to both counter modernity and offer an older and deeper way of knowing and being. There was, therefore, a convergence for many in their turn to the ancient past in the West and East.

The question was this, though: what and whose interpretation of the Classical Western and Eastern should be heeded and why? There can be no doubt, though, that both the more ancient Greek and Indian traditions had a certain charm and appeal for those that saw through the pretensions and limitations of liberalism and modernity.

Many of the more thoughtful Germans in the 19th century were quite keen on pondering how the Orient could and would walk them beyond the failing and faults of both Christianity and Science. Arapura's article, 'Modern thought and the transcendent: Some observations based on an eastern view' discussed Nietzsche and Paul Deussen (the German Vedantic scholar).

Deussen and Nietzsche were friends and both had an interest in India as a way of transcending both a faltering Christianity and the limitations of science. Deussen argued that Parmenides, Kant and Sankara had much in common. Nietzsche read Deussen's *Das System des Vedanta* and some of the *Upanisads*, and he opposed both. The Dionysian spirit did not live with an energetic passion in such texts. Apollo was too present.

Grant thought that Nietzsche and Heidegger had done more than most thinkers to make 'the modern western project conscious of itself'. Both men turned to the Classical way (both interpreting it selectively and bringing many modern assumptions with them). Nietzsche, like Grant, had an interest in Hinduism, but their interest and interpretation took them down different paths and trails.

Grant lived, moved and had his being in the 'Hindu wing of Christianity'. This means Grant's interest was much more in the contemplative wing of Hinduism. There was no doubt that Grant was drawn to Nietzsche and Heidegger. Both men, in their different ways, showed Grant how modernity could be challenged, the flaws and fallacies within it, and, following Heidegger, the problems with empiricism and rationalism as a way of knowing. But, Grant did not follow Heidegger or Nietzsche in their interpretation and turn to the Classical Eastern and Western traditions. This is where Simone Weil entered the drama for Grant.

George Grant, in many ways, saw Simone Weil as his Diotima. Grant thought that Weil's read of the Classical Greeks in *Intimations of Christianity Among the Ancient Greeks* was much sounder, saner and comprehensive than Nietzsche and Heidegger. The same sensitivity that Weil applied to the Greeks she applied to reading Oriental and Indian texts.

Simone Weil had a contemplative understanding of the philosophic journey that threaded together the inner and the outer journey, contemplation and justice. This is what brought Grant and Weil close to Gandhi and Tagore.

There is little doubt that Nietzsche and Heidegger did much to assist Grant in his analysis of the modern project, and that John Arapura and Bithika Mukherji did much to walk Grant deeper into the world of the Vedanta and Sankara. But, Gandhi, Tagore and Simone Weil did even more to guide Grant into a more integrated understanding of the Classical Greek and Indian way of integrating contemplation and politics. Grant, to his reflective and activist credit, embraced such wise sages and lived forth such an integrative way within the Canadian context.

ಙ ಚ

10

THE NEW SOCIOLOGICAL IMAGINATION, JNANA YOGA AND THE WEB OF LIFE: GANDHI, GRANT, MILLS, PEIRCE[1]

J. I. (Hans) Bakker

Introduction: on Gandhi, Grant, Mills and Peirce

This essay seeks to re-conceptualize aspects of the thought of Gandhi and Grant in light of what I would like to call "the new sociological imagination." I will compare and contrast Grant and Gandhi as "gnostic" thinkers who utilize "jnana yoga." (The terms gnosticism and jnana yoga are used here in the scholarly sense and not in the more limited and misleading popular sense.) I will do so utilizing a perspective which draws heavily on C. S. Peirce and C. Wright Mills. Hence, this paper can be nothing more than a sketch of complex ideas that could use book-length treatment.

A longer discussion, for example, might start with the rise of modern science (Bakker 2007). Mitchell (2006: 1-50) re-interprets the rise of modern Western European science as based in part on freedom of inquiry and a re-discovery of esoteric "Faustian" practical magic in alchemy and astrology, as well as occult theories of every kind. He bases his ideas on a recent book by Giovanni Filoramo (1990) concerning the wide-ranging types of gnosticism that existed in the first century of the C.E. The key fact about the Hellenic and Roman world of the first century is the multiculturalism and cross-fertilization of ideas among the various religions and philosophies of that time (Collins 1998: 80-133, 387-428). The cultural contexts was one of: "... multicultural exchange on the south-eastern periphery of the Roman Empire, where Hellenistic, Jewish, Iranian and Egptian ideas found an intellectually sophisticated meeting-place in Roman controlled Alexandria" (Mitchell 2006: 27). It is well known, for example, that Neo-Platonism influenced both early Christianity and various forms of gnosticism. The claim to spiritual exclusivity by the Roman Catholic Church meant that only the Church's magical nexus was acceptable. When Renaissance and Reformation era thinkers re-discovered the old "mysteries" it was an impetus toward modern science (Collins 1998: 429-569). Christopher Marlowe's play "*Faust*" (which was written circa 158-90) is viewed by Mitchell (2006: 41-50, 51-77) as highly symbolic of the transition. Many early natural scientists, like Isaac Newton, were more than a little bit like the legendary Faustus. An element of "gnosticism," in the first century multi-cultural sense, is still important for science today.

But recognition of a gnostic legacy in sociology would have been unacceptable in the early days when sociology was keen to become a Comtean positive science. What makes this paper possible is the intellectual context (or *Zeitgeist*) made possible by the "cultural turn" in sociological theory (Bonnell and Hunt 1999), especially since World War II. Bonnell and Hunt (1999: 8) divide the period from 1950-2000 into three major phases in the cultural turn in social science. The first two phases are more deeply connected to anthropology: (1.) the Semiological Revolution of Claude Levi-Strauss, based in part on Ferdinand de Saussure's comparative linguistics and *semiologie*, (2.) the Semioitic

Approach of "thick description" associated with Clifford Geertz and (3.) the more sociological phrase. The last phase involves complex sub-phases during the 1980s and 1990s, particularly the rise, popularity and fall of French Post-Structuralism and, eventually, Post-Modernism.

In the 21st century we are in a new, different phase, but the emphasis on Culture Studies and on the sociological re-discovery of "culture" has not abated. In the 1950s and in the 1970s the study of either Grant or Gandhi would not have been considered central to sociological theory. But now, I will argue, it is. In the *Post*-Postmodernist phase of cultural sociology (Smith 1998, Bharadwaj 2007) and "sub-cultural sociology" (Gelder 1997), sociological theory is expanding in new directions and it is possible to think of a "new sociological imagination."

Gandhi and Grant are important for the expanded intellectual horizons of the new sociological imagination. They are very much alike in certain striking ways. They are both the product of the later stages of the nineteenth century hegemonic British world capitalist empire, a major phase in what later came to be known as "globalization." India and Canada as contemporary nation-states are unthinkable without the British imperial presence in the nineteenth century. World War I was the "Great War" for the British, but it involves "British colonial" troops from all over the empire, making it truly a *world* war. Gandhi's political and sociological understanding was shaped by his periods of time outside of India, including South Africa and Great Britain, as well as his time in India. He became "cosmopolitan" and a "heretic" by isolationist, nineteenth century Hindu standards (Bakker 1993a). In a Postmodern Era when many French intellectuals have argued against all forms of "foundationalism" it is clear that the British laid a certain kind of legal and administrative foundation in India and Canada that has not entirely disappeared. There might still have been an India, but it would have been quite different than the current nation-state. Both countries are democracies and both have a vibrant intelligentsia, with many writers of both fiction and non-fiction who are internationally respected. Many of those writers and intellectuals come from a rich cultural background, due in part to family influences. Gandhi and Grant were products of the British Empire in all its glory.

George Grant might well not have become the public intellectual he was had it not been for his family background. His family is illustrious, although not rich. He was blessed with "cultural capital" (Bourdieu 1977: 63, 89, 183-187, 236), or what is also called "social capital" (Halpern 2005), but not with great family wealth. His family had what Weber calls "status" (*Stand*) but not necessarily economic class position (Weber 1968). Ancestors in Ontario and Nova Scotia were members of the local elites. Similarly, Gandhi came from an important Gujarati family, but he was not extremely wealthy. Gandhi was not from the Brahmin or Kshatria (*ksatriya*) caste, but his *Bania* caste status was not – in the final analysis – a major obstacle to getting a law degree in England. It was a difficult decision for him to go to England and leave India, thereby losing his caste status, but in the long run it was the right thing to do. He would not even have had the opportunity to make the choice to study law in England had it not been for his family background (Bakker 1993a). He had a nodding acquaintance with the *Bhagavad Gita* at an early age, but he really only started to study it intensively and memorize it studiously as a result of experiences he had with Theosophists in England (Bakker 1993b). Gandhi is a complex figure and it is difficult to summarize his worldview (Weltanschauung) in a few words. But it is clear that he was deeply "conservative" and progressively "radical" at the same time. He was a bundle of contradictions and no simple "naked fakir." He was a *sadhu* ("good man") and a yogin, in the most profound sense. In contemporary English the term "yogi" has gotten watered down. But the kind of "integration" with that which is higher and deeper (i.e. that which is considered "divine" and "noumenal") that characterizes true *jnana yoga* is certainly characteristic of Gandhi's profound understanding. To some extent he was a "heretic" with regard to the outward forms of Hinduism, but at a deeper and higher level he was a Mahatma (i.e. *maha-atman*, great soul).

Both Gandhi and Grant command respect among those who know their work. Grant is not a household name outside of Canada, but for those Canadian scholars and intellectuals who know about Canadian history Grant is an important contributor (Davis 1996). Similarly, while many people outside of India have heard of Gandhi, few have any detailed knowledge of what he did or what he wrote. I believe that anyone who studies the written work of Gandhi or Grant will gain a feeling of respect for their intellect and their deep grasp of major theological, philosophical, political and sociological issues.

Grant mentions Gandhi in some of his writings and in at least one letter. He wrote in a letter of June 1948: "Gandhi's death was a blow – but his being was of the quality that makes it possible for less clear lights like us to know where to go" (Grant 1996: 148). In a critique of the New Left written in 1966 he mentions Gandhi again. "The greatest figure of our era, Gandhi, was interested in public actions and in political liberty, but he knew that the right direction of that action had to be based on a knowledge of reality – with all the discipline and order and study that that entailed" (Grant 1998;). Grant wrote that sentence after having just mentioned "the central Christian platitude" that the "truth shall make you free." The kind of Biblical "truth" that Grant is referring to is not Enlightenment scientific truth but a deeper and higher type of insight, a "knowledge of reality." It is fascinating that the way in which Gandhi and Grant conceptualized the idea of knowledge of reality is very similar. Their epistemological positions are not precisely the same, but they are on a very similar wavelength. That is why it is reasonable to consider the extent to which Grant was also a kind of *jnana yogin*, even though he himself might have resisted that label. He might have resisted the non-Christian reading of the term, but he probably would have accepted it as a kind of cosmopolitan allegory of more universalistic qualities.

Nevertheless, while there are many aspects of their outlooks that I find stimulating and thought-provoking, they are not necessarily as well-rounded in their views as one would wish. The key aspect of their thought – taken at a very abstract theological and philosophical level (Collins 1998) – that I have a bit of difficulty with is that they frequently do not take a comparative and historical *sociological* view of key issues. They were not sociological theorists. But their ideas do have clear implications for sociological theory in the 21st century. Due to the background of debates of the 1980s and 1990s, we are able to understand their sociological relevance to interdisciplinary social science more clearly now

> *They are no longer alive and therefore they are not able to keep up with twenty-first century trends in* Post-Post Modernist *avant-garde theory. Their work is timeless, but it is no longer at the cutting edge, especially in terms of the basic formulation of the ideas. But, even more fundamentally, they sometimes lack what I call "the new sociological imagination." It will be part of the burden of this chapter to try to make it clear what I mean by that. Essentially I have in mind a new philosophical and meta-theoretical approach to the social sciences, especially my own discipline of sociology, an approach that leans heavily on Neo-Pragmatist epistemology. Gandhi and Grant have important contributions to make; but, it would be a mistake to limit our understanding to a literal reading of their ideas.*

The phrase "the sociological imagination" is usually associated with a famous book by a well-known sociologist, C. [Charles] Wright Mills. But here the emphasis is not on following that thinker. Instead, we must move beyond him and his limited formulation of the sociological imagination. He was too caught up in disproving other directions and died too early to fully articulate his own vision. We must move, I believe, in a direction associated with Neo-Pragmatism and the underlying epistemological ideas associated with Charles Sanders Peirce's semiotics. Obviously that is a tall order for a relatively short essay. To fully elaborate the notion of a new sociological imagination will require a book length treatment.[2]

It will not be possible to discuss everything in detail. That would require discussing epistemological, ontological, axiological, teleological, and other issues, in depth. But I would like to at least sketch some basic ideas that will, I hope, help not only to illuminate some of the similarities and differences between Grant and Gandhi but also help to provide a somewhat broader framework for understanding. Seeing Grant and Gandhi through a lens that has been shaped by Mills and Peirce is a difficult thing to do. It would be far easier to simply rehearse the well-known facts of Gandhi's life and thought and compare and contrast Gandhi with the Canadian philosopher George Grant. But I would like to do more than that. I would like this essay to be part of an initial exploration of the deep theological and philosophical issues that Grant and Gandhi explore. Instead of approaching those issues as a theologian or as a philosopher I will approach them as a sociologist.[3]

I believe that we must approach sociological questions with a renewed awareness, for example, of the "body" (Roberts 2006) and the "soul" or "spirit" (*Geist*) (Reimers 2006). It is not just a question of "mind" or "Reason." That is not a popular position to take. Most sociological theory – and even most sociological "meta-theory" – is based on axioms that stem from a somewhat simplistic materialist view. The European Enlightenment – which Grant considered a mistake and which Gandhi also rejected – is not the basis for a holistic understanding. However, the term "Enlightenment" can be extended to cover the "Radical Enlightenment" associated with Spinoza (Israel 2001). I believe that both Gandhi and Grant would have been more favorably disposed to that later phase in European thought. A strictly materialist ontology is based on Neo-Cartesian notions of scientific "objectivity." We have to move beyond a simplistic seventeenth century mind-body dualism (Dicker 1993). In order to do that, we have to re-examine many meta-theoretical, sociological questions. That process started during the Radical Enlightenment and continued during the rise of modern science and modern disciplines. Even the rise of philosophy as a separate university discipline – completely separate from theology – is a major step toward what we now think of as the social sciences. It can be argued that many of the important ideas that we associate with the 21st century sociological articulation of the global "culture" concept can be found in embryo in Hegel's early work and hs later dialectical phenomenology (Russon 2004: 198, 216, 227-28).

Part of that re-examination involves thinking with a willingness to move from Baruch ("Benedict") Spinoza's "least parts" to "greatest wholes" (Sacksteder 1991). We must move rapidly from part to whole and from whole to part in our thinking. Moreover, we need to think what the "whole" is really all about. That expanded horizon requires a Neo-Pragmatist outlook suitable for changed circumstances in the global twenty-first century.

In part the re-conceptualization of the sociological imagination discussed here goes well with Robert K. Merton's discussion of "serendipity" in science (Merton and Barber 2004158-198). If we are truly going to utilize the whole intellectual "web" to match the "web of life" we have to be open to fortuitous, serendipitous discoveries.

This analysis of George Grant and M. K. Gandhi stresses their views on the "web of our life." They had an ecumenical approach to religious beliefs and worldviews (*Weltanschauungen*). They utilized a form of *gnosis* or *jnana*. Their open-minded ways of thinking are deeply "conservative" in the sense that they wish to maintain all that is good from the past. But both thinkers are also radical in the way in which they conceptualize the future. One way that Grant and Gandhi can be understood is by utilizing the "new sociological imagination" that incorporates not only C. Wright Mills' original (1959) ideas but also more recent theories concerning a web approach to sociology and the part/whole relationship in hermeneutics and semiotics. It is argued here that despite their brilliance both Grant and Gandhi lacked certain theoretical resources which would have made their theories even more relevant for the twenty-first century.

Mills' famous book (1959) is mentioned here in order to set the stage. His discussion of the craftsmanship involved in utilizing the sociological imagination is based on his intuitive grasp of sociology as a calling. In Part Two that sense of craftsmanship is then applied to understanding in the social sciences and history. What is the relevance of a re-conceptualized sociological imagination for social change? Grant and Gandhi tend to emphasize a more intuitive approach to knowledge than is currently accepted by somewhat simplistic views concerning the scientific method. Intuition goes together with metaphysical worldviews (Davis 2004). Part Three extends the idea to education more generally, with some thoughts on the education of body and spirit as well as mind. The new sociological imagination requires incorporating insights from Gandhi, Grant, Mills and contemporary Peircian semiotics in order to move back and forth from "least parts" to "greatest wholes" (Scheff 2007) in any sociological inquiry.

The distinction that Mills makes between stereotypes of Grand Theory (e.g. Talcott Parsons) and Abstracted Empiricism (e.g. Paul Lazarsfeld) is well known in outline in sociology. However, few sociologists take his recommendations concerning a sociological imagination involving the craftsmanship of Classical Theory and Methods (e.g. Marx, Weber, Durkheim, Simmel, Mead) seriously. For Mills there is only one kind of sociology, the kind associated with the Classical approach. He presents this idea as an intuition and does not really defend it through a deeper analysis. A broader horizon is required. We can grasp that broader viewpoint if we add the "radical conservative" and "heretical" views of Grant and Gandhi to the equation.

Somewhat surprisingly, since he is often considered a Neo-Marxist, Mills' approach tends to be limited to the more "metaphysical" and intuitive as well. In a word, he is concerned with *gnosis*. In Sanskrit the same concept is referred to a *jnana*. The sociology student, particularly the graduate student, is conceptualized by Mill as more like an apprentice than a "theorist" who speculates without data or a "methodologist" who puzzles over data without thinking about ultimate theoretical goals. For Mills both tend to only fit in with "bureaucratic" and organizational agendas. There is a grain of truth to that. But, for Mills the mature scholar is primarily an independent thinker and "public intellectual" (Possner 2003). Such a thinker is not, by definition, a positivist scientist or a social philosopher and "theorist." In the conclusion it is recommended that a re-conceptualized "sociological imagination" involving a *combined* "Part/Whole" and "Web" Approach involves mind, body and spirit. A theory that does not pay attention to all three is bound to be unnecessarily limited and limiting. Hence, a complete synthesis of approaches to social science and history should not necessarily be restricted to Mills' specific meaning of the sociological imagination as *the* one approach. We should consider ways in which the sociological imagination can be expanded to provide a broader horizon encompassing the whole web of theories and methods, not merely a kind of "middle range" between ungrounded GT and reductionistic AE. Such an expanded vision is what I call "the new sociological imagination."

In a recent essay on one such Neo-Pragmatist approach (labeled "Pragmatist Hermeneutics") Dmitri Shalin (2007) points out that a disembodied view of the sociological imagination leads to error. The body and the spirit are as important to knowledge as the mind. Cognition (in the narrow sense) is never adequate if it is not "embodied." Greek philosophers like Socrates and Plato expressed the idea that thinking can be contaminated by the body. Descartes' mind-body dualism (Dicker 1993) is based on the argument that what a human being really is (i.e. one's soul) must be entirely distinct from the corporeal body. Masculine "Rationality" is a "faculty" often seen as the opposite of "feminine emotionality" by many rationalist philosophers (e.g. Kant 1996).

Some authors have tended to think that "structure" (e.g. de Saussure's *langue*) is much more important than "process" (e.g. *parole*). Indeed, in the study of language as a human phenomenon it has often been the rational grammatical structure that has been given precedence

(Bakker 2007a). The Scientific Revolution involved emphasis on rapid-discovery science and that form of science was often perceived as only possible through the application of "mind" in a strictly rational manner (Bakker 2007c, 2007d). Yet, a "meta-analysis" of the epistemological and ontological issues involved (Bakker 2007b) can lead to a different outlook, one that stresses mind and body. Without the full spectrum of mind, body and soul one is likely to have less that a full understanding. A "Web Approach" requires making linkages among all three (Phillips 2001). If we merely think in a way that is disembodied and that is "bureaucratically" lacking in "soul" then we are not likely to arrive at pragmatic answers to burning social issues.

But how precisely can one accomplish the utilization of mind, body and soul all at once? William James (1958: 146-148), in his "Talks to Students," advocates that a certain "strenuous relaxation" is necessary. The key idea in this paper is that a Web Approach requires us to be open to the complex inter-relatedness of various kinds of knowledge and learning. Hence, while C. Wright Mills is in some ways a model for pedagogy, we should also be aware of some of the limitations of Mills' approach. Mills comes close to the Web Approach and the Part/Whole Approach, but he cannot be considered a good guide to a full understanding of the inter-relatedness of all three. The importance of this topic was underlined long ago by Durkheim (1956, 1977).

Mills' Sociological Imagination

Mills was not a balanced person who could see the value of perspectives that did not entirely agree with his own. He was not, in the best sense of that word, a *yogin*. His gnosis was not tempered by a meditative awareness. He was not deeply in touch with body and spirit. To some extent we can say metaphoridcally that he was all "mind." He had a Socratic gadfly function as a public intellectual in a time when Marxist ideas of any kind were dismissed and when American intellectuals were less and less prone to go public

(Posner 2003: 1-220).[4] He was strident in his criticisms of practically everyone. His combativeness is revealed in his highly rhetorical dismissal of what he called "abstracted empiricism" (AI) and "grand theory" (GT). His views on what the sociological imagination consists of are limited and partial. The new sociological imagination would not dismiss all versions of "grand theory" or "abstracted empiricism" in the broader sense implied by mind, body and spirit. We can be wary of extreme forms of GT and AE without necessarily accepting all aspects of Mills diatribes against straw man characterizations of the work of Talcott Parsons and Paul Lazarsfeld.

As stated, the phrase "sociological imagination" is associated with C. Wright Mills (1916-1962), but it does not have to be limited to that one historical individual. Baruch ("Benedict") Spinoza (Sacksteder 1991) and Charles Sanders Peirce (Scheff 2007) are particularly important for the new sociological imagination. The new sociological imagination requires paying attention not only to the mind, but also to the body and the spirit.

When I invoke the "sociological imagination" I do not mean the specific sociological imagination associated with Mills. In other words, the sociological imagination is not just what Mills said. It is a spirit or an ethos; it is a gnosis or jnana. The mature scholar exercising the sociological imagination is an independent thinker and public intellectual. That is true, for example, of both Gandhi and Grant. Mills' gnosis/jnana about the role of the sociological imagination in the life of a sociologist is not, however, complete. A complete understanding of either Gandhi or Grant involves a complete use of body, mind and spirit to fully appreciate all that they have to offer.

When *Charles* Wright Mills (1916-1962)[5] put out his famous book *The Sociological Imagination* in 1959 he had already had seven books published. He also had published two major "classic" articles (Mills 1940, 1943) when he was still a graduate student. Two of his books were co-authored with Hans H. Gerth. The Gerth and Mills (1946) volume is frequently cited by those who wish to refer to the work of Max Weber, and it is clear that some of Weber's ideas concerning "domination" (*Herrschaft*) influenced Mills significantly in his analysis of the power elite. However, the other Gerth and Mills book, published in 1953, *Character and Social Structure*, is not nearly as famous or widely-read and cited today. *THE* Gerth and Mills (1946) book is the Weber volume. The translations would have been mainly done by Gerth, since Mills does not do any further scholarly work involving translation from German into English. Mills' three most famous single-authored books are *The New Men of Power* (1948), *White Collar* (1951) and *The Power Elite* (1956). They examine labor leaders, the new middle class and the elite.

Since Mills died early, at age forty-two, he did not leave a large number of additional works after *The Sociological Imagination* came out. (He died in 1962 and the book was published in 1959). Collins and Makowsky (1998: 238) call *The Sociological Imagination* Mills' "most important contribution." But that judgment could be challenged. It *is* his definitive statement on the nature of theory and methodology. Even if he had lived to a ripe old age it is not likely that he would have significantly modified the views expressed in that a fairly succinct (234 page) book. It does present his views on the "craft" of sociology. But it is more of a work of polemic than a balanced assessment of others' views. It is not, of course, a contribution to pedagogy per se. Mills was in some ways a "utopian" thinker (Horowitz 1983), an American variant of Ancient Greek thinkers like Plato. He was very much in his "mind" (i.e. his "symbolic-discursive" self) and not particularly well attuned to his "body" or "spirit." His progressive, radical ideology was based on an intuition (gnosis) of justice and not necessarily a carefully thought out philosophy (i.e. not a gnosis involving a fully-balanced integration of mind, body and spirit; see Shalin 2007).

The principal contention that Mills presents is that sociology as a discipline was suffering from two evils. He labeled those two destructive tendencies "Grand Theory" (GT) and "Abstracted Empiricism" (AE). He did not utilize those words in any kind of neutral manner. Instead, they are terms of derision. Mills uses the two labels in a thoroughly rhetorical manner as terms of approbation He has nothing good to say about either GT or AE. The terms, used in Mills' unqualified and rhetorical manner, are thoroughly mis-leading to students. Mills writes about GT and AE to warn students concerning the wrong ways to do sociology, and social science and history generally. A student who is sucked into either GT or AE, Mills argues, is likely to go off the right path and never find his way back again. He used them as terms of derision and he did not pull any punches in his mockery of them. That is part of the reason the book caught on. It packs a punch. It is easy reading, especially the first few chapters. It is good rhetoric but bad social science.

However, what is missing from Mills' analysis of "Grand Theory" (GT) is any attempt to apply some of the same rhetorical techniques to some of the classical social and sociological theorists: Kant, Hegel, Nietzsche, Marx, Max Weber, Simmel, Pareto, Durkheim, Mead, DuBois, Addams, Nightingale, Martineau, Marianne Weber, Adorno, Horkheimer, Benjamin, Gandhi, Grant, and so forth. The one and only example of the excesses of GT is Talcott Parsons. So, Mills is not entirely fair. He cites Franz Neumann's (1942) *Behemoth* as an example of how to do it right; but, Neumann's analysis has not been all that influential in sociological theory. It is an excellent historically-based analysis of the financing of the National Socialist (Nazi) Party, but today it is mostly known by specialists. Few sociologists would list Neumann as a leading classical sociological theorist, even though his work is cited by authors like Barrington Moore, Jr.

Indeed, when Mills chooses his heroes he chooses some of the better known classical sociological theorists. But he never makes that more sophisticated argument that at times Marx, Weber and Durkheim are just as obscure as

Parsons. Marx's *Capital* (Volumes I, II and III) and *Theories of Surplus Value* (Volumes I, II and III) are often summarized in one short volume. Weber's (1968 [1920]) *Economy and Society* consists of two major Parts, with Part II actually the one that was written first and with Part I sometimes contradicting Part II. Durkheim is often quite straightforward in his writing style, but it would be possible to summarize the central thrust of *The Elementary Forms of Religious Life* (Durkheim 1995 [1912]) in one short paper. Mills does not bother to point any of that out. Hence, the confusion which still exists as to exactly what the term grand theory is supposed to mean.

When we discuss "The Whole" it is possible to conceive of many different ontological views (Feuer 1958). As used by Mills the term GT is a rhetorical label and nothing but a rhetorical label. It is "the Other" in Mills' schema. As such it serves a useful purpose if, and only if, we can accept Mills' positive statement of belief in "Classical Theory."

It is a form of *gnosis*. I will discuss the spirit of his key idea in terms of a more refined understanding of "Gnosticism" (King 2004) and that will lead into a fuller conceptualization of gnosis. A complete education involves the body, for example in terms of *hatha* yoga, gymnastics, calisthenics and/or athletics. That is, if Mills is to be taken seriously then we have to view the sociological imagination in Socratic terms and situate Greek philosophy historically. I will not attempt to do that in any complete fashion here. Mills presents only a part of the picture.

Gandhi

When I collected together some essay about Gandhi in book form more than a decade ago (Bakkker 1993a, Bakker 1993b) it was not a matter of sitting down to write a unified book. I had composed various papers and they seemed to fit together. I had learned a little bit about satyagraha from various teachers affiliated with the Gandhi Peace Foundation and the *Sarva Seva Sangh*, many of whom had known Gandhi personally. I did not really set out to write a great deal about Gandhi but learning more about Gandhi's social theory became an exciting exploration. My students had read photocopies of the papers and said to me that they were pleased to learn more about Gandhi. They had been taught about all of the standard sociological theorists (Ritzer 2008), but they had never learned anything about Gandhi in their sociology courses. To this day, Gandhi is not considered a significant contributor to the academic discipline of sociology in Australia, Canada, the United States, or the European Union. He is not given more than passing mention in most textbooks in social science. When he is discussed it is usually in the context of his political stand against British Imperialism. He is not viewed as a social scientist and his ideas are not seen as an aspect of social scientific theorizing. To say the least, that is short-sighted.

Gandhi's social philosophy and social theory is relevant to many contemporary issues. One of the most significant issues confronting everyone on the planet is the potential for environmental disaster. The bio-physical environment is slowly becoming less and less sustainable. Global warming is now recognized by all reputable physical and life scientists as more than a myth. In a recent address the Canadian public intellectual Gwynne Dyer remarked that while at one time he had thought it was just a matter of a threat to a few polar bears in the Far North he now realizes that environmental catastrophe is just around the corner. He explained how carbon-based fuel pollution carried by international wind currents are creating larger and larger deserts, cutting into arable land.[6] While there is considerable controversy about the details, the general thesis that global warming is a serious problem is accepted by most responsible scientists and philosophers. One of the key problems is the increased demand for consumer goods and services, including items that were considered to be only luxuries even in the countries that have been industrialized for a long time.

Gandhi was very clear on the issue of appropriate technology. He was not inalterably opposed to all modern technological innovations. But he did feel strongly that new technologies and new forms of consumer goods and services must be developed in such a way that the majority of people will benefit. If global warming leads to environmental disasters related to cycles of excessive heat and cold and strange fluctuations in rain and drought then ordinary people will not benefit in the long run. Clearly the effects of global warming on food production, combined with even minimal levels of increase in world population, will eventually lead to significant problems. The Gandhian perspective has often been considered to be old fashioned. But as circumstances change the relevance of Gandhi's thinking concerning *swadeshi* becomes crystal clear once again.

The issue of hunger – and various other aspects of general "food in-security" – is a very real issue. Secure access to nutritious food will continue to be a problem for millions of people. The problem has not been solved and is not going to go away. Technological solutions will only get us so far. When we are not dealing with famine and hunger, malnourishment is often a serious concern. Families that earn a dollar a day often cannot afford to buy the kinds of food required to avoid major health problems, like diabetes in women who have had several pregnancies. A young diabetic mother can go blind. That makes her much less able to do what is necessary to raise her small children. The phrase "the world food crisis" was given a great deal of mass media coverage in 1973-74. Major international initiatives in the later 1970s helped to alleviate some of the most pressing problems; but then the Sahelian drought and major famines in several parts of the world hit the headlines in the 1980s (Bakker 1990: 5). There have been waves of public interest and public apathy. But in light of global warming the idea of a world food crisis occurring in many parts of the world sometime in mid-century is not at all unreasonable to consider. Floods and droughts disrupt food production. By the year 2050 the international production of food will not supply the global need for quality food at a standard that will suit rising expectations. If everyone were satisfied with a bowl of rice and a few vegetables the problem could be postponed for a long time. But more and more consumers wish to eat meat products that require a great expenditure of petro-chemical resources. The grain that feeds the cattle, pigs and poultry is utilized in such a way that far fewer human beings can be fed than if that same grain were utilized directly.

Gandhi was not just an ivory tower intellectual. While his knowledge of econometrics and tectonic plate theory was probably very limited, and he could not claim to be an expert in geomorphology, he nevertheless understood many things about basic human needs (Bakker 1993a). Ironically, at the same time that in many parts of the world the needs of most people have to be met by a dollar or two a day, there is a glut of material goods in many industrialized nations. One of the most ironic aspects of the global situation is the rise of obesity. There is an epidemic of poor nutrition in countries where the average per capita income is ten or twenty times higher than in less developed nations. While over one hundred million people suffer from malnourishment every day, a vastly greater number of people suffer from excess. What we need is a balance between needs and wants. That requires more than the expertise that comes from such specialized academic subjects as macro economics or the sociology of organizations.

One aspect of Gandhi's thought that makes him difficult for many people in North America is that Gandhi's cultural context is not perfectly familiar. Unless one has spent at least three or four months in India the whole subcontinent is a bit mysterious. Even a year or two is really not enough unless one learns at least one Indian language and makes a sincere effort to experience many different life styles, rural as well as urban, poor as well as middle class and elite. Popular mass media sources, including nineteenth century British novels and twentieth century Hollywood films, make India seem foreign. There is a great deal of what Edward Said called "Orientalism" in the average person's perceptions of everything related to India, Pakistan and Bangladesh. For the average North American intellectual it is far easier to understand many aspects of the work of Grant.

Grant

Grant writes in the context of Western European intellectual history. Unlike Gandhi, he is not someone who has explored Indian religions in great depth. For Grant, Pato is far more important than Shankaracharya and the Christian *Bible* is more directly a source of inspiration than the *Bhagavad Gita* (Bakker 1993b). While he was very well read and explored many religions on the basis of a comparative understanding of different faiths, he had not direct experience with *jnana yoga*. His *gnosis* was Greco-Roman and Christian. (It may not even have been "Judeo-Christian" and it certainly was not "Judeo-Christian-Islamic.") As a Canadian nationalist he was not keen on the United States but it is not clear that he had a deep knowledge of America. (Many Canadians know a great deal about America, but only at the level of the outside observer.)

William Christian has done a great deal to clarify our knowledge of Grant. Most of what little I know about George Grant comes from Professor Christian's excellent books. What I gather from those books is that Grant was not necessarily a profound philosopher. He does not seem to have developed a consistent philosophical system. He is not comparable to, say, Immanuel Kant or Georg Wilhelm Friederich Hegel. We can, of course, criticize Kant and Hegel for all kinds of good reasons, but their vast outpouring of philosophical writing commands almost universal respect, even from harsh critics like Nietzsche and Heidegger. Grant is not a philosopher of the same caliber as the most highly respected and most frequently discussed contributors to the discipline of philosophy. It is quite possible that in another hundred years his books will be largely forgotten. (It is less likely that Gandhi will be forgotten in another century, but his written work is not the main basis for his fame.) Yet, even if he is not a super star, Grant is a powerful voice.

What Grant argues very clearly is that the history of Western Civilization needs to be analyzed on the basis of a clear conceptualization of intellectual history. He goes back to the earliest Greek philosophers, particularly Plato, and makes it clear that certain Platonic (and Neo-Platonic) ideas mean a great deal to him, both intellectually and personally. He is an independent thinker. His iconoclastic views run counter to the commonly held opinions that undergraduates are taught in most lecture courses on the history of philosophy. His deeply held, but largely idiosyncratic, religious faith is quite contrary to the more materialistic aspects of Post-Enlightenment European – and consequently North American – thinking. Grant would not have any difficulty, for example, in seeing the merit of a book like the recent contribution by Adrian Reimers (2006) entitled *The Soul of the Person*.

Body, Mind and Spirit: Gnosis and Jnana

If we do not simply accept Mills' statements at face value but extract from his classic book that which is of lasting value – somewhat in the same way as Croce tried to distill that which was still living in Hegel – then we find an enthusiastic argument in favor of a sociological imagination that is not merely a matter of using one's analytical skills. Sociology, for Mills, is not just a cognitive task, a limited "bureaucratic" role (in the negative sense).[7] It is not simply an alienating "9 to 5 job" such as that of a temp worker. For Mills it is a calling. The word "calling" (Weber's *Beruf*) does not appear in the Index. But it seems clear enough that for Mills there is almost a religious significance to being a social scientist. He caustically derides all those who would approach research as merely a matter of applying existing techniques. Part of the reason the book caught on with so many graduate students of my generation in the 1960s was precisely that it severely criticized the very things we were so painfully required to learn: non-parametric statistical tests, regression analysis, factor analysis and other such techniques. They were *de rigueur*. You could not be a sociologist without those tools in your backpack. Seemingly the only way out was to either become a "theorist" (i.e. know a lot about the history of classical theory) or opt for cultural/social anthropology (where quantitative methods were less emphasized in those days).

Many of us "baby boomers" did accept the idea of sociology as a calling. After all, we could almost as easily have become something else. We could have studied any of the humanistic disciplines, like philosophy or art history. We could have studied one of the professions, like medicine, law or library science. We could have done M.B.A.s. There were many avenues open to the better than average students of sociology in the 1960s in North America and Europe. But we chose sociology. If we did not choose it in order to do AE or GT then we often chose it in order to do some kind of sociological imagination-based sociology.[8] I myself was not interested in being a technician. Indeed, when I had the opportunity to specialize in urban planning and architecture I returned to general sociology.[9] I wanted to pursue the sociological imagination. It is even somewhat surprising to me that I really have managed to support myself and my family, while still always engaged in the pursuit of that calling.[10]

While there is much that is rewarding about pursuing social science as a calling, it is not always easy to strive to fulfill the sociological imagination. Even if one were to restrict one's attention simply to the SI in the stereotypical fashion that Mills sometimes reverts to, it would not be easy. But to strive to broaden the sociological imagination even beyond the point that Mills was able to reach is quite challenging. Yet it is a challenge that is worth it. It may be easier under some circumstances to get tenure or promotion by pursuing AE, or even GT (in certain specialized circumstances), the lasting value of striving for the ideal of the sociological imagination is that it makes one's life better. Mills' discussion of the craftsmanship involved in utilizing the sociological imagination is based on an intuitive grasp of sociology as a calling. The distinction that Mills makes between the stereotypes of Grand Theory (e.g. Parsons as a GT) and Abstracted Empiricism (e.g. Lazarsfeldians as AE) is well known in sociology. But, few sociologists seriously examine his intuitive recommendations concerning a sociological imagination. We can apply the expanded sense of craftsmanship to education in the social sciences and history. A very broad vision is required, one that is even broader than Mills' vision. We need to have a very wide horizon and be willing to go up and down the ladder of abstraction (Part/Whole) while also scanning all inter-relationships (the Web).

The other structure of thinking is web-like. The key to the web approach is to examine ideas as having many linkages. It is a more "ecological" or "evolutionary" approach that involves looking at the ways in which ideas branch out over time. The simplified form of the web approach to thinking involves bifurcation. The term is derived from the Latin (*bi* + *furca*) and means "two-pronged" or "forked." In other words, the simplest web is a fork in the road. But a web involves not just one fork; it involves many forks, like the branches on a tree. It is an approach that emphasizes the "genesis" or "evolution" of ideas or things. It tends to have an historical component.

The key difference between a web-bifurcation approach and a dichotomized approach is that dichotomies tend to appear to come out of nowhere, while a web or bifurcation involves paying attention to inter-linkages. At the very least, if we have a fork in the road we know where we have come from; we know the path that led us to that split. The two-prongs are not simply polarities in some kind of absolute "space." As the saying goes, if you come to a fork in the road, take it! But when you take it you know where you have taken it, and (usually) why. Even if it was just a whim (like tossing a coin), you know a reason why that particular choice was made. It is concretely situated. A fuller discussion of the sociological imagination by Mills might have involved tracing the way in which classical theorists like Max Weber sometimes often got involved in theoretical speculations that are somewhat "grand". Mills could also have examined more carefully how the importance of empirical research and inductive use of evidence might lead to a somewhat specialized appreciation of empiricism. It is simply not the case that all detailed empirical studies are merely AE. Ideas are contextual. A fully "pragmatic" understanding puts the evolution of ideas into an embodied historical context that includes the somatic and "performative" as well as the discursive (Shalin 2007: 198).[11]

William James' 1892 lectures to teachers and to students convey that kind of pragmatic outlook. Ideas do not just float in space. They are concretely situated in practical choice. James (1958; 149-169) warns us against what he calls "a certain blindness in human beings." He makes it clear that no one has the whole of the truth or manifests the whole of goodness. We should, James argues, make the most of what we have and not presume to dictate to others what they should do. We should not regulate a whole field of inquiry or teaching. To some extent it might have been wise for Mills to have paid attention to James' "Talks." Yet, surprisingly, Mills does not really become deeply involved in American Pragmatist thinking (Shalin 2007).

Mills was mainly interested in teaching as a form of "Drawing Out." That is, he wanted to get students to rely on their intuitive understanding. To put it in one word, Mills advocates the goal that the Greek philosophers refer to as *gnosis*. The term is difficult to translate. Mills is ultimately a great deal more like Socrates, who is reported to have said, "Know Thyself!" (*gnothi seauton*). Mills' "Socratic" approach to knowledge is both his strength and his weakness. We can get an appreciation for the way in which Mills' emphasis on intuitive knowledge is inter-connected with other forms of knowledge – and of teaching – if we do not think in terms of simple dichotomies but instead focus on branches of the complex web that was American social science in the 1950s. A Web Approach will reveal more about Mills' implicit pedagogy than a more linear approach.

The new sociological imagination requires a certain degree of reflexivity and self-awareness. If we think of ourselves primarily as "talking heads" that move around from place to place on top of a much neglected physical body conceptualized as a stick figure then we are not as likely to be able to utilize a well integrated sense of body, mind and spirit (Phillips 2001). Most academic education is based on cultivating the mind. Many academics neglect the fact that they are not merely disembodied minds. A more holistic view of "self" helps to integrate body and mind. It can also lead to a re-conceptualization of the concept of "soul" (Dicker 1993).

Anecdote: Learning Through Experience

A concrete, personal example of a learning experience involving body, mind and spirit is a learning experience that took place recently at Kripalu Yoga Center in the beautiful Berkshire Mountains. The last workshop I was assigned to as a program assistant was a "Quest for the Limitless You" led by long-time Kripalu resident Atma Jo Ann Levitt. It was a rich and rewarding five days. Although there was considerable "gopher" work in that workshop as well (e.g. getting supplies ready), I was nevertheless allowed to also participate in many of the activities. Of course, when not in the workshop I was doing my yoga exercises at 6:00 AM and 4:15 PM and occasionally swimming and jogging. I was eating very nutritious food and getting to bed, dead tired, at 9:30 or 10:00 at night. I consumed no caffeine and no alcohol. To say the least, that is not my regular lifestyle when I am "at work" doing my normal teaching and administrative duties. It allowed me to connect with my body and "soul." To some extent I was able to be more than a "mind" attached to a stick figure.

A meaningful educational experience for me took place toward the end of the workshop. We were asked to suspend disbelief and do a visualization exercise. The exercise involved deep breathing and then guided imagery. I went through with it, setting aside my doubts about such work, and had a wonderful imaginary "trip." No drugs were involved, just deep breathing. I imagined, at the end of the half hour, that I was in Shangri-la (*Shambhala*). I was in paradise. It was an entirely enjoyable experience. I was there in my mind, but it also felt as if I was there in body and spirit. For a brief period of time I had a very interesting visualization, a fleeting glimpse of paradise.

No doubt some of you have seen the old black and white movie Shangri-la. The movie is based on a famous novel, once widely read, by James Hilton, which is called *Lost Horizon*. I incorporated elements from the novel and the movie in my imaginary voyage of self discovery. But I actually did "see," at least in my mind's eye, a very improved, twenty-first century version of Shangri-la/ Shambhala. It was, in a sense, the "city on the hill" that a famous Puritan divine, John Winthrop first mentioned and that Ronald Reagan (as well as many other politicians) spoke of. But it was hardly a "puritanical" place. Nor was it a particularly Buddhist or Hindu place either. It was something akin to the "liberal" and "republican" idea that Spinoza envisaged (Feuer 1958). It was a "Peaceful Kingdom," but not the kind of kingdom or princely domain we get in operetta. The closest thing to what I experienced may be Martin Luther King, Jr.'s "I have a dream" speech. It was a brief but powerful insight into a better world. It was the kind of better society I had hinted at in my book on Gandhi's social theory (Bakker 1993a) though hardly "scientific" (Bakker 2007d). Ultimately such a vision requires a "Part/Whole Approach" (Sacksteder 1991).[12] One might even say it requires an awareness of the "web of existence." To arrive at such an insight, or gnosis, is a matter of being in the body and not just in the mind. That, in turn, is part of an open-ness to serendipity (Merton and Barber 2004).

Origins of Sociology in Revolutionary Change

Now, that anecdote may seem out of place in an essay on re-conceptualizing Mills' sociological imagination – even if we accept the idea that serendipity plays a big role in the sciences, physical, biological and social. Let me attempt to explain why I feel that my narrative account is not extraneous. In order to make that clear we have to take a brief look at why there is a discipline called sociology (French *sociologie,* German *Soziologie*).[13] If we are discussing the "sociological" imagination, then what is that? Why is it a specifically *sociological* imagination?

One of the main reasons that there is a discipline called sociology is because the Industrial and Agricultural Revolutions of the eighteenth century greatly transformed Europe. Those who became sociologists were concerned about changes in their own society. Eventually the intense interest in the nature of social order in times of revolutionary change in the Netherlands, France, Germany or Great Britain led to the comparative study of different societies (Weber 1968 [1920]; Durkheim 1995 [1912]). As is well known the United States Constitution of 1783 is based in part on the European Enlightenment traditions that were formulated by Dutch, French, German and British thinkers in the eighteenth century. Those aspects of the Constitution which were considered to not be adequate in terms of Enlightenment values were, in part, "repaired" by Thomas Jefferson and other "men of 1801," a little known part of the story (Ackerman 2005: 14-30, 266). Now the United States still tries to uphold those Enlightenment beliefs to some extent, but there is considerable political confusion (Ricks 2007).

The Jeffersonian ideals have become largely just a memory as agriculture has become the main occupation of less than three percent of the population. The yeoman "family farmer" of the eighteenth century exists today largely only in the imagination of writers like Wendell Berry. For the most part it is not in everyday reality in New Hampshire or Iowa. There are a few real family farms left in Vermont and Idaho, but by and large agro-business has taken over. This is not the place to launch into an extended discussion of the ways in which the United States of the twenty-first century could not possibly have been imagined by the founders in the eighteenth century. Nor should the details of the Enlightenment values of those involved in the Presidential election of 1801 (Ackerman 2005) be rehearsed here, but clearly much has changed.

Yet what has not changed about America (and Canada) is an optimistic sense of open opportunity: "the American Dream." Everyone, it is felt, can rise in the stratification system, from rags to riches. America is still often spoken of as the land of opportunity. For some it has been and still is. The more general reality, as indicated very well by C. Wright Mills (1951, 1956) may be quite different. Mills was one of the few "public intellectuals" (Possner 2003) to speak out about the importance of social class and inequality in American life. But the "American Dream" remains. That is a dream of individual human dignity and worth. The current political and economic climate is one of deep division in part because many people disagree fundamentally as to how best to accomplish that dream. For some it requires going back to fundamental spiritual values. For others it requires changing with the times. But regardless of whether an American citizen lives in a so-called blue or red state, or in a state which some may regard as a "purple" mixture, the Goal is much the same. The struggle is about means and not ends. Do we stay with the Protestant Ethic and the Puritan version of the city on the hill? Or do we move to a New Age Ethic and a Post-Modern version of the city on the hill? Do we radically conserve or do we radically change? Do we continue to pursue a war (or several wars) or do we draw back from armed conflict (Ricks 2007)? How can the realization of the American Dream be accomplished by ordinary middle-class and working-class citizens?

Part V: The New Sociological Imagination

The larger context is always going to be part of the necessary background to any meaningful analysis of a sociological phenomenon like insight (e.g. insight into the nature of "society and the individual" the takes the "Part/

Whole Approach" into account). It is a matter of seeing all of the historical branches and not just making analytical dichotomies (Davis 2004). A "pragmatic" approach is required to really comprehend the meaning of terms like Gnosticism and gnostic insight or Christianity and messianic leadership. King cites Abelson (1967:322):

> *Definitions are good if and only if they serve the purpose for which they are intended. Thus, an evaluation of a definition must being with the identification of the point or purpose of the definition, and this requires knowledge of the discursive situation [context] in which the need for the definition arises ...*

Before we can settle on what any sociological phenomenon "really is" (or was) we need to become fully aware of *why* it is we are asking the question. What are we seeking to discover? What road are we on when we ask the question? What options (branches) are we contemplating? Are we trying to make a choice among several forks in the road? That requires "Part/Whole" thinking about the "Web" of possibilities, macro to micro and structural to agentic. Just as Spinoza attempted to utilize a Part/Whole and Web approach to the sociological imagination in the seventeenth century (Feuer 1958), we have to utilize a similar expanded and re-conceptualized version of the sociological imagination in the twenty-first century.

It is clear that Mills did not approach his discussion of the sociological imagination entirely in order to discover something new. He had settled convictions. He believed in his intuitive judgments. He had his own gnosis, albeit a somewhat limited one. Like a lawyer making a brief, he wanted to convince the jury, his academic peers as well as the educated non-specialist. Mills wrote as a public intellectual who was concerned with academic research bureaucratization (AE) and with empty theorizing based simply on logical pigeon holes (GT). He recommended an alternative he called the sociological imagination. But we do not have to accept *his* definition of that phrase. Instead, if we are truly seeking to build a general sociology that overcomes the unnecessary degree of super-specialization that exists today we can build on Mills to refine the idea of a sociological imagination. The situation has changed since the 1950s. His discussions of GT and AE were to some extent an attempt to destroy straw men of his own making. We need to have a broader vision of the whole web of possibilities for good general, paradigmatic theory and good empirical research.

We need to be able to visualize both a discipline and an object of study that will make sociology more cogent and more practical. The vision has been opened up by thinkers like Bernard Phillips and Thomas Scheff. But each of us can contribute to it in our own way, utilizing our own specific version of the expanded sociological imagination. The cumulative effect could be quite significant. Heaven knows there is a crying need for the kind of "common sense" that goes beyond the run-of-the-mill common sense that C. Wright Mills complained about. It is crucial not to reify our concepts by giving them a meaning that they may never even have had when they were first formulated. It is extremely important that we view theories and methods as "tools" that serve specific purposes in a certain cultural and political-economic context. The social worlds that humanity occupies are a worthy subject for sociological study not limited by unnecessary and premature closure but nevertheless disciplined by a craftsperson-like degree of precision. If we approach sociology as a calling that requires of us participation in body and spirit as well as mind we will accomplish far more than if we think of sociology as merely a job or a career.

Part VI. Conclusion: "Open Air"

Whitney Griswold was the President of Yale University. He wrote a little book (1962) entitled *Liberal Education & the Democratic Ideal*. The book ends with an interview. The last words that Griswold says in the interview are interesting. He says: the American student is "... in reality, struggling upward from the depths for a breath of air and something solid to hang onto." It is a mixed metaphor, but it helps to summarize the paradoxical nature of the conclusion that not only scientific and technical knowledge (*episteme* and *teckne*) are required, but also a certain degree of intuitive insight (*gnosis*). At the worst purely technical knowledge can become mere abstracted empiricism (AE) and intuitive insight can become mere grand theory (GT). But a healthy "breath of air" can resolve such false extreme. At its best the sociological imagination provides a healthy, balanced approach that ranges across all levels of abstraction and does not block the further development of insights *and* scientific reasoning.

Mills (1959: 93) cites Walt Whitman's phrase "man in the open air." That is the un-alienated man or woman. Mills cites Whitman mostly in the context of a polemic against the large-scale hierarchical organization of work. (Surprisingly, Thoreau does not get mentioned.) [14] For Mills the opposite to being in the open air would be "in the factory." The blue collar or white collar worker, particularly the shift worker, is very far indeed from the Jeffersonian ideal of the independent, yeoman landowning cultivator. But nevertheless, the idea of being in the open air can be taken as a metaphor for the kind of education that a combined Web and Part/Whole Approach could logically favor. It would mean being open minded and never restricting one's approach to any narrowly conceived specialization. That does not mean never specializing. Indeed, all sciences, physical and social, require a certain degree of selectivity. One simply cannot study everything at once. But premature closure and blind obedience do not make for good social science, or, for that matter, good natural science. There has to be a lot of "fresh air." The approach to the topic should always be open to serendipity (Merton and Barber 2004:158-198, 230-238). A narrow constriction of either theory or methods to a fine-tuned technique would result in nothing much more than a repetition of past errors.

Mills has allowed us to open a window to the fresh air that a sociological imagination can provide and the combined

Web and Part/Whole Approach of Phillips and Scheff will continue to improve our robust and healthy outlook. It is a question of integrating body and spirit and not just mind in the narrow sense. The new sociological imagination has yet to be fully developed. The next generation of students will have the opportunity to "stand on the shoulders" of such giants as Gandhi, Grant, Weber, Parsons, Lazarsfeld, Mills and many others still alive and working today. [15] We will have open to us an ontological framework that is "metaphysical" and "gnostic." It will be a framework which borrows from ancient *jnana yoga*. [16]

Recapitualization and Final Words

Charles Wright Mills was an important contributor to sociology. But when we use the phrase "the sociological imagination" we should not forget that his specific usage of that phrase may not have been based on as full understanding of the importance of theory and methods as is necessary in the long run. When we teach undergraduates and graduate students in sociology (or other social sciences) about the sociological imagination we should do so with a broad horizon in mind. We need to be able to think about complex questions in terms of the parts and the wholes and in terms of the wholes and the parts. That is not just a matter of the integration of the ideas of "structure" versus "agency" in the debate among European theorists, or the "macro" versus "micro" debate in American theory, as complex as the full integration of those ideas may be (Ritzer 2008: 499-546). It is a deep philosophical-epistemological problem that relates to "Pragmatic Hermeneutics" (Shalin 2007) and to a gnosis similar to that attained by Baruch (Benedict) Spinoza (Sacksteder1991). A deeper and fuller comprehension of the sociological imagination requires us to not only think about the question ("mind") but also integrate our thinking with embodied wisdom ("body") and the "spirit" ("soul" or *Geist*) of a crafts-person. Body, mind and spirit are required to actualize the sociological imagination in such a way that theory and methods become relevant for pragmatic action and praxis in times of crisis. In a general way, both Gandhi and Grant lead in the right direction. They do not emphasize a narrow version of the "moderate" Enlightenment and the "reductionist" aspects of the Scientific Revolution. Instead, they presume a more "radical" Enlightenment and a more holistic view of scientific knowledge as *scientia* (*Wissenschaft*). Such knowledge is ultimately based in part on an intuitive awareness. If one is going to rely on intuitive knowledge and somehow escape the potential danger of delusion it is necessary to stick close to the real world and to empirical, factual knowledge. A balanced approach of that kind requires a new sociological imagination.

References and Works Consulted

Note that internal references refer to readers and collections; I have not repeated all information for items that are found in general readers and collections of letters (e.g. Beiner 1996 is in Davis 1996; Grant 1998a in Christian and Grant 1996, etc.). Every work listed was consulted, but space does not allow a full discussion of each and every source used. A full discussion would require a book-length manuscript.

Abelson, Raziel. 1967. "Definition." *The Encyclopedia of Philosophy* 2: 314-324. Edited by Paul Edwards. New York: Macmillan.

Ackerman, Bruce. 2005. *The Failure of the Founding Fathers: Jefferson, Marshall, and the Rise of Presidential Democracy*. Cambridge, MA: The Belknap Press of Harvard University Press.

Bakker, J. I. (Hans). 2007a. "Language" and "*Langue* and *Parole*." Pp. 2533-2539 in Ritzer, George (ed.) *The Blackwell Encyclopedia of Sociology*. Oxford, U.K. and Malden, MA: Blackwell.

Bakker, J. I. (Hans). 2007b. "Meta-analysis." Pp. 2963-2964 in Ritzer, George (ed.) *The Blackwell Encyclopedia of Sociology*. Oxford, U.K. and Malden, MA: Blackwell.

Bakker, J. I. (Hans). 2007c. "Scientific Networks and Invisible Colleges." Pp. 4107-4108 in Ritzer, George (ed.) *The Blackwell Encyclopedia of Sociology*. Oxford, U.K. and Malden, MA: Blackwell.

Bakker, J. I. (Hans). 2007d. "Scientific Revolution." Pp. 4116-4117 in Ritzer, George (ed.) *The Blackwell Encyclopedia of Sociology*. Oxford, U.K. and Malden, MA: Blackwell.

Bakker, J. I. (Hans). 2005. "Trust and the Civilizing Process." Paper presented at the Symposium on Trust, Risk and Civility. Toronto: St. Michael's College, University of Toronto. Available on line.

Bakker, J. I. (Hans).1993a *Toward A Just Civilization*. Toronto: Canadian Scholars' Press.

Bakker, J. I. (Hans). 1993b. *Gandhi and the Gita*. Toronto: Canadian Scholars' Press.

Bakker, J. I. (Hans). 1990. *The World Food Crisis: Food Security in Comparative Perspective*. Toronto: Canadian Scholars' Press.

Beiner, Ronald. 1996. ""George Grant, Nietzsche, and the Problem of Post-Christian Theism." Pp. 109-138 in Davis (1996).

Bharadwaj, Lakshmi Kant. 2007. "The Sociology of Culture." Pp. 130-142 in Bryant and Peck (2007).

Bonnell, Victoria E. and Lynn Hunt (eds.) 1999. *Beyond the Cultural Turn: New Directions in the Study of Society and Culture*. Berkeley, CA: University of California Press.

Bourdieu, Pierre. 1977 [1972]. *Outline of a Theory of Practice*. Tr. Richard Nice. Cambridge, U.K.: Cambridge University Press.

Bryant, Clifton D. and Dennis L. Peck (eds.) 2007. *21st Century Sociology: A Reference Handbook*. Two Volumes. Thousand Oaks, CA: Sage.

Christian, William. 1996a. *George Grant: Selected* Letters. Toronto: University of Toronto Press.

Christian, William. 1996b. "Introduction." Pp. vii-xiii in Christian (1996).

Christian, William and Sheila Grant. 1998a. *The George Grant Reader*. Toronto: University of Toronto Press.

Christian, William and Sheila Grant. 1998b. "Introduction." Pp. 3 – 32 in Christian and Grant (1998).

Collins, Randall. 1998. *The Sociology of Philosophies*. Cambridge, MA: Belknap Press of Harvard University Press.

Collins, Randall and Michael Makowsky. 1998. *The Discovery of Society*. Sixth Edition. Boston, Massachusetts: McGraw Hill.

Davis, Arthur (ed.) 1996. *George Grant and the Subversion of Modernity: Art, Philosophy, Politics, Religion, and Education*. Toronto: University of Toronto Press.

Davis, Brent. 2004. *Inventions of Teaching: A Genealogy*. Mahwah, New Jersey: Lawrence Erlbaum Associates.

Dicker, Georges. 1993. *Descartes: An Analytical and Historical Introduction*. New York: Oxford University Press. [Professor Dicker's first name is "Georges."]

Durkheim, David Emile. 1956. *Education and Sociology*. Tr. Sherwood Fox. Glencoe, Illinois: Free Press.

Durkheim, David Emile. 1977. *The Evolution of Educational Thought in France*. Tr. Peter Collins. London: Routledge & Kegan Paul.

Durkheim, David Emile. 1983 [1914]. *Pragmatism and Sociology*. Tr. J. C. Whitehouse. New York: Cambridge University Press. [Lectures delivered 1913-1914.]

Durkheim, David Emile. 1995 [1912] *The Elementary Forms of the Religious Life*. Tr. Karen E. Fields. New York: Free Press.

Feldman, Daniel Hale. 2001. *Qabalah: The Mystical Heritage of the Children of Abraham*. Santa Cruz, California: Work of the Chariot.

Feuer, Lewis Samuel. 1958. *Spinoza and the Rise of Liberalism*. Boston, MA: Beacon Press.

Fioramo, Giovanni. 1990. A History of Gnosticism. Tr. Anthony Alcock. Oxford, U.K.: Blackwell.

Gelder, Ken. 2005 [1997]. *The Subcultures Reader, Second Edition*. London, U.K.: Blackwell. [Sarah Thornton was a joint editor for the first edition.]

Gerhardt, Uta. 2001. Parsons's Analysis of the Societal Community.' Pp. 177-222 in Trevino, A. Javier (ed.) *Talcott Parsons Today*. Lanham, Maryland: Rowman & Littlefield.

Gerhardt, Uta. 2002. *Talcott Parsons: An Intellectual Biography*. Cambridge, U.K.: Cambridge University Press.

Gerth, Hans H. and C. Wright Mills. 1947. *From Max Weber: Essays in Sociology*.

Gerth, Hans H. and C. Wright Mills. 1953. *Character and Social Structure*. New York: Harcourt, Brace and World.

Gouldner, Alvin. 1970. *The Coming Crisis of Western Sociology*. New York: Basic Books.

Grant, George. 1996. "Letter to Maude Grant of 12 February 1948 from Dalhousie University, Halifax." Pp. 148-150 in Christian (1996).

Grant, George. 1998a [1945]. "Mass Society." Pp. 50-58 in Christian and Grant (1998).

Grant, George. 1998b [1954]. "What is Philosophy?" Pp. 33-39 in Christian and Grant (1998).

Grant, George. 1998c [1966]. "A Critique of the New Left." Pp. 83-94 in Christian and Grant (1998).

Grant, George. 1998d [1973]. "Introduction to Plato." Pp. 207-210 in Christian and Grant (1998).

Griswold, A. Whitney. 1962 [1959]. *Liberal Education and the Democratic Ideal, and Other Essays*. Second Edition. New Haven: Yale University Press. [The book consists of essays originally published between 1951 and 1961.]

Halpern, David. 2005. *Social Capital*. Cambridge, U.K., Malden, MA, USA: Polity Press.

Horowitz, Irving Louis. 1983. *C. Wright Mills: An American Utopian*. New York: Free Press.

Israel, Jonathan. 2001. *Radical Enlightenment: Philosophy and the Making of Modernity, 1650-1750*. Oxford, U.K.: Oxford University Press.

James, William. 1958 [1892, 1899]. *Talks to Teachers on Psychology: and to Students on Some of Life's Ideals*. New York: W. W. Norton.

Kant, Immanuel. 1996. *Practical Philosophy. The Metaphysics of Morals*. Cambridge, U.K.: Cambridge University Press. [The Cambridge Edition of the Works of Immanuel Kant.]

King, Karen L. 2004. *What Is Gnosticism?* Cambridge, Massachusetts: Harvard University Press.

Kincaid, Harold. 1996. *Philosophical Foundations of the Social Sciences*. New York and Cambridge, U.K.: Cambridge University Press.

Lazarsfeld, Paul F. and Rosenberg. 1955. *The Language of Social Research*. Glencoe, Illinois: The Free Press.

Lidz, Victor. 2001. "Language and the 'Family' of Generalized Symbolic Media." Pp. 141-176 in Trevino, A. Javier (ed.) *Talcott Parsons Today*. Lanham, Maryland: Rowman & Littlefield.

Mead, George Herbert. 1934. *Mind, Self, and Society*. Chicago: University of Chicago Press.

Merton, Robert K. and Elinor Barber. 2004. *The Travels and Adventures of Serendipity: A Study in Sociological Semantics and the Sociology of Science*. Princeton, N.J.: Princeton University Press.

Mills, C. Wright. 1940. "Situated Actions and the Vocabularies of Motive." *American Sociological Review* 5: 904-913.

Mills, C. Wright. 1943. "The Professional Ideology of Social Pathologists." *American Journal of Sociology* 49 (September): 165-180.

Mills, C. Wright. 1948. *The New Men of Power: America's Labor Leaders*. New York: A. M. Kelley.

Mills, C. Wright. 1951. *White Collar: The American Middle Classes*. New York: Oxford University Press.

Mills, C. Wright. 1956. *The Power Elite*. New York: Oxford University Press.

Mills, C. Wright. 1959. *The Sociological Imagination.* New York: Oxford University Press.

Mitchell, Michael. 2006. *Hidden Mutualities: Faustian Themes from Gnostic Origins to the Postcolonial.* Amsterdam: Rodopi B.V.

Neumann, Franz. 1942. *Behemoth.* New York: Oxford University Press.

Paranjape, Makarand. 2002. "The Third Eye and Two Ways of (Un)knowing: Gnosis, Alternative Modernities, and Postcolonial Futures." New York: unpublished paper presented at the Infinity Colloquium, 24-29 July 2002.

Phillips, Bernard. 2001. *Beyond Sociology's Tower of Babel: Reconstructing the Scientific Method.* New York: Aldine de Gruyter.

Phillips, Bernard, Harold Kincaid and Thomas Scheff (eds.) *Toward A Sociological Imagination: Bridging Specialized Fields.* Landham, Maryland: University Press of America.

Posner, Richard A. 2003 [2001]. *Public Intellectuals: A Study of Decline. With a New Preface and Epilogue.* Cambridge, MA: Harvard University Press.

Prus, Robert. 2003. "Ancient Precursors." Pp. 19-38 in Reynolds, Larry T. and Nancy J. Herman-Kinney (eds.) *Handbook of Symbolic Interactionism.* New York: Altamira Press.

Prus, Robert. 2007."Aristotle, Pragmatism and Symbolic Interactionism." Urbana, Illinois: Couch-Stone Symbolic Interactionist Conference, unpublished paper.

Reimers, Adrian J. 2006. *The Soul of the Person.* Washington, D.C.: The Catholic University of America Press.

Ricks, Thomas E. 2007 [2006]. *Fiasco: The American Military Adventure in Iraq.* New York: Penguin Group (USA). [The 2007 edition has a new "Postscript" Pp. 440-451.]

Russon, John. 2004. *Reading Hegel's Phenomenology.* Bloomington, Indiana: Indiana University Press.

Ritzer, George. 2008. *Sociological Theory.* New York: McGraw-Hill.

Roberts, Richard H. 2006. "Body." Pp. 213-228 in Segal, Robert A. (ed.) 2006. *The Blackwell Companion to the Study of Religion.* Malden, MA: Blackwell Publishing.

Sacksteder, W. 1991. "Least Parts and Greatest Wholes: Variations on a Theme in Spinoza." *International Studies in Philosophy* 23 (1): 75-87.

Scheff, Thomas J. 1990. *Microsociology: Discourse, Emotion, and Social Structure.* Chicago: University of Chicago Press.

Scheff, Thomas J. 1997. *Emotions, the Social Bond, and Human Reality: Part/Whole Analysis.* Cambridge, U.K.: Cambridge University Press.

Scheff, Thomas J. 2007. "Spinoza and Part/Whole." Society for the Study of Symbolic Interaction List-serve: SSSI-Talk. [various contributions, August, 2007, available at the SSSI-Talk archives on the web. See Sacksteder 1991, which is cited by Scheff and Feuer 1958, which sets a historical context for Spinoza.]

Shalin, Dmitri N. 2007. "Signing in the Flesh: Notes on Pragmatist Hermeneutics." *Sociological Theory* 25 (3): 193-224.

Sherman, David. 2003. "Critical Theory." Pp. 188-218 in Solomon, Robert C. and David Sherman (eds.) 2003. *The Blackwell Guide to Continental Philosophy.* Malden, MA: Blackwell Publishing Co.

Smith, Philip (Ed.) 1998. *The New American Cultural Sociology.* Cambridge, U.K.: Cambridge University Press.

Stouffer, Samuel et al. 1949. *The American Soldier.* Princeton, New Jersey: Princeton University Press.

Swedberg, Richard. 2005. *The Max Weber Dictionary: Key Words and Central Concepts.* Stanford, CA: Stanford University Press. [With the assistance of Ole Agevall.]

Trevino, A Javier (ed.) 2002. *Talcott Parsons Today: His theory and Legacy in Contemporary Sociology.* Lanham,

Maryland: Rowman & Littlefield. Foreword by Neil J. Smelser.

Upitis, Rena. 2003. "Making Art, Making Connections." *Journal of the Canadian Association for Curriculum Studies* 1 (2): 1 – 6.

Weber, Max. 1968 [1920]. *Economy and Society*. Tr. and ed. Guenther Roth and Claus Wittich. Based on earlier translations by Epohraim Fischoff, Talcott Parsons, et al. 2 Volumes. Berkeley, California: University of California Press.

Notes

1. Portions of this essay repeat the general thrust of ideas also discussed in a forthcoming publication on the web and part/whole approach to sociology. Some phrases will be approximately the same. However, that publication stresses education and does not mention either Gandhi or Grant. It also does not develop any aspect of the notion of Peircian semiotics and severely underplays the notion of gnosis or jnana.

2. In my seminar course on "Advanced Topics in Sociological Theory and Methodology" I have been trying for about a decade to sort out the relevance of hermeneutics and semiotics for sociological meta-theory and research theory. The term "*semiologie*" can be used to specifically designate the approach characteristic of certain French Post-Structuralist and Post-Modernist philosophers. They are basically Cartesian in their thinking, despite their alleged "anti-foundationalism." When read in context Ferdinand de Saussure's original contributions are not directly related to those subsequent writers who echo selective aspects of his views. He was well grounded in comparative, historical linguistics; they are not (Bakker 2007a).

3. Ultimately, of course, these issues will require intellectual contributions from professionally-educated theologians and philosophers, not only from India and Canada but from many other places.

4. Surprisingly, Possner does not emphasize Mills at all. He mentions Max Weber, Daniel Bell, David Riesman and Robert

Putnam (Possner 2003: 13). Mills name does appear in Table 5.1 (Possner 2003: 201) as one of twenty-seven living sociologists among 368 living public intellectuals classified. Mills does not make the "top one hundred" list (Possner 2003: 209-211). Henry Kissinger, Daniel Patrick Moynihan, George Will, Lawrence Summers, and William J. Bennett are the top five in terms of media mentions (in 2001). Indeed, no sociologist makes the top one hundred list. Margaret Mead is one of the few living social scientists mentioned, unless we count John Kenneth Galbraith and Marshall McLuhan. W. E. B. DuBois is also listed as having considerable media attention in 2000-2001.

5. C. Wright Mills did not use his first name, Charles. One could imagine that if he had a different personality he might have been addressed as "Charles W. Mills." But no one talks or writes about "Chuck" Mills. C. Wright Mills always wanted to be "right"!

6. Public Lecture at the University of Guelph, Guelph, Ontario, October 2, 2007.

7. Note that Max Weber makes a clear argument about the importance of modern "rational-legal bureaucracy" for large scale nation-state systems. Few people would want to go back to any of what Weber calls "patrimonial-feudal" or "patrimonial-prebendal" systems and pre-modern bureaucracies. See Swedberg (2005: 18-21, 194-196) for succinct clarification of these key terms.

8. The letters "SI" often represent Symbolic Interaction. Here, of course, I mean "Sociological Imagination" in Mills' sense. It is one of the deficiencies of his book that he pays scant attention to Symbolic Interaction or Interactionism generally. He mentions "symbol spheres" but his comments about George Herbert Mead are not laudatory. He mainly associates Mead with the psychoanalytic approach (Mills 1959: 160, 172). While very concerned with "practicality," Mills has nothing original to say about Pragmatism. He does not mention Dewey, James or Peirce!

9. As a student at the University of Toronto in the 1970s I first enrolled in a Ph.D. program in urban planning and architecture (1971-72). Although I am deeply grateful to teachers like Hans Blumenfeld and William Michaelson, I nevertheless felt a "calling" for sociological theory and

methods, due in part to such teachers as Larry Cross, Robert Perkins, Evan Vlachos, Thomas Berry, T. R. Young, Lewis Feuer, Irving Zeitlin, Wsevlod Isajiw, Paul Lazarsfeld, Jeffrey Reitz, Harold Orbach, Willem F. Wertheim, Robert Van Niel, Cees Fasseur, Russ Burnside, Lorne Tepperman, Raymond Breton and Lorna Marsden.

10. I add these reflexive comments since being "reflexive" about the roots of one's own ideas is part and parcel of the combined Web and Part/Whole Approach. Perhaps if I had chosen to make a career in urban planning or in AE I would today have a different view of the lasting value of Mills' ideas.

11. Shalin's (2007: 198) typology is more complex. He indicates three types: (1) symbolic-discursive, (2) somatic-affective and (3) behavioral-performative. They do not synchronize in any precise way with the notion of mind, body and spirit. However, it is not possible to summarize Shalin's complex thirty page paper without getting lost in too many fine points which are not directly relevant at this time.

12. The specifics of the "Part/Whole Approach" that Thomas Scheff culls from the discussion by Sacksteder (1991) of the "Part/Whole Approach" in Spinoza are not necessarily what is meant here. Spinoza was writing in the Netherlands during a period of rapid social change and upheaval in which the socio-political and economic circumstances were quite different from what they are today in the United States and Canada. Spinoza himself did not follow "a single path" but varied his approach during his lifetime (Feuder 1958). Nevertheless, Spinoza did follow a kind of "Part/Whole Approach" of a very general sort. We can disagree with Spinoza's ontology (or, "metaphysics") but still accept his epistemology (or, "scientific method") as valid, provided we pay careful attention to historical context. After the assassination of Johan de Witt Spinoza regarded sociological issues related to politics quite differently than he did before August 20, 1672.

13. Use of the German and French words is important when we discuss the historical origins of sociology because the current American English usage tends to cloud the fact that earlier views on what the sociological imagination is are not necessarily directly in line with current usage in North America. We can also, of course, use the term "sociology" in

a sense that is more universal, as Feuer (1958) does in his discussion of Baruch Spinoza's sociological insights *avant la lettre*

14. Mills (1959: 222) cites Whitman again in a different context but does not point out that Whitman wrote lovingly about Manhattan. Moreover, the fact that Whitman was inspired in part by his gay identity, albeit *avant la lettre*, is also not mentioned. Mills picks and chooses his quotations to make his points.

15. Robert K. Merton has elaborately researched the phrase, often attributed to Isaac Newton. The idea that we today are "dwarfs" compared to the "giants" of the past does not imply that there are no longer any giants. But it often takes several generations to fully realize the contributions made by thinkers in the past. To quote another famous saying, "the prophet is [often] not recognized in his [or her] own country [and time]."

16. Discussions (via email) with Bernie Phillips have helped to lead me to this conclusion. I have reached this view after giving a great deal of thought to the limitations of the European Enlightenment (particularly the French versus the German *Aufklarung*). The epistemological break with metaphysical beliefs may not be the final answer. In another paper I would like to further explore the ways in which Immanuel Swedenborg's mysticism may have influenced Immanuel Kant's *Critique of Pure Reason*.

ಐ ಛ

11

WERE MOHANDAS K. GANDHI AND GEORGE GRANT NEO-LUDDITE NATIONALISTS?

James Gerrie

Introduction

There is a little recognized but very important similarity between the thought and work of Mohandas K. Gandhi and George Grant. Both are recognized to be exemplars of nationalist fervor. Yet for both, a central symbol of such fervor is the rejection of a specific technology. It is easy to focus on what Gandhi embraced in terms of technology. He embraced the spinning wheel as a symbol of Indian national independence. But it is important to understand the flip side to this positive symbol. Behind its adoption is a negative judgment. Gandhi was also rejecting the industrial system of the production of linens. So, in a way, the focus of his efforts for national revival was the rejection of a specific kind of technology in favour of another, which he felt was more conducive to the proper support of Indian national life. Similarly, Grant, in his most famous writing on Canadian nationalism, *Lament for a Nation*, placed the rejection of a technology at the centre of his defense of a Canadian identity. In this case, it was nuclear weapons and their repudiation that he felt was absolutely essential to the very survival of Canada as a nation. The following chapter will investigate this little commented similarity in the lives of these two men. I will reflect on the question posed by this similarity and argue that it is based in their acceptance of fundamentally Neo-Luddite ideas.

The first question that must be considered is whether their repudiation of aspects of modern industrial society was merely based in some form of religious conservatism or naïve religious romanticism. This is a question posed by the American philosopher of technology James Dewey about those who base their criticism of technologies in some kind of religious outlook. Hickman and Schradd describe Dewey's view as follows:

In that same essay Dewey mentioned a third threat to technological and social inquiry. It is consequent on the activities of contemporary Luddites, especially of the theocratic variety. They resist the application of scientific and technical methods to the field of human concerns and human affairs both because they tend to think of themselves as outside of and above nature, and because they prefer a return to the medieval pre-scientific doctrine of a supernatural foundation and outlook in all social and moral matters. He further suggested that this group erroneously believes that the methods of science and technology have been applied to every area of human concern—and have been found wanting.[1]

Are Gandhi and Grant religious reactionaries in Dewey's sense? Is their promotion of the rejection of technologies merely an instance of a preference for a return to a "medieval pre-scientific doctrine" or is it representative of a radically modern kind of social critique? My position is that their views do not simply represent an anti-technology attitude born of religious conservatism or romanticism. Rather, their political reflections represent ground-breaking insights into the understanding of the nature of technology that will likely come to predominate in the politics of the 21st century, which I call Neo-Luddite Nationalism.

Neo-Luddite Nationalism Defined

Neo-Luddite nationalism is nothing more than the rejection of nebulous concepts of national character, identity or "consciousness of a given set of people"[2] as the defining characteristics of nationhood in favour of an understanding that sees nationhood as being defined by the choices people make about the technologies they use. A basic conclusion to be drawn from this understanding is that it is incoherent to speak of "two nations" that are essentially indistinguishable in terms of the technologies used by those peoples. As Grant puts this point succinctly in reference to the relationship between Canada and the United States: "Nearly all Canadians think that modernity is good, so nothing essentially distinguishes Canadians from Americans."[3] Nations are constituted as nations by the distinctive technologies and combinations of technologies that allow them to be differentiated from other nations, not by nebulous notions of national character, identity or consciousness.

Neo-Luddism is a term popularized by Chellis Glendinning, in her influential article "Notes toward a Neo-Luddite Manifesto."[4] Glendinning outlines three central points that define the Neo-Luddite outlook. First, Neo-Luddites are not anti-technologists, but simply call for greater ethical selectivity regarding our technological choices. Second, they view all technologies as inherently political. Third they reject what Glendenning calls "the personal view of technology" as "dangerously limited"[5] and argue instead that any ethical analysis of technological choices must account for the power of technology to influence one's decisions. These three points are born of the fundamental outlook on technology of Neo-Luddites, which is characterized by what Andrew Freenberg calls the "non-neutrality thesis."[6] This outlook rejects the more "common sense" view that technologies are mere neutral artifacts, for the view that all technologies both embody and express fundamental values.

According to the non-neutrality thesis, any act that involves using a technology inevitably contributes to the creation of some negative effects that cannot be separated from the good effects sought in normal use. A currently prominent example is one's choice to use a car, which people are now recognizing has effects beyond those of one's immediate intentions. Such intentions can be quite varied, from highly sinister to highly benign, but regardless of the specific ends one seeks they all contribute to the problems of air pollution and global warming. Such inevitable ethical impacts of technologies are based in 4 kinds of inevitable consequences of using any technology discussed at length by Neo-Luddites:

1. INFRASTRUCTURE/INPUT

Every technology inevitably requires a system of supports in order to function, for example, cars require the existence of factories, suppliers, parking lots, gas stations, roads, etc. When one uses a car one also uses these supporting technologies and technological systems.

2. FUNCTION/OUTPUT

Every technology inevitably enhances some desired function and such enhancements have inevitable environmental and social consequences that arise from the enhancement. In addition, technologies often have unintended outputs that are a result of their ordinary operation.

3. CONDITIONS OF ATTENDANCE

Any technology requires certain kinds of physical and mental actions and emotional dispositions and reactions from its users in the course of using that technology. The media theorist and critic of technology, Neil Postman, calls such requirements, "conditions of attendance."

4. NEW SOCIAL GROUPS/"KNOWLEDGE MONOPOLIES"

Since no one can master every technology (or master them all equally well), experts are always an inevitable part of the use of technologies and the running of technical systems. The dynamics of the creation and interaction of such groups has been detailed by the Canadian Economic historian, Harold Adams Innis, who calls such groups "knowledge monopolies."

These four aspects can lead to a fifth kind of consequence, which although not inevitable, is an ever-present possibility as long as a technology is used:

5. CHANGES IN VALUES

These preceding 4 consequences can encourage changes in values in 4 distinct ways. Infrastructures clearly define the social and physical environment in which we must live and thus help define the kinds of skill sets to be preferred for the successful navigation of such an environment. Functions are by definition desires that technologies satisfy, which present the possibility for increased satisfaction through increased use. The conditions of attendance by definition train us into forms of behaviour and inevitably provide models of action for others to follow. And finally, technology clearly plays a key role in empowering and dis-empowering social groups, thus vitalizing or devitalizing the abilities of these groups to promote the value specific to the activities of those groups, thus creating new points of possible conflict in the social order.

The implication of such inherent ethical and political aspects of all technologies has led the majority of contemporary philosophers of technology to advocate for a general moral obligation for the continuous reassessment of our technological choices. As Langdon Winner puts it, all "artifacts have politics."[7]

Gandhi and Grant are early promoters of such a perspective towards technology, and are unique in applying the insights of such a perspective to questions of national identity. Technologies for them, as for Neo-Luddites, always manifest values, therefore all nations, which are defined by distinct matrices of technologies, also express distinct visions of the good and are thus proper objects for both moral analysis and allegiance. The perspectives of Gandhi and Grant on technology, thus, represent a form of nationalism based in a radically new perspective on technology that has only come to prominence in the philosophy of technology at the end of the late 20th century.

However, some suggest that their perspectives on modernity and nationalism emerge from commitments to religious conservatism. For instance, Neil Robertson comments as follow about Grant:

For Grant, the only possibility for getting 'beyond' technology is, on the one hand, through recollection of a pre-technological ethic evoked by those remnants of pre-modernity still present (this is Grant's conservatism), and, on the other hand, through the radicalizing of technological civilization to the point of its collapse from its own inner nihilism (here appears Grant's extremism).[8]

Gregory Baum says this of Gandhi:

> Steering between these two political trends (extreme and moderate), Mahatma Gandhi worked out his own ethico-religious nationalism. He shared with the Moderates the horror of violence and the desire for Hindu-Muslim solidarity; and he had a certain affinity for the policies of the Extremists, especially the call for religious renewal uniting the educated with the people and the search for strategies that would make Indians more independent of the empire.[9]

Raghavan Iyer suggests that "Gandhi's critique of modern civilization was not the typical response of theological pessimism or of despairing world-weariness."[10] But Iyer is unclear what Gandhi's positive alternative is, beyond an appeal "to the teachings of all religions that we should remain passive about worldly pursuits and active about godly pursuits."[11]

While I would certainly agree, as Gandhi and Grant obviously do, that such a spiritual teaching is true, I don't think such a perennial religious message can fully explain either the substance or ongoing appeal of the thought and work of these two great nationalists. If the core of their social and political thought does boil-down to the message that people should lead godly lives, then their thought really does simply represent a call to religious conservatism and a return to the past as the best response to the problems of modernity. Such a conclusion would add great support to those who would wish to discount the thought of Gandhi and Grant. As Madhuri Santanam Sondhi comments "For decades Gandhi has been regarded as eccentric in his rejection of modernity."[12] Similar denunciations of Grant have also been made.[13]

I believe the ongoing appeal of their thought is actually based in their ground-breaking acceptance of three main Neo-Luddite claims about technology touched on briefly already 1) Technology is not ethically neutral (The Non-Neutrality Thesis), 2) we must be individually more selective about our technologies (The Selectivity Imperative), and 3) technology manifests powers that can deflect individual attempts to control it so that we must work together with others politically in order to bring it properly under control (The Autonomy of Technology). This last view has been developed most fully by Langdon Winner. He draws this view from the work of Jacques Ellul, a French protestant sociologist, who was an important influence on Grant's early works on technology.[14]

Neo-Luddite ideas about technology are coming to dominate politics in the 21st century. We should therefore see Gandhi and Grant as important forerunners of the politics of the future. The most important political movements, such as environmentalism, new urbanism/smart growth, anti-globalization, and the critique "banalization or vulgarization of cultural life"[15] are all unified by their critical response to, and even rejection of, certain technologies and "megatechnologies."[16] This perspective on the work of

Gandhi (and Grant) rejects the view of those like Madhuri Santanam Sondhi who see the fundamental core of Gandhi's critique as being based in the rejection of a "cluster of ideas which shaped the humanist revolution, revolving round the axis of individualism."[17] My perspective also rejects the notion that Gandhi's (and Grant's) view is best understood as arising out of a "position as an arcadian within the 'dialectic of Enlightenment'."[18] The uniqueness of the critiques of Gandhi and Grant are not based primarily in their rejection of enlightenment ideas about individualism, science or nature. Instead the uniqueness of their critiques rests in their embrace and early expression of a unique and new understanding of the nature of technology, which these days is being expressed most forcefully by Neo-Luddites.

Gandhi's View of Technology

The idea of non-neutrality is based primarily in a broad definition of technology that emphasizes its practical nature rather than its nonessential and incidental connection with artifacts. Morton Wintson expresses this understanding as follows: "Technology is not a collection of things, but rather is a systematic and rational way of doing things; it is, in general, the organization of knowledge people, and things to accomplish specific practical goals."[19] This practice-based view of technology has only recently gained wide spread academic acceptance with the development of Science and Technology Studies (STS) programmes,[20] and the research of "twenty years of increasingly critical history and sociology of technology."[21] However, such a holistic practice-based view seems an integral part of Gandhi's outlook:

Swadeshi is that spirit within us which restricts us to the use and service of our immediate surroundings to the exclusion of the more remote. Thus, as for religion, in order to satisfy the requirements of the definition, I must restrict myself to my ancestral religion. That is, the use of my immediate religious surroundings. If I find it defective, I should serve it by purging it of its defects. In the domain of politics, I should make use of the indigenous institutions and serve them by curing them of their proved defects. In that of economics, I should use only those things that are produced by my immediate neighbours and serve those industries by making them efficient and complete where they might be found wanting.[22]

In this citation we find Gandhi's reflections on "use and service" (i.e. means and practice) sweeping together the practices of religion, political institutions and the mundane products of one's local economy. Nor does he distinguish between the processes of finding and removing "defects" in areas of human activity that most people think are quite distinct. Clearly Gandhi would agree with Winston's view that the "monetary system, the banks, and the stock and commodity markets are technologies" and "even governmental systems, ranging from varieties of representative democracy to theocracy and dictatorship, are competing technologies for managing concerted societal action and resolving political conflicts...[about which] people ask 'Is there a better way to run a government?' no less frequently than 'Is there a better way to design a mousetrap'."[23]

The Non-Neutrality Thesis in Gandhi's Work

Gandhi also clearly holds a non-neutrality view of means. He believes that ends are an integral part of all means when he states that "the means may be likened to a seed, the end to a tree; and there is just the same inviolable connection between the means and the end as there is between the seed and the tree."[24] Sondhi calls this Gandhi's "principle of the convertibility of means and ends."[25] Ganguli also comments that "ethical neutrality is obviously outside the universe of discourse of a man like Gandhi" and "Gandhi never acknowledged the duality of means and ends or values."[26] It is an integral part Gandhi's notion of non-violent resistance that "social ends or values were viewed as interfused with means objectified in social institutions, social practices and social relations of various kinds which form a seamless web, so to speak,"[27] or as Horsburgh puts it, "ends arise out of means."[28]

But such a reading of Gandhi's conception of technology raises the contention that his views are simply based in an "arcadian sensibility" for simpler more natural times. Some such as David Hardiman, despite some misgivings, feel obliged to fit Gandhi into such a category. For Hardiman Gandhi is similar to western romanticists in their views about the revitalization and even deification of nature. However, this interpretation throws up some immediate apparent contradictions. For example, as Hardiman himself points out "[Gandhi] did not however seek this pantheisitic deity in the wild, as Thoreau and other Western romantics did—implicitly accepting a divide between 'nature' and 'culture'."[29] As Hardiman notes "Gandhi was rooted too firmly within human society to be attracted in any way by such as life."[30] Gandhi is not noted for being highly focussed on nature but more with the concerns of people living in villages. Nor was he particularly disinclined to speak positively of science or to use scientific or technological metaphors, such as when he states: "We are destroying the matchless living machines, i.e. our bodies by leaving them to rust and trying to substitute lifeless machinery for them."[31] To see Gandhi's intense critique of Western society laid out in *Hind Swaraj* as being based primarily in some form of romantic rejection of modern science or enlightenment views of nature does not fit.

But how else can we make sense of the apparent profound repudiation of Western society expressed in *Hind Swaraj*? Understanding his fundamental Neo-Luddite insights provides a way to explain his deep misgivings with certain aspects of Western culture, without having to jam him into the procrustean bed of Western religious romanticism. It also allows one to explain why he was so adamant in expressing that the Swadeshi movement was neither simply a form of temporary protest *against* the British nor based simply in a wholesale repudiation of all things Western. It is in this ongoing struggle to properly define the movement that we can find his belief in the importance of selectivity when it comes to technology most clearly expressed.

Again and again he reiterates to his followers that the reason for embracing Kadhi has nothing to do with harming the British. He also continuously defends against his critics that his position is simply born of a sweeping repudiation of all things Western. For example, in *Young India* he states emphatically: "I have tried to show times without number that no one need think of civil disobedience in connection with Khaddar. Civil disobedience has no direct connection with Khaddar."[32] The reasons for using and making Kadhi were not based the needs of the struggle for independence. They were based in an analysis of the intrinsic ethical merits of Kadhi production methods for a primarily rural society like that of India with a large population and the demerits of industrial production methods for such a society. It is this moral analysis of the intrinsic moral impact of particular production methods that is key.

Part of this analysis involves an understanding of the specific needs of people in a specific kind of society. This kind of moral analysis of systems and products at work in their distinctive cultural and environmental context is a moral obligation of all people, everywhere, and stands above issues of national independence struggles, which is why Gandhi can state:

> The economics and civilization of a country where the pressure of the population on land is greatest, are, and must be, different from those of a country where the pressure is the least. Sparsely populated America may have need of machinery. India may not need it at all.[33]

The fact that people keep misinterpreting this point of Gandhi, such that he must restate it "times without number" simply represents the oft made complain of Neo-Luddites that people are enthralled to the notion of the inherent neutrality of means. The reticence of those followers of Gandhi, who keep suggesting that once the independence struggle is finished they can go about dressing and producing in whatever way they like misses Gandhi's essential commitment to a form Neo-Luddite nationalism. It is by way of distinctive technological practices that nations differentiate themselves from others. This effort is not based in idiosyncratic notions of difference but in the relevant moral differences between people living in different kinds of societies and different environments. But, if people should have the same moral duties, Gandhi would insist that they should choose the same morally appropriate means. If India were as sparsely populated as America, it would have different moral obligations in regard to the kinds of methods of production that its people should adopt.

This is why he also insists again and again to critics and perplexed followers, that the Swadeshi movement is not about simply rejecting all things Western. All people, according to Gandhi, must do their moral duty. The only reasons that might justify people doing things differently are differences in relevant moral circumstances based in geography and/or social conditions, or because of the limited moral understanding of inherently flawed human beings, which requires some room for moral experimentation by individuals and peoples. As Gandhi states:

Evolution is always experimental. All progress is gained through mistakes and their rectification. No good comes fully-fashioned ... but has to be carved out through repeated experiments and repeated failures by ourselves. This is the law of individual growth. The same law controls social and political evolution also. The right to err, which means the freedom to try experiments, is the universal condition of all progress.[34]

Swadeshi was not a boycott movement but a moral principle to be followed by all. This included the British, such as when he mentions "I have read some treatises which show that England could easily become a self-contained country growing all the produce it needs."[35]

The essential point is to bring a complex moral analysis to bear on the means one employs or is involved in, which is the main principle of the Neo-Luddite movement. Also, like Neo-Luddites, he was quick to point out that adopting such a critical stance to technologies did not imply that he was "anti-technology." In his efforts to ameliorate village life Gandhi placed a great deal of emphasis on productive efficiency and the improvement of the quality of village based industries. Nor did it imply that he was simply in favour of indiscriminately preserving all traditional means. For example, "He was asked whether he would like to take up any handicraft. He replied: 'not necessarily. I should examine each of them, find out their place in the economy of the village. If I see that they must be encouraged because of *inherent merit*, I shall do so'."[36] And elsewhere he was willing to consider the selective use of certain kinds of industrial production, as long as an emphasis on supporting employment for the mass of rural workers was maintained. As he states: "Provided this character of the village industry is maintained, there would be no objection to the villagers using even modern machines and tools that they can make and can afford to use. Only they should no be used as a means of exploitation of others."[37]

Gandhi insisted again and again that "without the cottage industry, the Indian peasant is doomed."[38] Such a statement was the same claim voiced by the original Luddites in regard to the distressed cottage workers of the English Midlands. The conflict there was overcome, as Kirkpatrick Sale makes clear in his history of the Luddites,[39] by the possibility open to England at that time to transport its excess population. But the worry about employment and the new phenomenon of mass unemployment originally voiced in that time has never really gone away. It remains today in the widespread worries about globalization in the West and worries about the increasing gap between low skilled mass labourers and the rising "symbolic analyst" class.[40]

The Selectivity Imperative in Gandhi's Work

H.J.N Horsburgh reflects intensely on the following remark of Gandhi: "we have always control over the means and never on the ends."⁴¹ Horsburgh takes this remark as an indication of a detailed Gandhian critique of utilitarian ethics that can be reconstructed from an analysis of Gandhi's written work. However, it seems more likely to me that it simply represents Gandhi's acceptance of the non-neutrality thesis. Taken in this way, such a remark indicates two important points about Gandhi's position. First, our moral values or "ends" are not relative to us, but are a part of reality that must somehow be discovered by "experimenters with truth." Second, our choice of appropriate means is an important way we can manifest our understanding of our moral obligations, because it is through the application of such obligations to the creation and selection of means, that these obligations can become manifest. This is a reiteration of the basic premise of Neo-Luddites, that since technologies inevitably manifest values, it is imperative that we make sure our choices are made consciously and with a proper moral analysis of the complete manifold of values that will be expressed.

Gandhi believed that hand spinning, combined with weaving on hand looms, was the only logical way for the people of India to become self-sufficient and independent. He also claimed that if India employed his methods, poverty would be greatly reduced. Among Gandhi's arguments for intrinsic merits of home spinning were that it required a few simple low cost implements, was easy to learn, was suitable as part time employment for rural people and could prevent the drain of wealth from the country.⁴² It is easy to find in such observations Gandhi's concern with the implications of the infrastructure and outputs of home spinning as opposed to industrial production, as well as concerns about the relative power the distinct kinds of social groups set up by different production systems. But the activity of spinning was much more than an exercise in economic analysis for Gandhi. The practice of spinning also had moral and spiritual implications as well. As Ganguli notes: "There was a tendency to encourage Khadi as a ritual or sacrement (Gandhi has himself stressed this aspect)."⁴³

One of the "conditions of attendance" of the activity of the wheel is that it allows the spinner precious time to reflect and think, even meditate or pray. During the process of spinning the mind is free to dwell on things other than one's personal worries and cares. Gandhi believed that to the extent that the spinner was able to turn away from self-centred thoughts and became more other-centred he or she would reach a higher sense of purpose and become more spiritually aware.

Grant's View of Technology

Grant essentially held an understanding of technology as process. For him the most noteworthy aspect of technology is the increasingly prominent role that technological problem solving has come to play in Western political life. He sees this characteristic as a phenomenon warranting our deepest consideration. In his essay "Thinking about Technology," Grant tried to make his readers aware that technology, rather than being simply "the whole apparatus of instruments made by man and placed at his disposal for his choice and purposes," is also a distinct way of approaching the world.[44] This understanding of technology, which emphasizes it practical nature, is revealed in the following description Grant gives of modern life:

> I never forget returning home to Toronto after many years in Halifax. Driving in from the airport, I remember being gripped in the sheer presence of the booming, pulsating place which had arisen since 1945. What did it mean? Where was it going? What had made it? How could there be any stop to its dynamism without disaster, and yet, without stop, how could there not be disaster?[45]

Grant defines the term "technology" as the "endeavour which summons forth everything (both human and non-human) to give its reasons, and through the summoning forth of those reasons turns the world into potential raw material, at the disposal of our 'creative' wills."[46] Technology involves a certain attitude to the world, an attitude of control.

For Grant, technology results from the bringing together of two distinct types of human activity, knowing and making, in which "both activities are changed by their co-penetration."[47] According to him, in ancient societies a strong distinction was drawn between practical knowledge and the kind of theoretical knowledge necessary for understanding the good. This distinction helped protect and preserve the integrity and distinctiveness of both of these types of thinking. However, Grant argued that for modern people the idea of theory had come to encompass only the kind of instrumental reasoning necessary for technological activity and not the kind of contemplation necessary for understanding the good. To quote him:

It may perhaps be said negatively that what has been absent for us [as moderns] is the affirmation of a possible apprehension of the world beyond that as a field of objects considered as pragmata—an apprehension present not only in its height as 'theory' but as the undergirding of our loves and friendships, of our arts and reverences, and indeed as the setting for our dealing with the objects of the human and non-human world.[48]

Therefore, the union of knowing and making that technology represents changes both activities because within technological practice instrumental knowing is all that is required. Edwin and David Heaven argue that Grant's view of technology is that "reason as calculation has replaced thought in the classical sense as 'steadfast attention to the whole'."[49] For Grant, this opens a possibility for modern people to allow contemplative knowing of the good to be excluded from a life, which comes instead to be dominated by technological practice. Thus the exercise of human creativity can increasingly become limited to the wilful manipulation of the world.

The Non-Neutrality Thesis in Grant's Work

It is easy to find expression in Grant's of the kind of analysis of technologies regarding infrastructure, outputs, conditions of attendance and new social groups recommended by Neo-Luddites. In his essay "The computer does not impose on us the ways it should be used" Grant explicitly sets out to reject the characterization of the computer (or any technology) "as neutral instrument."[50] Grant's analysis quickly turns up the 4 main categories of inevitable ambiguous effects. In regards to Infrastructure he notes:

> *[Computers] have been put together from a variety of materials, consummately fashioned by a vast apparatus of fashioners. Their existence has required generations of sustained effort by chemists, metallurgists, and workers in mines and factories. It has required a highly developed electronics industry and what lies behind that industry in the history of science and technique and their novel reciprocal relation.*[51]

In regard to the category of Function/Output he notes, "Abstracting facts so that they may be stored as 'information' is achieved by classification, and it is the very nature of any classifying to homogenize what may be heterogeneous."[52] In regard to Conditions of Attendance he comments that: "To be awake in any part of our educational system is to know that the desire for these machines shapes those institutions at their heart in their curriculum, in what the young are encouraged to know and to do."[53] And finally in regards to the creation and empowerment and dis-empowerment of different groups, he states:

> *The computer has required that the clever of our society be trained within its massive assumptions about knowing and being and making which have made algebra actual. Learning within those such assumptions is not directed towards a leading out but towards organizing within. This entails that the majority of those who rule any modern society will take the purpose of ruling increasingly to be congruent with this account of knowing.*[54]

To be a member of the new elites of contemporary society requires not only mastery of the new electronic technologies, but for the users of those technologies to identify with the new kinds of activities they make possible.

The Selectivity Imperative in Grant's Work

Grant argues that the tendency in modern civilization is toward an increasing expectation that everyone should focus on seeking only the kind of knowledge that is applicable to the creation and application of useful instruments and techniques rather than on seeking to apprehend the moral implications of such activity. It is not only natural scientists who are looked to for the knowledge necessary for technological activity. As Grant points out:

> Much of the new technology upon which we are going to depend to meet the crisis in the 'developed' world is technology turned towards human beings... so that we can be shaped to live consonantly with the demands of mass society.[55]

This broadness of the understanding of technology is one of the central aspects of his understanding of technology. The knowledge involved in technology need not be restricted to the knowledge of non-human nature of natural science but can also include knowledge of human nature that emerges from the social sciences and humanities. As he puts it: "In North America we have divided our institutions of higher learning into faculties of natural science, social science and humanities, depending on the object which is being researched. But the project of reason is largely the same, to summons different things to questioning."[56] According to Grant, in technological activity there is no distinction between sources of knowledge and no distinction between the types of objects to which this knowledge can be applied.

Gandhi and Grant's Views of the Autonomy of Technology

Grant's reasons for looking at technology primarily as a distinctive type of activity are rooted in his concern that it can supplant ethical forms of knowing and acting. As Grant puts it, "The pursuit of technological advance is what constitutes human excellence in our age and therefore it is our morality."[57] This was a concern also expressed by Gandhi, "Western Nations are groaning under the heels of a monster—the God of materialism. Their moral growth has become stunted."[58] Grant also felt that technology was, in some ways, even beginning to take on the characteristic of a religion in the form of a faith in progress, the aim of which was "the domination of man over nature through knowledge and its application."[59]

Grant ultimately regards technology much as Neo-Luddites do. It is the natural expression of human freedom and creativity through the activity of seeking to control one's environment through the application of knowledge, but there are always ethical consequences that inevitably flow from it. Most importantly for Grant, technology as a form of activity, can be contrasted with other activities, such as contemplation, reflection, and recollection and can also influence these activities through the imparting of a guiding attitude of control. Therefore, for Grant, technology should be viewed as "a mode of being."[60] That is, he sees technology as an approach to life the guiding attitude of which can supplant the attitudes of other ways of approaching the world, and in so doing, can transform these activities into technological activity. According to Grant, such a characteristic is an aspect of the very genesis of technology, which is the co-penetration of knowing and making—theoretical reflection and formal practice. Technology is a type of making which involves taking on the attitude that through the application of knowledge and reason human beings can create a world better fitted to human purposes.

To put Grant's position most simply, technology is for him a type of problem solving. As Peter C. Emberley notes, "every society has a regime of truth. Ours, Grant reminds us, is sustained by the account of knowledge where a wilful subject confronts a material and metaphysically neutral environment which can be represented as 'resource' or as a 'problem.' Such a confrontation is one where knowing and making co-penetrate to secure the object."[61] Problem solving in general is the attempt to overcome an aspect of the world that is not to one's liking, but technology involves the improvement of the ability of people to deal with general types of problems. Grant argues, therefore, that technology embodies an "account of knowledge which is homogenising in its very nature."[62] Technological products are the result of the application of knowledge and reason to solve problems. Therefore, it solutions can never be idiosyncratic. It is only in terms of our understanding of the good, which is how we can come to define problems as problems, that variation in human societies can occur. According to Grant, technology is the ongoing quest to provide the "one best means" for solving problems. Homogenization threatens when such action consistently supplants contemplation and deliberation about what our proper ends (i.e. problems) should be. Heterogeneity can only result when ends are deliberated and vigorously contested by individuals and peoples. But if technologies are simply accepted without proper moral analysis, such as can occur in the circumstances of colonialism, or in Canada's case, with the simple enthralment to technological change in its American guise, this can ultimately lead to the "universal homogeneous state" as foretold by Hegel and expounded upon by Alexandre Kojève.[63]

Because technology is for Grant a form of activity it is intimately related to the will. "We are confronted with three primals [in Grant's thought]: contemplation, love, and will."[64] Choosing to put an instrument to use involves ceasing the search for understanding about the problem which that instrument is meant to address and choosing to act on one's knowledge. Technology always involves one in practice. Consequently, technology is not for Grant an activity which can itself encompass contemplation and deliberation about end because it is always an endeavour to satisfy ends taken as already given. It can be coupled with the activity of discerning and assessing ends, but it need not.

There are three aspects of technology that Grant found most significant. 1) While technology can supplant contemplation or deliberation about ends, technological action always involves seeking to satisfy given desires or ends and, therefore, cannot be said to be value neutral or separable from human evaluation. 2) Technology cannot be limited to the material world or the world of material objects, and therefore any understanding of it must allow for the inclusion of technologies which are directed toward the control or self-control of human beings and the social world and technologies which are embodied through formal activity. 3) Technology demands adopting an attitude of control that can influence the way that one engages in other types of human activity such as contemplation and deliberation about ends.

This final characteristic is where the possibility of the "autonomy" of technology raises its head for Grant. He expresses his concern about this possibility of technology this way: "We move into a tightening circle in which more technological science is called for to meet the problems which technological science has produced."[65] Two factors contribute to this possibility. First, as already mentioned, technological practice can compete with, and thus squeeze out of our lives, the opportunity to reflect on our moral obligations and the good, especially in regard to our technological activities. As Grant describes this dangerous quality of technology: "The ambiguity is that technology, which came into the world carrying in its heart a hope about justice, has in its realization dimmed the ability of those who live in it to think justice."[66] Second, technology involves us in habitual practices, one could even say, ritual practice, such that it becomes second nature and thus, can hide from our conscious consideration. We can, for instance, become so reliant on technological innovation itself, as a universal tool for dealing with the challenges we face as individuals or societies, that this approach can become the automatic response to every predicament we face. Technology, in a way can force out all potential competition, in the form of the skeptical ethical consideration of its limits. So as Grant states: "When we, as Western people, put ourselves the question of what can lie 'beyond industrial growth,' we are liable to be asking it as a problem within the package which is that destiny. It is taken as a problem of the same order as that which we are currently meeting because of our dependence on oil and the Arab awakening."[67] In other words, the problem is one to be met with the traditional means of the application of military power or technological solutions, such as the hydrogen car or compact-florescent bulbs, etc. As even Grant himself admits "human beings may still be able to control the ways that cars are used by preventing, for example, their pollution of the atmosphere or their freeways from destroying the centre of our cities."[68] But all such efforts, no matter how successful or well intentioned, ignore the essential possibility that some of the crises we are facing are not rooted in a lack of sufficient means, but a lack of efforts at the proper assessment of means in terms of their complex effects. As he says, "Fifty years ago men might have said 'the automobile does not impose on us the ways it should be used.' This would have been a deluding representation of the automobile."[69]

The recommendation of both Gandhi and Grant is to question longstanding technological habits by engaging in a more thorough moral analysis of the technological activities and practices in which we partake. For Grant the most important of such was the use of nuclear weapons. But he was also willing to question the computer, and the car culture, as when he says with some hope, "Indeed in Canada, we may be able to deal better with such questions [about the car], as the history of the Spadina expressway may show."[70] The Spadina Expressway was a proposed highway through the centre of the city of Toronto that would have destroyed many neighbourhoods. It was cancelled after protests led by activists like Jane Jacobs and with the support of Canada's media theory intellectual superstar, Marshall McLuhan.

Gandhi also advocated for such direct actions. Especially actions that would allow people to break out of established technical norms and into new experiences that would allow them to understand the moral implications of the instruments and systems of the world from which they had come. For instance he states:

> I fully stand by [what] I have described in Hind Swaraj...My experience has confirmed the truth of what I wrote in 1909. If I were the only one left who believed in it I would not be sorry...I believe that if India, and through India the world, is to achieve real freedom, then sooner or later we shall have to go and live in the villages—in huts, not in palaces... We can have the vision of truth and non-violence only in the simplicity of the villages.... The sum and substance of what I want to say is that the individual person should have control over the things that are necessary for the sustenance of life.[71]

Gandhi was deeply influenced by Henry David Thoreau, one of the first intellectuals to explicitly voice a concern about technological dependency and the autonomy of technology, such as when he asserted that "we do not ride on the railroad it rides upon us." Like Grant, Gandhi was also continuously vexed by those who sought to transform his call for moral responsibility regarding means, into a political ideology or legislative programme. For example, we can find a commenter conclude something like the following immediately following an analysis of Gandhi's defense of swadeshi and the need to wear khadi: "In the rest of the chapter we propose to deal more specifically with the positive core of *swadeshi*, i.e. employment of the masses of the population through deliberate regulation of consumption and productive technique in the national interest."[72] But as Rashmi Sharma notes, for Gandhi it was only "as a last resort, [that] statutory measures or legislation could also be used. But the statute that Gandhi has in mind was not one imposed by the state. That represented violence in its concentrated and organized form."[73] As Gandhi himself puts this principle, "such a statute will not be imposed from above. It will have to come from below. When people understand the implications of trusteeship and the atmosphere is ripe for it, the people themselves, beginning Panchayats will begin to introduce such statutes."[74] In a similar fashion, Grant's lament at the moral failure of Canadians to refuse American nuclear weapons, became a rallying cry among the New Left for legislative programmes to reform the "the branch plant" economic relationship between Canada and the United States. Indeed, the brief push towards economic nationalization undertaken by Canada in the 1970s is seen by many as being the main legacy of Grant's *Lament for a Nation,* rather than Grant's rejection of nuclear weapons and Canada's involvement in the American military system.

Conclusion

Although they did not use the term, I think the best phrase to describe the political outlooks of Gandhi and Grant is Neo-Luddite nationalism. Gandhi's Swadeshi programme was born primarily of his desire to seek technologies that manifested important moral values in a specific context. It was not born of a chauvinistic belief in the superiority of all things Indian. Grant's *Lament for a Nation* arose not from a love of all things "Canadian" but from the decision of a government of the time to accept nuclear weapons onto Canadian soil. In other words, their impassioned calls to national duty represent a universal duty everyone has to be selective about the means one chooses, while acknowledging that this will inevitably manifest itself as differences between individuals and groups in the kinds of choices that are most appropriate. In other words, people do not choose to be a nation and then make choices based on such an abstract choice. It is because people make (and must inevitably make) different moral choices about the best way of living in diverse circumstances and according to diverse human attempts at "experiments with truth" that nations come into existence. In Grant's words "the way we come to love the God is by first loving our own."[75] Such as task is perennial and enjoined on all people. This is a major reason why the teachings of Gandhi and Grant have such continuing universal appeal.

Notes

1. Larry Hickman, "Doing and Making in a Democracy: Dewey's Experience of Technology," in *Philosophy of Technology: The Technological Condition*, ed Val Dusek, and Robert C. Scharff (Oxford: Blackwell, 2003), 375.
2. Howard Aster, "Nationalism and Communitarianism," in *Nationalism, Technology and the Future of Canada*, ed. Wallace Gagne (Toronto: McMillan, 1976), 53.
3. George Grant, 1970; quoted in H.D. Forbes, "The Political Thought of George Grant." Journal of Canadian Studies 26, 2 (1991): 54.
4. Chellis Glendinning, "Notes Toward a Neo-Luddite Manifesto," in *Philosophy of Technology: The Technological Condition*, ed Val Dusek, and Robert C. Scharff (Oxford: Blackwell, 2003), 375. From *Utne Reader 38.1 (1990)*: 50-3.
5. Ibid., 604.
6. Andrew Feenberg, *The Critical Theory of Technology* (New York: Oxford University Press, 1991) pp. 5-8. Also see: pp. 163-198.
7. Langdon Winner, *The Whale and the Reactor: A Search for Limits in an Age of High Technology* (Chicago: University of Chicago Press, 1986), 19-39.
8. Neil Robertson, "Freedom and the Tradition: George Grant, James Doull, and the Character of Modernity in *Athens and Jerusalem: George Grant's Theology, Philosophy, and Politics*, ed. Ian Angus, Ron Dart and Randy Peg Peters (Toronto: University of Toronto Press, 2006), 148.
9. Gregory Baum, *Nationalism Religion and Ethics* (Montreal: McGill-Queens University Press, 2001), 41.
10. 0 Raghavan N. Iyer, *The Moral and Political Thought of Mahatma Gandhi* (New York: Oxford University Press, 2000), 26.
11. Ibid.
12. Ibid., 35.
13. H.D. Forbes, 1991, 47.
14. William Christian and Sheila Grant, eds., *The George Grant Reader* (Toronto: University of Toronto Press), 394.
15. Madhuri Santanam Sondhi, *Modernity, Morality and the Mahatma* (Delhi: Haranand, 1997), 35.

16. Stephanie Mills, ed., *Turning Away From Technology: A New Vision for the 21st Century* (San Francisco: Sierra Club Books, 1997), xiii.
17. Sondhi, *Modernity, Morality and the Mahatma*, 35.
18. David Hardiman, *Gandhi in His Time and Ours: The Global Legacy of His Ideas* (New York: Columbia University Press, 2003), 74.
19. Morton Winston, "Children of Invention," in *Society, Ethics, and Technology*, 3rd ed., ed Ralph D. Edelbach and Morton Winston (Toronto: Thomson Wadsworth, 2006), 1.
20. Ibid., xi.
21. Andrew Feenberg, *Questioning Technology* (New York: Routledge 1999), 201.
22. M. K. Gandhi, speech delivered before the Missionary Conference, Madras, 14 February 1916; quoted in Rashmi Sharma, *Gandhian Economics: A Humane Approach* (New Delhi: Deep and Deep, 1997), 146.
23. Winston, "Children of Invention," 2.
24. M.K. Gandhi, *Hind Swaraj*, 60; Quoted in H. J. N. Horsburgh, *Non-Violence and Aggression: A Study of Gandhi's Moral Equivalent of War* (Toronto: Oxford University Press, 1968), 43.
25. Sondhi, *Modernity, Morality and the Mahatma*, 69.
26. B. N. Ganguli, *Gandhi's Social Philosophy: Perspective and Relevance*: Toronto: John Wiley and Sons, 1973), 98.
27. Ibid.
28. H. J. N. Horsburgh, *Non-Violence and Aggression*, 42.
29. Hardiman, *Gandhi in His Time and Ours*, 76.
30. Ibid., 75.
31. M. K. Gandhi, *Young India*, 1.1.1925, p. 52; quoted in Rashmi Sharma, *Gandhian Economics*, 37.
32. M.K. Gandhi, "Liberals and Khaddar" in *Young India*, 12 June 1924 (New York: Viking), 603
33. M.K. Gandhi, 1934; quoted in Ganguli, *Gandhi's Social Philosophy*, 299.
34. M.K. Gandhi, *Speeches and Writings of Mahatma Gandhi*, 3rd ed. (Madras: Natesan, 1934), p. 245; quoted in Iyer, *The Moral and Political Thought of Mahatma Gandhi*, 354.

35. Quoted in Ganguli, *Gandhi's Social Philosophy*, 286.
36. Ibid., 288.
37. Ibid., 300.
38. Ibid., 287.
39. Kirkpatrick Sale, *Rebels Against the Future* (Addison-Wesley, 1996)
40. Jeremy Rifkin, *The End of Work: The Decline of the Global Labor Force and the Dawn of the Post Market-Era* (New York: Jeremy P. Tarcher/Penguin, 1995), 35.
41. Horsburgh, *Non-Violence and Aggression*, 42.
42. Sharma, *Gandhian Economics*, 155.
43. Ganguli, *Gandhi's Social Philosophy*, 301.
44. George Grant, *Technology and Justice* (Toronto: Anansi, 1986) 19.
45. George Grant, "Conversation with George Grant" in *George Grant in Process*, ed. Larry Schmidt, (Toronto: Anansi, 1978), 86.
46. George Grant, *English-Speaking Justice* (Concord, ON: House of
46. 1. Anansi Press, 1985), 88.
47. Grant, *Technology and Justice*, 13.
48. George Grant, *Technology and Empire* (Toronto: Anansi, 1969), 35.
49. E. Heaven and D. R. Heaven, "Some Influences of Simone Weil on Grant's Silence" in *George Grant in Process*, ed. Larry Schmidt, 69.
50. George Grant, "The Computer Does Not Impose on Us the Ways It Should Be Used" in *The George Grant Reader*, eds. William Christian and Sheila Grant (Toronto: University of Toronto Press), 423.
51. Ibid., 422.
52. Ibid., 424.
53. Ibid., 422.
54. Ibid.
55. Grant, *Technology and Justice*, 16.
56. Ibid., 37.
57. George Grant, *Philosophy in the Mass Age* (Toronto: The Copp Clark Publishing Company, 1966), iv.

58. M.K. Gandhi, *Mahatma*, Vol I, ed D.G. Tendulkar (New Delhi: Publications Division, Ministry of Information and Broadcasting, Gov't of India, 1951), 196; quoted in Sharma, *Gandhian Economics*, 32.
59. Grant, *Philosophy in the Mass Age*, 4.
60. Grant, *Technology and Justice*, 17.
61. Peter C. Emberley, "Values and Technology: George Grant and Our Present Possibilities," 472.
62. Grant, *Technology and Justice*, 24.
63. Ibid., 86.
64. Bernard Zylstra, "Philosophy, Revelation, Modernity," in *George Grant in Process*, ed. Larry Schmidt, 155.
65. Grant "The Computer Does Not Impose..." in *The George Grant Reader*, eds. Christian and Grant, 432.
66. Grant "Justice and Technology" in *The George Grant Reader*, eds. Christian and Grant, 437.
67. Grant "The Computer Does Not Impose..." in *The George Grant Reader*, eds. Christian and Grant, 432.
68. Ibid., 424.
69. Ibid.
70. Ibid.
71. M.K. Gandhi, "Hind Swaraj" *Young India*, 26 January 1921, in *The Collected Works of Mohatma Gandhi* ed. K Swaminathan (New Delhi: Publications Division, Ministry of Information and Broadcasting, Gov't of India, 1958-94), 277; quoted in Vivek Pinto, *Gandhi's Vision and Values: The Moral Quest for Change in Indian Agriculture* (New Delhi: Sage Publications, 1998), 17.
72. Ganguli, *Gandhi's Social Philosophy*, 289.
73. Sharma, *Gandhian Economics*, 41.
74. M.K. Gandhi, *Harijan: A Journal of Applied Gandhism*: 1933-55 (New York: Garland, 1973), 31.3.1946, pp. 63-64; quoted in Sharma, *Gandhian Economics*, 41
75. Dennis Lee, "Grant's impasse," in *By Loving Our Own: George Grant and the Legacy of Lament for a Nation*, ed. Peter C. Emberley (Ottawa: Carleton University Press, 1990), 11.

☼ ☾

12

GEORGE GRANT AND GANDHI: A LIVE INTERVIEW WITH MRS. SHEILA GRANT

Arati Barua

George Grant, the well-known Canadian nationalist, philosopher, political scientist and an active activist is relatively unknown in Indian intellectual milieu. He is considered to be one of the most original and profound nationalist thinkers of Canada though was often misunderstood[1]. George Parkin Grant, popularly known as George Grant, was born in November 13, 1918 in Toronto to William and Maude Parkin Grant, a renowned family of Canada.

George Grant comes from an academic background. George Monro Grant his paternal grandfather, was the Principal of Queen's University from 1877 until his death in 1902. Sir George Parkin on the other hand was his maternal grandfather and he was the founding secretary for the Rhodes Scholarships[2]. In May 1926 Grant first entered Brown school and then in the next year he went to prep school. In 1932

Grant entered upper school at UCC (Upper Canada College). Grant lived with his family in the Principal's residence (his father being the Principal of Upper Canada College) in the Southeast Wing of the main building of UCC. 'Grant's education was influenced by his father's enthusiasm for Canadian history, his defense of French Canada, and his view of war as senseless'[3]. But in February 3, 1935 when his father died, Grant had to move out from the official residence and he had to live elsewhere, a situation he detested.

In 1936 Grant graduated from UCC and entered the same year Queen's university in Kingston, Ontario. In that year Grant's mother Maude became the Dean of Women at McGill's Royal Victoria College. Grant won 2 scholarships in 1938, which allowed him to take travel in England and Europe. His family wanted him to be a public figure like his grandfathers and for that reason he was sent to Oxford to study Law [4]. But somehow he did not want as his mother, who was a very strong woman, expected him to be the Prime Minister [5] of Canada. He chose to be an educationist, a philosopher, a professor of religious study and political philosophy and to work for the betterment of Canada and the Canadians wholeheartedly. So in 1939 he joined Law at Balliol College, England as a Rhodes Scholar [6]. However Grant later on changed his subject to Theology and got his D. Phil in theology in 1950. Before he had got his D. Phil, Grant married Sheila Allen in London in 1947.

In 1961 Grant was appointed in the Department of religion at McMaster University in Hamilton, Ontario where he continued to teach for 20 years. In 1964 he became the Chairman of the Mcmaster Department of religion and a Fellow of Royal Society of Canada. On March 27th 1965 Grant's "*Lament for a Nation*" was published which immediately drew the attention [7] of all readers. In 1980 Grant resigned from McMaster and was appointed Killam Professor in the Department of Political Science at Dalhousie, Halifax but he retired from Dalhousie as soon as he became 65 [8].

His magnum opus, the *"Lament for a Nation"*, is still considered to be a masterpiece [9] in twentieth century Canadian writings on nationalism. In this influential work, Grant appeared to be a great patriot, a nationalist in fire, an idealist conservative, a philosopher and above all a political activist. He reestablished himself as a profound original thinker in his subsequent and more fundamental work, *"Technology and Empire"*. The highly surcharged George Grant with emotions and feelings for conserving Canadian national identity in the *Lament for a Nation* turned into a more sober, logical and rational thinker in the *Technology and Empire* to arrive at the same conclusion. The conclusion is that Canada must not be in the rate race to catch up the American technological levels at the cost of its own national identity. For him the concept of modernism as used today is based on a particular value judgement that modernism means achieving the highest technological standard set by the Americans. Modernism does not necessarily mean saying good bye to our past. And modern technological development is essentially based on a gale of "creative destruction", justifying the destruction of the past knowledge and technology to pave the way for the new technology. New technology means the only way to move on the unending path to development. George Grant vehemently opposed to this view of modernism and technology in his *Technology and Empire* because it destroys the past – the valuables we inherit from our forefathers. Modern technology not only destroys the past but also it imposes a terrible homogenizing[10] effect on every culture forcing all nations to follow the Americans burying its own identity. A fervent nationalist George Grant did not want this to happen to Canada.

I have accumulated this much knowledge about this wonderful gentleman by going through his biography as portrayed by William Christian of Guelph University and as it is given in T.F.Rigelhof's 'chronology of George Grant' in his book *"George Grant redefining Canada"*(2001). There may be many gaps in my understanding of Grant as I am exposed to his profundity only by an accident. It just happened that one fine morning as I approached the issuing desk of books in the library my eyes suddenly got struck at the *Biography of Grant* by Christian, which was lying on the issue desk. Perhaps some user has just returned the book. Sheer curiosity instantly propelled me to draw the book towards me and I just wanted to read about George Grant. As I was reading about the life of this remarkable Canadian gentleman it turned out to be great revelation to me. I felt as if I am reading Mohan Das Karamchand Gandhi of India.

To my knowledge I have not come across any study or comparison between Grant and Gandhi. I wanted to know the foundational propositions giving rise to the convergence of the ideas of these two great souls of Canada and India. Interestingly, during the same time I also came across the web site of SICI and its fellowship facilities. I was so much enthused to study a comparison between Grant and Gandhi that I immediately sent an email to Prof. William Christian asking for his views[11] on the scope of research on the issue and also placement possibility at Guelpf University. I wrote to Prof. Christian because I did not know about any other authors on Grant at that point of time. Professor William Christian encouraged me to submit a proposal in SICI, giving me hope of a placement possibility at the Political Science Department of the Guelph University and confirming to be my research advisor in the event of my success in crossing the selection barriers for the fellowship. Eventually I was selected for the fellowship and in due course of time I landed up at the Guelph University.

Before I reached the Guelph University it was necessary for all Shastri scholars to attend orientation course on Canadian Studies which was organized at Halifax. It was a great opportunity for me, as if the entire program was instituted at Halifax to benefit me alone! Professor William Christian wrote to me that George Grant's wife[12] lives in the city of Halifax only. Nothing could perhaps be more dramatic than this news to me. I wrote to Mrs. Sheila Grant, the widow of George Grant, expressing my desire to have an interview with her and I also wrote to her the purpose of my visit. She welcomed me and so on 21st May, 2003 I knocked at the door of Mrs. Grant (1622,Walnut street, where George Grant used to live till his last days) for an interview[13]. She is a very warm lady and appreciated me for taking up the project. I realized that the bookish knowledge could not give me true aspects of George Grant's views on Gandhi. And there could not have been a better person than Mrs. Sheila Grant to educate me on that. Therefore it is befitting to my purpose that before my commentary on the Grant-Gandhi issue I must place before the readers what Mrs. Sheila Grant thinks about such a comparison. The following is a transcript version of my interview with Mrs. Sheila Grant:

Interview with Sheila Grant

AB. Did George Grant ever meet M. K. Gandhi?

SG. No, he did not have an occasion to do so.

AB. When did he come to know about Gandhi? Did he read any of Gandhi's books or books authored by others on Gandhi?

SG. I don't know exactly but I imagine that he came to know about Gandhi before I met him [in 1945]. But both of us admired Gandhi very much. Maybe Grant came to know about Gandhi before our marriage. Grant must have read some of Gandhi's books, probably he read Gandhi's Autobiography. I have read Gandhi's Autobiography and I saw a movie on Gandhi made by Richard Attenborough.

AB. Which aspect, if any, of Gandhi's philosophy was most appealing to Grant?

SG. Certainly "Non-violence". Grant was a pacifist and did not like the outcome of war, so he accepted Gandhi's concepts of Non-violence and pacifism.

AB. Did Grant ever realize that there were similarities of views between him and Gandhi?

SG. No, I sometimes had that question to my mind. I have great reverence for Gandhi and I love my husband and I admired him much but I won't put my husband on the same level with Gandhi [because Gandhi was a thinker and a holy man and Grant was merely a thinker].

AB. There is apparent commonness of views between the two, particularly, on technology and modernism. Did Grant ever conceive of these ideas independently or only later did he found some?

SG. No, I think it is quite independent. What George Grant was doing in a small way while writing his book 'Lament for a nation" was similar to what Gandhi was doing earlier.

AB. Who are other Indian thinkers who in your opinion had profound influence on Grant?

SG. He did get a chance to go to India, he was offered a chance to lecture somewhere in India, but he did not go as it was too late for him. He would have loved to go to India.

AB. What are the influences of Grant on the contemporary political and economic thinkers in Canada? Is that influence of the same dimension with that of Gandhi in India?

SG. Not the same dimension. His "Lament for a Nation" did have an influence on Canada and the Canadians. It was also the time when the Canadians began to realize that their country is being taken over by others and hardly it could be called an independent country. But nothing formal had been done.

AB. Do you think Grant's views on technology and modernism is feasible in the complex modern world? If you have any reason then would you elucidate on how to make it feasible?

SG. Yes, I certainly, I think he was right. In his book "Technology and Empire" he did feel that.

AB. How do you think of India today? Do you have any message for Indian people in general?

SG. Humility - my heart beats for them. I don't know much but my husband knew better. He would have known what political things were going on and what India was going for etc but I don't know.

AB. Do you consider him a philosopher, a humanist, an idealist or a political ideologist?

SG. I consider him a Philosopher. I never heard of any criticism [from him] about Gandhi. He [Grant] could not have failed in any precision [on that subject]. He was a great subtle man, a philosopher.

AB. In today's concern for environmental problem many of the views of Grant and Gandhi seem relevant. For example, it is impossible to sustain the present level of development without having serious impact on earth's resource availability and environment. So there are some views on limiting the growth which could be attained by limiting our desires and wants. Here lies the relevance of the views of the technology and modernism of Grant and Gandhi. What is your opinion? Any comments on this?

SG. I think that is true. I think that is very well put.

AB. Unfortunately Grant's philosophy is not a part of existing curriculum of studies in India. My endeavor would be to see that his views are introduced in our academic course in India. Do you maintain the same view for Gandhi in Canadian academic milieu as well?

SG. I don't know whether he (Gandhi) is taught. I would have hoped but I have no way of knowing about it, as [because of my age] I don't see a lot of people these days.

Appendix

First of all I wish to express my sincere gratefulness to the Shastri Indo-Canadian Institute to facilitate me with the fellowship due to which only I could pursue my research on Grant and Gandhi in Canada. This is the first part of my research work on Grant and Gandhi mainly based on an interview with Mrs. Sheila Grant (wife of George Grant) on her view about Grant and Gandhi.

Professor William Christian of Guelph University who was my formal supervisor for the research on the topic was of immense help for me in every respect and my thanks are due to him.

Finally without a few words about Mrs. Sheila Grant-the widow of George Grant, my research article on Grant and Gandhi would not be complete. Sheila Grant was not only the wife of this famous patriotic philosopher of Canada but she was also herself a highly educated, an Oxford educated lady and her husband was much influenced by her personality. In fact George Grant himself has said in the preface to his *"Technology and Justice"* that she was a co-author to this book as he says:

"*All that I write proceeds from sustained discussions with my wife. In that sense, she is the co-author of my writing and explicitly named such in the articles about euthanasia and abortion*". (p –10).

Even after his death Sheila Grant is still working with Prof Christian and other scholars on Grant and is helping them in the works of publishing Grant's writings on different areas. For example, she is a co-editor with Prof Christian for the book "*The George Grant Reader*" from university of Toronto press 1998 besides contributing her own papers in different books. Regarding her contribution towards the publication of Grant's works, it is noteworthy what Prof Christian the biographer of G Grant says, " It is no more than the truth to say that without Sheila Grant this book (*Biography of George Grant*) would not exist. At the simplest level, she made George Grant's papers freely available to me, shared her reminiscences, read each draft of the manuscript, corrected untold errors, and made many suggestions for improvement. More important, she kept her husband more or less sane for over forty years. She valued his work and actively worked with him to make it as good as it was. Without her he undoubtedly would have been a profound thinker, but his published work would not have been as good."(p. XI, *Biography of George Grant*).

Now she is quite old and she dose not keep often well too. So this interview is not a very easy and ordinary interview in the sense that with difficulties I could arrange a meeting with her within those three days of my stay in Halifax where I was attending my orientation course on Canadian studies in the St Mary's university. It was Dr. Edna Keeble the Director of the summer institute's course, who immediately arranged a video camera (in fact she gave her own video-camera and a small tape recorder without which my interview would not have been possible and so my heartfelt thanks to Dr Keeble) and Ms Pauli the program organizer who made an appointment with her (Mrs. Grant) for me the moment I expressed my desire to meet Mrs. Grant.

Mr. Vinay Gupta from JNU a student who was also there for the same course helped me in taking the video recording of the interview with Mrs Grant in Halifax, my thanks are due to him also.

Mrs. Grant could walk with difficulties to open the door for us but still gave me her time, listened to my questions with patience and tried to answer them one by one with smile. After coming back to India, I tried to take out the excerpts of the recorded interview by listening repeatedly to the taped conversations and then this article took place. So my heartfelt thanks to this fine lady for helping me in my humble effort.

Notes

1. "George Grant (1918-1988), author of *Philosophy in the mass age* (1959), *Lament for a Nation* (1965) and *Technology and Empire* (1969), was one of Canada's most significant thinkers- but was often misunderstood." In a review by Mark Wegierski of *"George Grant- in Conversation"* (ed.) by David Cayley.

2. "George Grant....... was born into a renowned family. Both of his grandfathers devoted their lives to the reform of education. Sir George Parkin started up the Rhodes Scholarships at Lord Milner's request; George Monro Grant turned the struggling Presbyterian school of Queen's in Kingston into a university. George Grant's father, William Grant, rescued Upper Canada College (a private boys' school in Toronto) from mediocrity and made it an important educational institution. P. 304, *"George Grant and the Subversion of Modernity: Art, Philosophy, Politics, Religion, and Education"* (ed.) by Arthur Davis, University of Toronto press, 1996.

3. p-158, *"George Grant, redefining Canada"*, by T. F. Rigelhof, 2001, XYZ publishing.

4. Co-incidentally, like Grant, M.K. Gandhi also had been to England to study Law only.

5. "George Grant (being)....the nephew of Vincent Massey, Canada's first native-born Governor General....Yet he did

not become a prime minister of Canada as his mother had hoped for". "*George Grant redefining Canada*", back cover page.

6. "As a Rhodes scholar at Oxford, he started out in Law and ended up in theology". William Christian, in *Kitchener-Waterloo* column.

7. "It is interesting to look back ....at the reviews '*Lament for a Nation*" received upon publication. About a third were complimentary, most were mixed, and more than a few were downright hostile". p-44, "*By loving our own : George Grant and the legacy of Lament for a Nation*" , (ed.) Peter C. Emberley, Carleton library series 161, Carleton University Press.

8. "The decision to return to Dalhousie having been in some measure a mistake, Grant retires as soon as he turns sixty-five, but he remains in the public eye. He appears on radio and television and speaks against Free Trade, testing cruise missiles, and abortion." P-171, "*George Grant redefining Canada*", T.F.Rigelhof,2001, XYZ publishing.

9. 'His (Grant's) masterpiece *Lament for a Nation*, was a ninety-seven page combination of philosophy, political analysis, religion and rant the like of which was seen before in Canada and has certainly not been seen in the almost forty years since it appeared in 1965", William Christian, Kitchener-Waterloo Column.

10. "*Lament for a Nation* (1965), a meditation on the implications of the Diefenbaker period, attracted wide attention for its somber conclusion that Canada- a nation with conservative roots-was doomed to disappear in the American-led empire of modern liberalism, which for Grant is an inexorable force leading to a universal and homogenous state of almost certain tyranny." By Charles Taylor, P-766, "*The Canadian Encyclopaedia*", Vol. II, 1985.

11. Prof. William Christian of Guelph University who has written a number of books on George Grant including the *Biography of Grant* confirms the fact of similarity between Gandhi and Grant. He even talked to Mrs. Sheila Grant (the Oxford educated widow of G. Grant) in this context and she says to Prof. Christian that "there might be some similarity between Grant's meditations on the relation between the eternal and transitoriness of the political and Gandhi's, but she emphasizes that she thought that Gandhi's authority

was immeasurably greater because he was a saint and her husband most certainly was not" (in a personal letter to me by Prof. Christian).

12. Mrs. Sheila Grant, the Oxford educated wife of George Grant had a great influence on Grant's life as she was from an English tradition of education.

13. I have an audio- cassette of the interview with Mrs. Grant as well as a video- cassette on it but unfortunately it did not cover the interview fully.

ಙ ಛ

13

GEORGE GRANT ON ORDER AND CREATIVITY

(Andrew Kaethler)

Indeed it is easy to think that in the long haul it may be the Vedanta which is most resistant to destruction by technology.[1]

The idea of order, which is embedded in the notion of natural law, is found throughout George Grant's writings. The most explicit use of this language is seen in *Philosophy in the Mass Age*, and is implicitly written within the pages of his final book *Technology and Justice*. In *Technology and Justice* natural law is implicitly seen with his adamant rejection of ultimate freedom in the name of order. We as humans are part of something greater than ourselves—"to exist is a gift."[2] Limits are set by belief in cosmos rather than chaos. In order to understand Grant's emphasis on order it is necessary to see Grant's thought in context with the thoughts of those with whom he grappled, particularly Friedrich Nietzsche.[3] This compelling German stood in contradistinction from Grant rejecting a pre-existing order or horizon by stating that God is dead. Grant found Nietzsche's thoughts so powerful, persuasive, and consistent that it loomed over him like a threatening storm. Fearful of succumbing to Nietzsche, Grant shaped his philosophy and theology in a way that safeguarded him from falling into the Nietzschean 'will to power'. One of these effects, made more visible by his subtle interest in the Vedanta, is his emphasis on an existing unchanging order, and an inevitable fear of willing, which radically limited his view of creation and creativity. Unfortunately, because of this Grant was forced to ignore the biblical Old Testament and its notion of God as creator and one who wills. Furthermore, it limited Grant to hint at intimations of deprival and disabled him from offering something other in response to technology. This essay will expound on Grant's idea of order and creation, and attempt to find a way in which those of us who are deeply influenced by his thought can heed his warnings of technology without sacrificing creativity. This response is foreshadowed in Grant's own writings on myth and perhaps it is the profound depth of myth that draws Grant to the East.

In *Philosophy in the Mass Age* (1959) Grant defines the theory of natural law as "the assertion that there is an order in the universe, and that right action for us human beings consists in attuning ourselves to that order."[4] This assertion, in a similar form, is found among the pre-scientific civilizations. Greek, Hindu, and Christian thought are riddled with it. Within Christianity, Grant's religious faith, natural law theory has had many proponents, from the ancient writings of Augustine and Thomas Aquinas to the modern thoughts of Jacques Maritain and C. S. Lewis; however, these writers did not share in Grant's struggles with a God who wills and creates. They did not see a conflict between cosmic order and creation. In fact, it is just because the universe is created that it can be seen as cosmos. Augustine claimed that humans were created with the law written on their hearts.

Grant also perceives the connection between God and cosmos, but there is a subtle change in his later thought. In the 1985 interview with David Cayley he appears hesitant to link God and order with a concept of creation; instead, he ties it to the very essence of God. When asked about his conversion experience Grant stated, "it was a kind of affirmation that beyond time and space there is order... And that is what one means by God, isn't it? That ultimately the world is not a maniacal chaos...."[5] By itself this statement is at best vague, and does not take shape until it is combined with what is stated further in the interview concerning his doubts with creation: "A lot of the great question are frankly just beyond me. I am certain in speaking about God, for instance, but I am not at all certain about whether God is a creator. I can believe in the eternity of the world very easily."[6] It seems that for Grant natural law is not so much written in the hearts of humanity[7] or in the Pauline sense of nature (Romans 1), but is gleaned from contemplation of what is beyond—order outside of creation.[8] This sounds like Aristotle's notion of God:

> *The Aristotelian god like the biblical God is a thinking being, but in opposition to the biblical God he is only a thinking being, pure thought: pure thought that thinks itself and only itself. Only by thinking himself and nothing but himself does he rule the world. He surely does not rule by giving orders and laws. Hence he is not a creator-god: the world is as eternal as god... For Aristotle it is almost blasphemy to ascribe justice to his god; he is above justice as well as injustice.*[9]

Yet Grant does not construe God in the Aristotelian fashion? Grant unambiguously connects justice to God. He believes that Christ's death on the cross is the ultimate depiction of justice. Is God simply Grant's idea of perfection? David Cayley mentions Grant's debt to Simone Weil for his understanding of the relationship between necessity and the Good (the Good and God were synonymous for Grant), and asks Grant to speak about it. In his reply Grant appears to postulate God as the mere ideal for moral perfection:

> *The order of the good enters the human world when human beings are moved by their love of perfection. There have been in our tradition arguments for the being of God, and Weil's argument, if you want to use that word, is always the argument from perfection... 'the ontological argument,' namely that it is clear that human beings cannot get better by their own efforts, they can only get better insofar as they have partaken in an idea of perfection.*[10]

This seems to assert that God is merely the idea of perfection, but for Weil God is not a simple contemplative ideal. Weil believed that she actually encountered Christ: "Christ came down and took possession of me... In my arguments about the insolubility of the problem of God I had never foreseen the possibility of that, of a real contact, person to person, here below, between a human being and God."[11] Weil did not postulate an abstract God to fill the ethical need for perfection. 'Perfection' should be understood as a philosophical non-abrasive way of referring to God. Nonetheless, Grant's uncertainty about creation generates problems as it is not only inconsistent with his faith, but it elevates cosmic order in such a way that it dangerously teeters over the precipice of ethical abstraction.

Grant's hesitancy in regards to order and creation largely stems from his disagreement with the modern extreme existential notion of freedom espoused by Nietzsche. According to Nietzsche, we are beyond good and evil; therefore, freedom is not simply the freedom to choose but necessitates active creativity—one creates his/her own values. Grant, on the other hand, believes that freedom is a gift that is given in truth: "The truth shall make you free" (John 8:32). Unlike Nietzsche, Grant believes in the existence of good and evil (evil being the negation of good), yet Grant's notion of freedom gives him the atypical response that one does not choose between good and evil like they are competing truths, but rather one has the liberty to be indifferent to good.[12] Grant's view of freedom is passive rather than active, and thus there is no conflict between freedom and order since freedom is engulfed by order.

Grant desperately wants to avoid falling into the Nietzschean way of willing, absolute freedom and complete creativity. He realizes that justice cannot exist if we are beyond good and evil. Nietzsche's *übermensch* is absolutely free to create as he/she wills, and there is nothing that guides the *übermensch's* choice. Will to mastery is the essence of the technological paradigm. Grant believes that without transcendence there is no justice. True justice is unchanging and does not necessarily coincide with our desires; therefore, justice must be other.

Unfortunately, the radical undermining of freedom in the name of order severely limits creative willing. Receptivity is the Grantian antonym for existential freedom. Receptivity is the act of orienting oneself to the Good (Grant, like Simone Weil, uses the Good interchangeably with God) and waiting for God—waiting for grace. Simone Weil, Grant's saint, words this beautifully:

> Above all our thought should be empty, waiting, not seeking anything, but ready to receive in its naked truth the object that is to penetrate it... We do not obtain the most precious gifts by going in search of them but by waiting for them. Man cannot discover them by his own powers, and if he sets out to seek for them he will find in their place counterfeits of which he will be unable to discern the falsity.[13]

Weil hints that self-negation is the ideal, unlike the polar opposite Nietzschean elevation of the self. Weil writes that God has given us our being in order that He can beg it back from us. God lives most fully through us in our choice to die to the self.[14] Without the self there is no will. Interestingly, Grant uses Mozart as his example of receptivity par excellence, whereas, for most classical music enthusiasts Mozart is seen as a creative musical genius. Why the different outlook? Grant believes that Mozart is fulfilling his intended purpose as a vehicle for the torrent of music that God is revealing through him. But can we realistically see Mozart as a passive receptor for God's music? Is Mozart so emptied of his self that his totality has become the vehicle for God's melody? Perhaps Grant has gone too far. One would be hard pressed to find a historian who would depict Mozart as the embodiment of holiness. Nevertheless, there may be a way to balance this in which Mozart is both creator and receiver.

Here we must ask if there can be creative willing that is not technological—creativity that does not fall prey to the will to power. Grant hints at the answer in a course lecture concerning myth. Grant wisely maintains that one must first participate in myth in order to fully analyse it. Objective analysis works well for science, but does little in the extensive realms of morality and religion. Myth like all great art brings together the particular and the universal. Philosophy, the study of the whole, represents the absolute universal; however philosophy is restricted by our own limited personal abilities. It is tremendously difficult if not impossible to completely immerse oneself in the truths of the universal:

> *If we are (as I think we are) particular beings with the capacity for the universal—but with a tremendous stake in our particularity—then it is very hard for us to partake directly in the universal—either intellectually or morally—but it is in the beautiful—which in its perfection is the complete unity of the particular and the universal—that we can begin to grasp the universal.*[15]

The beauty of myth is a vehicle for the deepest of truths in which pure factual abstract thought is highly limited, if not incapable of expressing. Grant, comparing art and myth, claims, "The great works of art in some sense teach us of existence in its totality and even of our own mode of being in the world."[16]

It is possible to see the coming together of the particular and the universal as the joining of order and creativity. Order is represented by the universal and creativity by the particular. Myths are embedded with particular people, gods, and geography, which the teller of the myth has creatively made, while revealing deep universal truths (of course there are exceptions). Murray Jardine points out that when examining myths we are not to ask, "'Are they literally true?' but rather, 'What do they mean?'"[17] This sort of questioning seems to fit with Grant's preferred mode of reasoning in which meaning outweighs cold fact. Myth is not a detailed systematic description of the way things are; the deepest truths cannot be systematically described. Instead, myth demands participation in the mysterious.

Openness to mystery and accepting the primal truths of mystery seems to be more of an Eastern perspective than Western. Eastern Orthodox theology claims that the mystery of the triune Godhead is the primal truth in which all other truths originate—the beginning point is mystery. The Western demand for systematic thought struggles with such openness, whereas, for Eastern Orthodoxy the most important aspects of Christianity are not written down, but have been the subject of oral and symbolic transmission. This is why Christianity cannot systematically compose a single philosophy (contrary to Western insistence).[18] It is no surprise that Grant leaned strongly towards Eastern Orthodoxy, and was greatly influenced by Eastern thought as a whole, including Vedantic thought.

Why does Grant postulate that the Vedanta is the most resistant to technology? The Hindu philosophy of the Vedanta did not grow out of the origins of technological thought and it remains resilient to its forceful ways because it resides in a culture of myth. India or the East as a whole is inundated with stories about gods, demons, heroes, and villains. The West also has its myths; however, it has expended much of its energy on debunking such stories in the name of scientism. In this regard the West has been successful: the majority of Westerners define myth as false story, rather than a narrative that relays the deepest truths. This is the regrettable result of the fact/value distinction, something that Grant adamantly rejected.

If the cosmogonies of both the Old Testament and the Rig-Veda are read in the same manner as myth, they can offer a way in which creativity and order are able to come together. The mystery of creation is found in both Hindu and Christian scriptures and both emphasize the concept of the Uncreated bringing about the created. Philip Sherrard asserts that since God creates *ex nihilo* everything reflects an aspect of his divinity, yet God's character is unknowable; He is beyond being.[19] By taking these two points, God as creator and God as beyond being, Grant's fear of the willing God, the God who appears to be the epitome of technology, can be eradicated. First, the creation account depicts humans as created, thus placing them beneath God. Second, if God's character is unknowable and he is beyond being the 'is' of God is removed. God cannot be systematically characterized, but rather He must be constantly sought after in relationship. The unknowablity of God causes humans to be utterly dependent upon Him. Although humans are creators, as we are made in the image of God, our creativity cannot be systematically drawn from our notion of *imago dei*. God's image is elusive and any notion of creating must be done in fear and trembling, rather than with the assurance of one who has a clear and concise handbook.

In light of this Grant's view of Mozart can be balanced out. Mozart, like Grant asserts, is a model of receptivity as he orientates himself to God in order to fill himself with music. This is the recognition of our 'createdness', as one who is constantly dependent on the Creator. Mozart's disciplined training and personality also flow into the music, and therefore Mozart is a finite creator, a creator dependent upon the uncreated infinite One. He creates within the boundaries set by the Creator and these provide both purpose and limit to his creative capacities without erasing his identity.

God is the creator and He wills His creation, but willing and creating for us, as created ones, is limited since we are constantly dependent upon God. The creation narratives of Christianity and Vedantic thought must be read with an understanding of myth and narrative and not through the scientific lens of technology. The format of narrative itself has a beginning and end in which creativity is sandwiched between purpose and limit. It is unfortunate that Grant's Eastern leanings did not reveal this way of reading the Old Testament, as it would have balanced out his sense of order with creativity.[20]

Grant's insistence on the primacy of order led to the rejection of creativity. Without mythical understanding Hindu culture will either fall prey to technology or will similarly fall into an over inflated understanding of dharma. By understanding myth and its role, and reading creation narratives accordingly creativity can exist without sliding into excess. Perhaps the technological 'bringing forth' because 'we can' or 'must,' can be changed to bringing forth because 'we should.' Grant points out that 'should' implies 'ought' and asking 'ought we to' drastically changes the creative process, reflecting the genesis narrative. 'Ought' questions embody both personal dependence upon God and the law that is hidden within our hearts, but that law within us must never overshadow He who made the law. Perceiving God as creator implicitly provides limits to the created.[21] Absolute creativity posited by Nietzsche is certainly dangerous, but so is absolute order. An overemphasis on order easily slides into hierarchical abuse, and ethical, religious, or political complacency. Furthermore, the technological paradigm will plough over the religious institutions of the West and East unless we can creatively respond. In the absence of creativity we are solely dependent upon order as our last line of defence. Order is a good defence, a fortified wall, but it is purely defensive, and a certain amount of offence is needed if we are to provide anything more than criticism.

Notes

1. George Grant, *Technology and Justice* (Concord: Anansi Press, 1986), 68.
2. Grant, *Technology and Justice*, 75.
3. Nietzsche and Heidegger were the most influential thinkers in Grant's life positively and antagonistically; however, in this essay it is sufficient to focus on Nietzsche.
4. George Grant, *Philosophy in the Mass Age*, ed. William Christian (Toronto: University of Toronto, 1995), 27.
5. David Cayley, *George Grant In Conversation* (Concord, Ontario: Anansi Press, 1995), 49.
6. Cayley, 76.
7. Augustine wrote, "as the law of deeds was written on tables of stone, so is the law of faith inscribed on the hearts of the faithful" (De Spir. Et Lit. xxiv).
8. This can also be deduced from Grant's take on Plato's cave analogy.
9. Leo Strauss, "Jerusalem and Athens: Some Preliminary Reflections," in *Faith and Political Philosophy: The*

Correspondence Between Leo Strauss and Eric Voegelin, 1934-1964, trans & ed. Peter Emberley & Barry Cooper, (University Park, Pennsylvania: The Pennsylvania State University Press, 1993), 129-130

10. Ibid., 175.
11. Weil, "Spiritual Autobiography," in *The Simone Weil Reader*, ed. George A. Panichas (Rhode Island: Moyer Bell, 1977), 16.
12. See the addendum to George Grant, "Two Theological Languages," in *Collected Works of George Grant*, ed. Arthur Davis (Toronto: University of Toronto Press, 2002), 2.
13. Simone Weil, "Reflections on the Right Use of School Studies," in *The Simone Weil Reader*, 49.
14. Weil, "Decreation," in *The Simone Weil Reader*, 350.
15. George Grant, "Lectures at McMaster in the 1960's: A Selection" in *Collected Works of George Grant*, ed. Arthur Davis and Henry Roper (Toronto: University of Toronto Press, 2005), 3:721.
16. Ibid., 720.
17. Murray Jardine, *The Making and Unmaking of Technological Society: How Christianity Can Save Modernity From Itself* (Grand Rapids, Michigan: Brazos Press, 2004), 142.
18. Philip Sherrard, *The Greek East and the Latin West: A Study in the Christian Tradition* (Limni, Evia, Greece: Denise Harvey, 1995), 28-29.
19. Ibid., 32.
20. Grant interpreted the Old Testament as triumphalistic, and following in the steps of Weil he avoided it almost to the point of marcionism.
21. Aristotle's God who does not create is impersonal, and is a God of 'isness' in which limits provided by a dependent relationship do not exist. Aristotle's God can be clearly labelled, whereas, the creating God by the act of creating is personal and therefore necessitates constant interpretation and reinterpretation, and thus dependence.

☯ ☪

14

SECULARISM – A GANDHIAN PERSPECTIVE

(Geeta Mehta)

Introduction

The word 'religion' is derived from the root to 'religare' i. e. to bind together. Once religion served the purpose of binding together people who were scattered in different tribes; essentially it acted as a cementing factor. Today, religion is being used to divide the people, hence the need for secular approach in the present context.

In the context of sectarian and dogmatic conflicts in medieval Europe secularism had come to mean separation of state from religion. Secularism emerged in Western Europe as a movement of protest against the excesses, the massacres and the wars waged in the name of religion. Its principles were derived from utilitarian ethics which shunned what was based on prejudice and passion and sought to achieve human welfare by applying the scientific method of induction and deduction to social realities.[1]

Secularism often denotes a way of life and conduct guided by materialistic considerations devoid of religion. The basis of this ideology is that material means alone can advance mankind and that religious beliefs retard the growth of the human being. Secularism in this sense is perhaps the basis of Marxism.[2]

To the secular mind, society and social conditions are the result of what men do and not of some divine dispensation operating from above and outside man. Poverty, inequality, exploitation, oppression, hunger, barriers of caste, class and creed, are seen as man-made and not as eternal and divine. Hence it is really a scientific and rational pursuit of industries as well as social welfare.

Secular State

The idea of a secular state appears to have been put forward by Marsiglio of padua in the 14th Century. In his famous book "Defensor Pacis", he pointed out the difference between divine and human law. He declared : " The rights of citizens are independent of the faith they profess; and no man may be punished for his religion". [3]

The secular state is a concept of Western origin where the church authority sought to claim priority over the state authority and the church came to dominate the state authority for almost one thousand years. For some time, the Christian state and the church worked in mutual cooperation; but later the conflicts between the Pope and the Emperor started. Some of the ideas which led to the Reformation contributed to the growth of state power, and rise of absolute monarchies of 15th and 16th centuries. State came to be regarded as distinct from loyalty to the church, Renaissance and Reformation separated the state from the church or temporal power from the spiritual power. By the end of the 16th Century the triumph of *regnum* over the *sacredotium* was complete.

In the west, Secularism is the logical climax of the movement of renaissance, Reformation, development of

Science, advancement of knowledge and the emergence of the Philosophy of liberal democracy. Scientific inventions and geographical discoveries of 15th and 16th century helped to widen man's worldly affairs. Thus western secularism demonstrated the significance of human reason in political affairs. Religion came to be discarded as the basis of legal status of the state.

Shri S.P. Sathe points out Four Models of state-religion relationship available from historical as well contemporary politics.

1. A theocratic state i.e. a state which professes its own religion e.g. Pakistan, Iran and Israel. A theocratic state is not necessarily bad or anti-democratic. In Indian history, we have a number of examples of theocratic politics which treated various religions and followers of such religions with equal respect. Akbar, Shivaji are such examples.

2. A state which treats all religions with equal respect, though it may not have its own religion.

3. A secular state which neither has its own religion nor promotes or obstructs any religion. The United states of America is the most prominent example of this model and

4. An Anti-religion state in which atheism is cherished. The soviet Union and other communist countries followed this model for a long time.[4]

The revolution- French, American, Russian and Industrial- strengthened the idea of Secularism. Jefferson called secularism the wall of separation between church and state. That has been regarded by many constitutional jurists as the basic principle of a secular state. This complete separation between church and the state has been steadfastly adhered to by the American nation throughout its history. Industrial Revolution being the most widespread all over the world has spread the idea of secularism with its materialistic outlook.

Secularism in the Indian Context

Though the concept of Secular state is of Western Origin, it does not mean that freedom of religion or religious tolerance are foreign to countries in the East. Freedom to practice and propagate one's own religion has been one of the basic ideas of secular state. Ancient Indian state accepted this notion in theory as well as in practice and left the individual to follow his or her belief and faith.

As Mr. M.C. Setalvad says, "The Hindu view of life, which attaches greater importance to the future evolution of man and the ultimate absorption of the human personality in the Absolute, necessarily leads the Hindus to attach lesser importance to individual religious beliefs and makes for toleration. A basic doctrine of Hindu philosophy holds that spiritual liberation of man can be reached in many ways and Hindu Society, therefore, embraces in its fold diverse, contradictory and even conflicting beliefs and practices".[5] Even Donald Eugene Smith writes that the freedom of thought in ancient India was so considerable as to find no parallel in the west before the most recent age.[6]

People of different races and cultures have come to our land from beyond the mountains and the seas. The old inhabitants and the newcomers, after they had struggled and fought, eventually forgot their enmities. There was fusion of culture. "This unity of history, her ideals and her humanity is the living spirit of India".[7]

There is fusion between pre-Dravidian and the Dravidian, and the Aryan cultures. There is also the synthesis between the Brahmanic, Sramanik and Lokayat ways of life. Then we had the Saka, Gujars, Pratiharas followed by the Arabs, Turks and Moghals; Islam and Hinduism which appeared so anti-thetical, at last intermingled and from their synthesis grew Sufism, the cult of love and devotion.

S.K. Sinha observes that our independence movement was profoundly secular but secularism as a word did not figure in the political vocabulary of that struggle. Our founding fathers gave us a very secular constitution yet secularism as a word did not figure in it. It was later incorporated in the preamble to the constitution through an amendment, in 1976, Ironically after this amendment, politics in India started getting increasingly less secular. Today Secularism is the most oft-repeated word by our politicians but it is least practiced by them. [8] The Indian secular state was envisaged to be non-discriminatory, interventionist to protect the individual from religion and non-interventionist to allow religion as well as the individual to be free .[9]

But M.N. Roy held that India was not a secular state. A theocratic society- one imbued with religious superstition and blind faith- can hardly be the soil of a secular state. A state which was merely neutral between religions, a non-communal state, according to Roy, was not secular in meaningful sense of the term. He believed that a secular state must afford its citizens not "the freedom to choose from among various religious doctrines but the freedom of the human spirit from the tyranny of them".[10]

The non communal approach of the congress promoted by leaders familiar with western liberalism and British tradition prevailed throughout the struggle for independence. The congress presidents were Christian, Parsi, Hindu and Muslims. The secularist view of life was repeatedly stressed by them so the religious matters came to be regarded as relating to the conscience of the individuals. As early as the year 1931, the congress at its session at Karachi passed the resolution that "The state shall observe neutrality in regard to all religions".

But the use of the word secular to describe the nature of the Indian state was not a very happy one. In the words of Pandit Nehru, it was being used for want of a better word'. Dr. Radhakrishanan has stated that "The religious impartiality of the Indian state is not to be confused with secularism or atheism. Secularism as here defined is in accordance with the ancient religious tradition of Inida".[11]

The ideal of a secular state in the sense of a state which treats all religions alike and displays benevolent neutrality towards them is in a way more suited to the Indian environment. In the Indian context. Secularism means equal respect for all; faiths and the state keeping itself impartial, in not preferring one to another. Secularism in India does not stand for the abolition of Religions but only for the separation of state and religions.[12] The accepted Hindi translation of secularism, Dharamnirapeksha (Religious neutrality) does not convey the real meaning of the word. It is translated as 'Sarvadharma Sahisnuta' tolerance for all religions in Indian languages but that was not acceptable to Gandhi. He writes," Tolerance may imply a gratuitous assumption of the inferiority of other faiths to one's own, whereas Ahimsa teaches us to entertain the same respect for the religious faiths of others as we accord to our own"[13] He further states, "Tolerance gives us spiritual insight, which is as far from fanaticism as the North Pole from the south. True knowledge of religion breaks down the barriers between faith and faith. Cultivation of tolerance for other faiths will impart to us a truer understanding of our own".[14]

Secularism of Gandhi and Nehru

Though Gandhi and Nehru both tended to the same conclusion, their approaches were different, Gandhi believed all religions to be true, he pleaded for universal religion which would comprise of the basic truths underlying all religions. The state, therefore, had to regard all religions as equal. Gandhi's approach was thus based on his intense belief in the truth of religion. "Gandhi's starting point was of a religious man, who believing all religions to be true accepted the theory of a state which fitted in with this *belief*: hence the secular state. Nehru's staring point was that of a practical political thinker and leader who, while personally believing all religions to be mostly untrue, had to provide for their freedom to function peacefully without prejudicing the democratic system; hence the secular state".[15] Gandhi was deeply religions but was non-communal. Nehru was agnostic and non-communal. Although they differed in their styles of polities, both shared a non-communal, Humanistic social philosophy.

For Gandhi, communal harmony was not a matter of his policy but creed. From his childhood, he had this one idea that between Hindus and Musalamans there should be no difference of opinions"[16] His experiences in South Africa strengthened this conviction. It is significant to note that during early phase of his movement in South Africa, Gandhi's followers were mostly Muslims.

Gandhian Perspective

Gandhi deliberately picked up religion as the basis of political action and national identity. True to the Hindu sensibility he said: " Those who say that religion has nothing to do with politics do not know what religion means".[17] He said: "I reject any religious doctrine that does not appeal to reason and is in conflict with morality. [18] Gandhi introduced religion which is capable of standing the scrutiny of science and reason on one hand and at the same time guide us to the new dimensions of the spirit in man. He made religion revolutionary enough to meet the challenges, both of science and social change.[19]

Gandhi equated religion with morality and so there was no conflict in following any religion. Vinoba enumerates four components of religion. One is worship' involving direct relationship with God, the second is ethics' connected with truth, non-violence etc. The third includes customs' and practices' which pertain to various rites performed at death, birth etc. The fourth is mythology, stories etc. Thus a religion has several components. [20] Gandhi emphasized the second component of religion where all religions agree with one another in their message of truth, love and non-violence. For Gandhi, religion was all comprehensive. "You must watch my life: how I live, eat, sit, talk, behave in general. The sum total of all those in me is my religion .[21] So he says, "In reality there are as many religions as there are individuals".

[22] Further he adds, "Religions are different roads converging upon the same point. What does it matter that we take different roads, so long as we reach the same goal?"[23]

He gives another simile, "Even as a tree has a single trunk, but many branches and leaves, so is there one true and perfect Religion, but it becomes many as it passes thought the human medium- The one religion is beyond all speech".[24] He sincerely believed in "equal respect for all religions" (Sarva-dharma samabhava). This is Gandhi's secularism. Gandhi says, "If we are to respect other's religions as we would have them to respect our own, a friendly study of the world's religions is a sacred duty".[25] He again says, " The key to the solution of the tangle lies in everyone following the best in his own religion and entertaining equal regard for the other religions and their followers".[26]

Thus we should have equal respect for all religions because

(i) All religions are like different paths leading to the ultimate Truth. In the words of Gandhi "The soul of all religions is one, but it is encased in a multitude of forms. Wise men will ignore the outward crust; see the same soul living under a variety of crusts".[27]

(ii) All religions are more or less imperfect. All the holy Scriptures admit that God is truth. But Mahatma Gandhi goes ahead and says that truth is God. Truth is one and various religions are the glimpses of the same truth. Being the reflection of the Universal Truth, they are initially one and, therefore, are equally true. But they are received and interpreted through human minds, which are imperfect, so all the religions are imperfect. They are only partial reflections of truth. He writes, "I believe that all the great religions of the world are true, more or less. I say 'more or less' because I believe that everything that human hand touches, by reason of the very fact that human beings are imperfect, becomes imperfect. Perfection is the exclusive attribute of God and it is indescribable, untranslatable. I therefore, admit in all humility, that even the Vedas, the Quran and the Bible are the imperfect word of God, and imperfect being that we are, swayed to and fro by a multitude of passions, it is impossible for us even to understand this word of God in its fullness".[28]

(iii) Though there is diversity of human nature yet religion is a constitutional necessity of man as such. Gandhi writes, "In theory, since there is one God, there can be only one religion. But in practice, no two persons I have known have had the same and identical conception of God. Therefore, there will, perhaps, always be different religions answering to different temperaments and climatic conditions. But I can clearly see the time coming when people belonging to different faiths will have the same regard for other faiths that they have for their won, I think that we have to find unity in diversity. We are all children of one and the same God, and therefore, absolutely equal".[29]

Gandhi believes that the religions are the various paths to reach the same destination. The historical and geographical conditions in which the different religions came into being are different, but they aim at all round evolution of their followers in particular and of mankind in general.

(iv) All religions are humane in their genesis though inspired by Divinity. Gandhi writes, "We are all children of the same father whom the Hindu, the Musalman and the Christian know by different names. The names do not indicate individuality, but attributes, and little man has tried in his humble way to describe Mighty God by giving Him attributes, though He is above all attributes, indescribable, inconceivable, immeasurable, living faith in this God means acceptance of the brotherhood of mankind. It also means equal respect for all religions.[30]

Gandhi does not see the possibility of unreligious world, because the truth is one, wise men speak in different ways. "I do not share the belief that there can or will be on earth one religion. I am striving, therefore, to find a common factor and to induce mutual tolerance".[31]

After long study and experience, Gandhi came to the conclusion that (1) all religions are true, (2) all religions have some error in them, (3) all religions are almost as dear to him as his own Hindusim.[32]

Unity of all Religions and Conversion

As Gandhi approbates the conception of the unity of religions, he is dead against the forcible conversions of the followers of one religion into another. He says, "I am against conversion, whether it is known as shuddhi by Hindus, Tabligh by Musalamans or proselytizing by Christians. Conversion is a heart process known only to and by God. It must be left to itself".[33]

Religion has nothing to do with nationality. Gandhi says, "Religion is no test of nationality. But a personal matter between man and his God. In the sense of nationality they are Indians first and Indians last, no matter what religion they profess".[34]

Shri. M.C. Setalvad observes, "The citizens also have to strengthen the secular state and its democratic set-up by their own whole-hearted efforts and by their deliberate and continuous cooperation in all efforts made by the state. Secularism, in the Indian context, must be given the widest possible content. It should connote the eradication of all attitudes and practices derived from or connected with religion which impede our development and retard our growth into an integrated nation. A concerted and earnest endeavor, both by the state and citizen, towards Secularization in accordance with this wide concept can alone lead to the stabilization of our democratic state and the establishment of a true and cohesive Indian nationhood'.[35]

Criticism

Gandhi's view of Sarva-dharma-sambhava seems to be idealistic and therefore may not be adopted by a common man. A common man's understanding of Religion is not moralistic and rationalistic but ritualistic. The answer to this criticism is that in these days of Science, man has to become rationalistic. As observed by the first saint of Nuclear Age, Acharya Vinoba Bhave, "The days of Parochial Religion and power- politics are numbered and now are the days of Science and spirituality". The saints are the seers; they can see the future world with proper perspective. Science has brought man-kind together and it will survive only if it is guided by Spirituality rather than Parochial Religion.

Conclusion

Secularism is essential for the preservation of freedom as well as social Peace and political stability. Secularism is neither no to religion, not any indifference to it. Swami Vivekananda has also pleaded for reconciliation by "Synthesis between the Vedantic mind, and the Islamic body which is the only ray of hope for our motherland".[36]

Religious exclusiveness is an anti-religious phenomenon, which has led to religious fundamentalism and fanaticism. Indian secularism is no atheism or materialism but it means equal respect for all religions, not mere tolerance but positive respect. Gandhi's approach to secularism is positive. It is an approach to the unity of religion. He prescribed eleven vows of which respect for all religious faiths (Sarva-Dharma- Samabhava) occupies an important place. [37] It also finds the first place in the scheme of his constructive programme. [38] He has enjoined upon us "to study text of other religion besides one's own which will give one a grasp of the rock bottom unity of all religions and afford a glimpse also of the universal and absolute truth that is beyond the dust of creeds and faiths".[39]

Acharya Vinoba Bhave went a step further to facilitate and motivate the people for the study of the essence of all religions, he studied the Original scriptures of all religions and gleaned the essence of Quran, Vedas, Manusmriti, Christian teachings, Japaji, Dhamma-Sara, Samana Suttam and so on. He used to say that the Bhagvad Gita itself is an essence. Instead of reciting the prayers of all religions as Gandhi used to do in his prayers, Vinoba composed three verses of the names of all Gods of different religions of the world which was recited during the prayer. In the public meetings Vinoba used to observe silence for two minutes guiding the people to recite the name of deity which one worships in one's mind. He said, "The more we concentrate on the fundamental oneness of humanity, the more do the different religions appear as enriching and strengthening one another. I regard the different religions as merely different forms of worship. Each form has its distinctive merit. When the different ways meet together all these merits gather together and make a rich and full pattern".[40]

Kaka Sahib Kalekar once argued with Gandhiji that Sarvadharma Mamabhaba (Considering all religions to be mine) is a better precept rather than Sarva-dharma-samabhava (equal respect for all religions) Gandhi answered, "Let us develop equal respect for all religions first, and then we may think of considering all religions as mine". Vivekananda said," If it is true that God is the centre of all religions and that each of us is moving towards Him along one of these radii, and then it is certain that all of us must reach that centre. [41] In the Biblical language, Gandhi says, "In God's house there are many mansions and they are equally holy".[42]

Notes

1. Beg M.H. *"National Integration: some Approaches"*, National Integration and Communal Harmony; (New Delhi: Gandhi Darshan Samiti, 1982) p.31.
2. Setalvad M.C. *Secularism* (Govt. of India Publication Division, 1965); p.3.
3. Quoted from Donald Eugene Smith, *India as a secular State* (Princeton University press, 1969);p.4.
4. Sathe S.P. *Secularism- Law and the Constitution of India* (Pune: Indian Secular Society, 1991); p.7.

5. Setalvad M.C. *Secularism*; op.cit; p.13.
6. Smith Donald Eugene: *India as a Secular State*;op.Cit.;pp.61-62.
7. Pande B.N. *National Integration- An Urgent need* (National Integration and communal harmony); p.81.
8. An Article on Concept and practice of secularism in the Book *Secularism-Concept and practice* edited by A.K. Lal (New Delhi: Concept publishing co.1998)p.19.
9. Sathe S.P., *Secularism Law and the Constitution of India*, op.cit.;p.8.
10. Sinha V.K. ;(ed) *Secularism in India*, (Bombay: Lalvani Publishing House, 1968) p.145.
11. Quoted from Setalvad M.C.; *Secularism*, op.cit;p.21.
12. Madam T. N.; *The Historical Significance of Secularism in India, Secularisation in Multi Religious Societies* (ed); ICSSR;p.11.
13. Narayan Shriman (General Editor) *The Selected works of M.Gandhi* Vol: IV (Ahmedabad; Navjivan publishing house 1969),p.240.
14. *Ibid*; p.242.
15. Smith Donald Eugene: *Nehru and Democracy: The Political Thought of an Asian Democrat*, (Calcutta orient Longmans 1958)p.156.
16. Gandhi's address at the meeting of the Muslims in Bombay; 9th May 1919. *The collected works of Mahatma Gandhi* vol. XV, (Ahmedabad: Navajivan Trust 1965) p.295.
17. Quoted by Singh Ramjee; *Gandhi and the Twenty-first Century*, (New Delhi, peace Publishers India, 1993) p.121.
18. Gandhi M.K. *My Religion*, compiled and edited by Bharatan Kumarappa (Ahmedabad: Navjivan publishing House, 1996); p.4.
19. Singh Ramjee., *The Relevance of Gandhian Thought*, (New Delhi: Classical Publication-1983)p.35
20. *Sarvodaya*, A Hindi monthly, June 1951;p.769.
21. Gandhi M.K. *Harijan*, 22-9-1946; p.321.
22. Gandhi M.K.,*Hind swaraj*, (Ahmedabad: Navjivan publishing House-1938), p.49.
23. *Ibid*. 50.

24. Gandhi M.K. *All Religions are true*: (Bombay:Bhartiya Vidya Bhawan, 1962) p.3.
25. *Ibid*; p.15
26. *Ibid*; p.13
27. *Young India* Sept.25.1924;p.318.
28. *Young India*; 22-9-1927;p.319.
29. *Harijan*; 2-2-1934;p.8.
30. Gandhi M.K. *All Religions are true*: op. cit.; p. VII.
31. *Young India*; 31-7-1924;p.254.
32. Gandhi M.K.; *All Religions are true*,op.cit.;p.241.
33. *Young India*; Jan.6,1927;p.2.
34. *Harijan*; 29-6-1947,p.215.
35. Setalvad M.C., *Secularism*; op.cit.;pp.28-29.
36. Vivekananda quoted in *Jati, Sanskrit aur Samajvada*; p.24.
37. Gandhi M.K.; *From Yervada mandir*, (Ahmedabad: Navjivan Publishing House 1932) pp.25-29.
38. Gandhi M.K.; *Constructive Programme*: Its Meaning and Place;(Ahmedabad: Navajivan Publishing House;1978).
39. Singh Ramjee; *Gandhi and the Twenty-first Century*; op.cit.'p.129.
40. *Harijan*; an English Weekly; 17-6-50;p.139.
41. Quoted by Singh Ramjee; *Gandhi and the Twenty-first century*; op.cit;; p. 128.
42. *Harijan*; an English weekly; 20April, 1934, p.73.

෴ ෴

15

George Grant and His *Lament for a Nation*: With a Special Reference to M K Gandhi's '*Hind Swaraj*': A Comparison

Arati Barua

Masterpiece is not a word to use lightly, but Lament for a Nation merits it—

William Christian,

Lament for a Nation should be respected as a masterpiece of political meditation—

Peter Emberley,

It is more than forty years since George Grant's Lament for a Nation: the defeat of Canadian Nationalism took wings and left the press. It is most appropriate, therefore, to reflect on this timely text and meditate on its perennial relevance for Canadian thought and political life—

Ron Dart

The name of George Grant and his philosophy- both are very new in the Indian academia. He is one of the most original thinkers of Canada, who was often misunderstood. George Parkin Grant, which is his full name, was born in November 13, 1918 in Toronto, in a renowned family of Canada.

Grant's best books "*Lament for a Nation*" and "*Technology and Empire*" established him as a great patriot, a nationalist, as well as an idealist philosopher of Canada. I got interested in the philosophy of George Grant especially through Prof. William Christian's *Biography of George Grant*, which is very illuminating in this sense. When I started reading Grant's "*Lament for a Nation*" it was quite surprising for me to see the similarity of Grant's views with that of Mohandas Karamchand Gandhi, especially with reference to his "*Hind Swaraj*" (Indian Home Rule). Like Grant in Canada, people in India also misunderstood Gandhi vastly and yet he was regarded as the only leader who understood them. From these similarities it appears to me that the best way to introduce Grant in India will be to call him a "Gandhi in Canada" or a "Canadian Gandhi". Interestingly Grant is already known as the "Father of the Canadian Nation" after the publication of his *Lament for a Nation*.[1]

George Grant comes from an academic background. His father was a Principal. George Monro Grant was his paternal grandfather who was the Principal of Queen's University from 1877 until his death in 1902. Sir George Parkin on the other hand was his maternal grandfather and he was the founding secretary for the Rhodes Scholarships.

George Grant was a University Professor who taught in the Mc Master University, Hamilton, in the department of Religious studies for 20yrs and in the University of Dalhousie till his retirement in the Political Science department. Later on he was a Fellow of the Royal society of Canada. But his family people wanted him to be a public figure like his grandfathers. So he was trained for a public life to carry on like his grandfathers and for that reason only he was sent to Oxford to study Law. But somehow he did not want to be the Prime Minister of Canada as expected by his mother who was a very strong woman and who had much influence on George Grant. He chose to be an educationist, a philosopher, a professor of religious study and political philosophy and to work for the betterment of Canada and the Canadians wholeheartedly, which gave birth to a series of books on freedom of Canada and the Canadians in terms of not only political freedom but also in spiritual sense of the term.

M. K. Gandhi was born in India, educated in England, working in South Africa but had a unique cultural background, unique in the sense that he was ever evolving personality in terms of cultural identity. Gandhi's contribution to public life and his capacity to reach to millions of people was much larger in comparison to George Grant. It is because George Grant, unlike Gandhi, is yet to be discussed in the global world. In this context even Mrs. Sheila Grant (wife of Dr. Grant) also says that "there might be some similarity between Grant's meditations on the relation between the eternal and transitoriness of the political and Gandhi's", but she emphasizes that she thought that Gandhi's authority was immeasurably greater because he was a saint and her husband most certainly was not. [2] Gandhi and Grant both fought throughout their lives for the protection and the preservation of the ancient wisdom, religion and culture as well as the great minds of the past. As a 'philosopher of religion' Grant always tried to preserve the 'revelation of Christ' but at the same time he had great respect for Hinduism also. Gandhi also despite being rigid Hindu greatly admired Christianity. [3]

Gandhi and Grant both fought against power, which impels human beings, to 'dethrone God' and spiritualism. Both of them fought against the power that exploits Nature and human nature for their own purposes. Both of them were constant pursuers of Truth. Both were the worshipers of Truth, Beauty and Goodness.

Both focused on the role of philosophy in imparting education. [4] Their views regarding the University, College and Educational Institutes are almost same. Their views on morality and values and their lament on the loss of old values in modern technological society are almost same. Their reactions towards the professionalism especially of medical practitioners and lawyers are similar. Above all their philosophy of humanism is also same and which is evident in both -*Lament for a Nation* and *Hind Swaraj*.

The more one goes through the works of Grant, the more one can find his thought comparable to that of Gandhi, especially on the themes of modernity and technology. Grant himself has referred to Gandhi with great respect in his works. He has compared Gandhi with Jesus Christ.

In the similar manner there are many differences amongst these two eminent thinkers who talked about limits of Modernity and limitlessness of human urges in a similar tone.

While Grant called himself as a Scottish Canadian, actually he was a Canadian in the true sense of the term. Gandhi was an Indian born, educated in England, working in South Africa but had a unique cultural identity. As we have discussed above that M.K. Gandhi's contribution to public life and his capacity to reach to millions of people was much larger in comparison to G. Grant. It is because Grant is yet to be discussed in the global world.

G. Grant was basically a University Professor, mostly being confined to classroom but who dared to speak at times against not only the Prime Minister of Canada but also against the President of United States. G. Grant being an educationist and a University Professor, his field was education and he had to deal with the educated people mainly.

But for M.K. Gandhi public life was his field. He came from a political background.

G Grant's background was academic. His father being a Principal, grandfather a minister/Knight, uncle Vincent (Massey) being the first Canadian born Governor- General, his background was quite different M.K. Gandhi was from a political background because his father was a prime minister [5] in Kathiawar state in Gujrat. So it was a quite different environment for Gandhi. He himself says about his father that '..To certain extent he (Gandhi's father) might have been even given to carnal pleasures. For he married for the fourth time when he was over forty".[6] Gandhi was the youngest son of the fourth wife of his father. But Gandhi's mother had left an outstanding impression of saintliness on him. She was deeply religious and a devout Hindu woman. So Gandhi had a different kind of background to lead his life in search of truth and to cultivate religious faith in his own effort. In this connection it is interesting to note that Dr. Grant's mother also had great influence on her son.[7]

Being from a political background there were special instructions so that Gandhi should not be beaten up in school, no punishment should be given to him and so on. However, he had repented all throughout his life for his bad handwriting. Another reason was his weak physical constitution for which he was often jealous of his brothers who were having better health. He was even under the illusion that the Muslims and the Christians have got strong body built because they eat meat and so he had even secretly started taking meat also with his friends to be physically strong. However he confesses all his wrong doings and explains beautifully in his "*The Story of My experiments with Truth*" [8]. Gandhi used to follow the method of meditating upon whenever there was something wrong and it helped him throughout his life. Even in his political career whenever he faced with such problems and felt that he should not have done this, then immediately he used to withdraw himself from everything and did introspection within himself and then tried to find out some solution to it. This helped him a lot. Hence Gandhi was from a totally different kind of background than Dr Grant.

But George Grant was a Rhodes Scholar at Oxford. He went to Oxford to study Law, (interestingly Gandhi also went to London to study Law) but later on he (Grant) changed his subject to Theology and did his D. Phil. on it. In fact Grant's father and his grandfather also were public figures. So naturally his family people had expected him also to be a future public figure for which he was actually trained. During the Second World War he worked in Adult Education Center and delivered a series of talks on CBC (Canadian Broadcasting Center) radio that was the forerunner of the current ideas program. So there are many differences among them. But still there are parallel interests among them.

Like Gandhi, G. Grant also was a nationalist, and a political and idealistic philosopher. Both of them reflected on the destiny of their nations in a peaceful and non-violent manner, through their writings to encourage their readers to protect the uniqueness of their own nations from external forces. This patriotic urge in Gandhi instigated him to write 'Hind Swaraj' in 1909 and the same urge made Grant to compose his masterpiece "Lament for a Nation" in 1965.

"His (Grant's) masterpiece *Lament for a Nation*, was a 97 page combination of philosophy, political analysis, religion, and rant the like of which was seen before in Canada and has certainly not been seen in the almost 40 yrs since it appeared in 1965" (William Christian-Kitchener Waterloo)[9].

While one book was written in 1909, the other was written in 1965 but still there are quite a lot of similarities between the two. These two masterpieces are still relevant to us in many ways. Gandhi is as relevant today to India and to the whole world as he was at that time; and similarly Grant is also as relevant for anyone who wants to understand the spirit of North America in general and that of Canada in particular.

However the only difference between the two classics is that —

> *George Grant's* Lament for a Nation *was a mournful lament for a nation, which seems to be pessimistic. But Gandhi's* Hind Swaraj *was an outlining programme for the future but not a lament. Gandhi was a futurist, not a historicist* [10].

Regarding Grant's *Lament for A Nation* it is said –

> *"Lament for a Nation is a true lament, a passionate expression of grief, regret, and sorrow. The Canada whose death he (Grant) mourns is the country that George saw personified in his own mother, a country tied to European values as it is to the physical realities of the New World in order to create a society of free and equal people who are less disordered, unstable, undemocratic, and violent than Americans. To be truly Canadian, we are forced to be more British than the British, more French than the French, and more American than the Americans in putting our ideals into practice. Growing up in Ontario when he did and coming to know Quebec as well as he does, George had taken it for granted that to be a Canadian is to be a unique kind of North American. Being northerners, being British and French and European, have made Canadian tough rather than pretty, have given us a greater loyalty to being good than to being free. This Canada, his Canada, has been extinguished by politicians who gave their allegiance to multinational corporations rather than their fellow citizens"*[11]

After discussing about the differences between Grant and Gandhi in different respects especially in their upbringing, family background, profession, social environment etc, it is quite interesting to know that finally they came to the same point of convergence.

Both the thinkers believed in the freedom of will politically as well as spiritually. Their views are quite similar regarding that one has to have the political freedom first in order to have spiritual freedom.

Like any other ethical thinker Gandhi also accepted the freedom of the will as a necessary postulate of morality. But he recognized that man is not absolutely free. Every man has certain limitations. According to Gandhi one should try to understand one's capacity and then to try to improve one's own capacities so that he or she can develop his or her own self to the best of his or her capacities. He accepts that we cannot totally overcome our all limitations. But in spite of all these limiting factors such as laws of nature, habits and tendencies, law of karma etc for Gandhi, we still have sufficient scope within the constraints to bring improvement in our environment, body, and mind. So, according to Gandhi one can improve his conditions and change his habits and shape his destiny accordingly as he or she wishes [12]

Logically and naturally spiritualism is concerned with the part of a larger togetherness than Science and technology. Gandhi says that what he had been striving and pining to achieve all his years is "self-realization, to see God face to face, to attain moksha" [13].

Gandhi says that whatever he was doing, he was doing in the pursuit of this goal. Even what he did in his political field also was directed to this aim only. Nothing he thinks can distract him from the spiritual value. The experiments that he was doing were spiritual. He tried to learn the eternal truths from different traditional religious and philosophical teachers of the world. But he used to select some of them and then combined those teachings in his own way. He selected only those that appealed to him as sound and worthy of application to life. Tolstoy, Ruskin and Thoreau were the great teachers of Gandhi who were the great source of encouragement for him all throughout his life.

Grant had a great experience of feeling God's existence in his life. Regarding the facts that formed his belief in Christianity, Grant talks about his divine experience of feeling 'God' once which he calls a 'prodigious moment' of his life which he cannot explain but can just feel and experience and this is what he means by Christianity [14].

Grant was influenced by Charles Cochrane, Harold Innis, Austin Farrer, James Doull, Leo Strauss, Simone Weil, Jaques Ellul, Nietzsche and Heidegger and also by his Oxford educated English wife Sheila Grant.

Both of them did not like orthodoxy of religion especially of Christianity and of Hinduism. Both had quenched for spiritualism. When in 19th century the whole world was under the spell of Science and Technology, Gandhi and Grant were against these two; and they believed that spirituality is the only means to free us from earthly problems including those of dogmatic church. Both Grant and Gandhi did not like Church related dogmas and magic and so on. Gandhi – was against -Hinduism that encourages untouchable. He said, " I regard untouchability as the greatest blot on Hinduism"[15].

What is the destiny of modern civilization, how far is it healthy, is it reproducible? What is the soul or background of the modern civilization? Is it expandable? These were the questions that stroke deeply these two thinkers in two different environments and situations. Whether modern civilization was to be committed or was it only a passing phase? Was this craze for Science and Technology a mere infatuation that will not last for long?

They were trying to find out a solution to such questions.

For G. Grant, to be Christian was to be a Christian in his own way, freedom of seeking the meaning of the intellectual faculties, dissociating from Orthodox Christianity in the pursuit of spiritualism.

Like Grant, Gandhi also made a viewpoint in *Hind Swaraj*. The point of Gandhi's moral and political thought in *Hind Swaraj* was provided by what he called "severe condemnation of modern civilization" [16]. This book has been named as a "spiritual classic, and even as the greatest book written in modern times". [17] "It was not just the moral inadequacy and extravagant pretensions of modern civilization, but its treacherously deceptive, hypnotic and self-destructive tendency that was the theme of *Hind Swaraj*" [18]

In the same way G. Grant the great Canadian Political philosopher has expressed critical analyses of Modernism and Technology in the context of Canada in his book *Lament for a Nation*. This is, therefore, an interesting issue to examine whether the philosophical foundation on which Gandhi spoke against Modernism and Technology in his *Hind Swaraj* is also the logical foundation for Grant to speak against Modernism and Technology in Canada. However, there is a possibility that Grant's views against Technology and Modernism may be based on an entirely different philosophical standpoint than that of Gandhi.

The answer to this question will be definitely, yes. Of course their political situations were analogous.

"The message of Lament for a Nation was a sad one: Canada would one day disappear, because increasingly little separated us from the Americans. Ironically, Grant played a large part of in the Canadian nationalist movement in the 1970s as we tried to prove him wrong. He hoped the nationalists would succeed, because he deeply loved his country and wanted it to survive" (William Christian on GG)[19].

But the difference between the Indian context and the Canadian context lies in the fact that – in Canada it was not a colonial dominance but an ideological dominance whereas in Indian context it was a question of a colonial dominance of India by the British. Gandhi in his *Hind Swaraj* calls modern civilization a disease, perishing humanity [20].

Further he writes: " This civilization takes note neither of morality nor of religion .... immorality is often taught in the name of morality" [21].

However, the best part is that Gandhi is not pessimistic and says that " Civilization is not an incurable disease" [22].

GANDHI on Machines and technology:

Gandhi said "What I object to is the craze for machine"[23]. He was not against machines. He was in fact against the machine age. He accepted that machines were inevitable. For him even the human body also is a machine, "it is ... the purest piece of mechanism, but if it is hindrance to the highest flights of the soul, it has to be rejected". While he was in favour of retaining the simple machinery like the Singer Sewing Machine he did not want the complicated machinery to be retained. The simple machines also he wanted to be nationalized.

However he made some exceptions to some machines like car etc. which he did not consider to satisfy the primary wants of man. But a needle for him serves a primary need for all . So Gandhi strongly felt that "machine is good when it serves man but not when it seeks to master him". For he believed that, "industrialization might lead to greater production of goods but not necessarily to greater moral progress". However he did not ignore the growing importance of machinery. He said, " Machinery has its place it has come to stay. I am aiming not at the eradication of all machinery but its limitation............" [24].

GRANT on Technology and Modernism

For Grant the so-called modernism is nothing but a product of our endless surge for technical progress. He followed Alexander Kojeve for whom " The whole world was moving relentlessly towards a universal and homogeneous state"[25] . While " such an outcome was desirable" for Kojeve (" since it was a prelude to an universal peace where war between classes and nations no longer existed"), but for Grant " it was not a cause to rejoice" [26]. In his *Lament for a Nation* (1965) Grant accepts such an understanding about the impact of technology. Grant pointed out to the geographical position of Canada which was next to the "dynamic center of technology and modernism, (of) the US" and hence Grant feared that this would lead to eventual disappearance (of Canada) as an independent country "because both Canadians and Americans shared the same commitment to technology and modernism"[27].

For Grant the impact of technology on our life and society is absolutely de-humanizing. He vehemently opposed the monstrous growth of technology in modern times and expressed his deep concern about the danger of the technological development rather more intensely in yet another book *Technology and Empire* (1969)[28] . Like Gandhi, Grant also believed that science is not only dominating the "non-human nature" but also the domain of human nature. He rejected the view that technology is a matter of choice. "For him, technology was not something of outside of us that we could choose to use for good or ill. We lived in a society in which society (and increasingly a world) in which technology determined all existence"[29] .

As we live in finite time and space, in a finite earth, the unlimited technological growth and development is infeasible and unsustainable. The impact of mindless growth of technology and surge for modernism is increasingly felt to be a major constraint on our limited environment and resource base. Our environment is in serious danger for the continuation of life and survival of mankind. Many rare and valuable species of the world are already at the threat of extinction. In this background we may find a lot of relevance of Gandhian ideals as an alternative model of development and the same perhaps may be said about George Grant in Canada today.

In his *"Technology and Justice"*, Grant expresses his view that technology, is not simply "the whole apparatus of instruments made by man and placed at his disposal for his choice and purposes" [30]. But it is also a distinct way of approaching the world. William Christian also believes that technology for Grant was not "just a way of making things or even of doing business. It was a way of thinking and it was becoming a way of being" [31].

Both Gandhi and Grant said that technology is inevitable, but we have to deal with it. Gandhi did not take an anti-technological stand but an extra-technological (outside) stand, an alternative which means life according to nature.

Gandhi made an ideology out of it but George Grant did not.

Gandhi says that we should try and we can do so, if we try, to live at par with nature, totally giving away technology. The lawyers, the doctors all can do so. But for George Grant the good effects of technology such as medicines etc are inevitable and very much acceptable. Grant often attributed to Robert Oppenheimer, a nuclear scientist, the words, "When you see something that is technically sweet, you go ahead and do it"[32].

Grant never denied that science had delivered the goods it promised. "Brilliant scientists have laid before us an account of how things are, and in that account nothing can be said about justice" [33].

Dr. Grant uses the notion "Techno mania" but not in the sense of pragmatic instrument for meeting our needs but in the sense that we cannot ignore the machines since in his precarious moments of life it was re-vitalised by modern technology only, once he was even rejected in the army also due to this problem.

He could recuperate life with modern machine only. So he was impressed by the usefulness of modern technology but he could not ignore the destructive power of technology that produced Nuclear bomb –the ultimate destructive weapon, the highest gift of science and technology that led to holocaust.

Similarly M.K. Gandhi also said that there must be a limitation to the science and its invention or discoveries.

Human Destiny:

Both M.K. Gandhi and G. Grant were primarily concerned with the question of human destiny. The great bond between them is the two axiomatic phrases of "Truth" and "Non-violence".

G. Grant was a pacifist, and he considered Gandhi to be a great pacifist. To quote from Christian's *Biography of Grant*, "...presumably the two great pacifists in history were Jesus and Gandhi-one was put to death in a miserable way and one was shot ....You have to be at the highest level of sainthood to think that you carry this through".[34]

M. K. Gandhi brings Buddha's notion of non-violence or *ahimsa* and applies it to all spheres of life. For him religion is religion of truth. For him Truth is God and God is Truth. It is not an abstract entity. According to Gandhi if God is to be God, He must rule the heart and transform it. For him religion means to accept God for life. Accepting God means to allow love, truth and reason to rule the heart and to remove the passion and other ill feelings from the heart. Therefore morality is the essence of religion for Gandhi. True religion and true morality are inseparably bound up with each other.

Originally the term *"Ahimsa"* meant a negative fact but M. K. Gandhi transformed it into an active force and for him there was no room for cowardice or weakness in *ahimsa*. Violence for Gandhi is rather an expression of fear of an inner sense. Gandhi interpreted the term *Ahimsa* as a virtue, which expresses love and good will. Hence Gandhi translates *ahimsa* by the word 'love'. According to Gandhi to love God is to love all His creations in whom God is incarnate. So says Gandhi, "When you want to find Truth as God, the only means is love or *ahimsa*."

Besides the differences of time, historical location, agenda, orientation, background, profession and destiny they were having much common interests.

One was shot dead and the other was retired as an icon, not popular in his own generation but adopted as pathfinder, a controversial figure to his own nation. But M. K. Gandhi was crowned as the "Mahatma" and by non other than Ravindranath Tagore that too within 8 years of his (Gandhi's) return to India [35]

M. K. Gandhi comes to his conclusion through trial and error method. He never had a proper education or training in Philosophy or theology whereas G. Grant had a D. Phil degree on Theology and that too from Oxford.

But Grant was from a virtuous background. Grant was born into a renowned family. Both of his grandfathers devoted their lives to the reform of education. Sir G. Parkin started up the Rhodes Scholarship at Lord Milner's request. G. Monro Grant turned the struggling Presbyterian school of Queen's in Kingston into a University. Grant's father William Grant rescued Upper Canada College (a private boys' school in Toronto) from mediocrity and made it an important educational institution.[36] Grant inherited the family business. He spent almost his whole life teaching or being taught. He took an undergraduate degree in History at Queen's University, where his concern for education reform first showed itself.

After he won a Rhodes scholarship at Queen's, Grant went to Balliol College, Oxford to study Law. He returned home to Toronto in Feb 1942. After the War Grant returned to Oxford to study for D. Phil. in Theology. Afterwards he taught at Dalhousie University in Halifax from 1947 until 1960. He returned in 1980 and stayed until his retirement from teaching in 1984. "As a Rhodes scholar at Oxford, he started out in Law and ended up in theology"[37]

While the modern Western thinkers like Ruskin, Tolstoy and Thoreau influenced Gandhi on the one hand; on the other hand he was highly impressed by the Vedas, Vedanta, Gita and Upanishads of Hinduism.

For M. K. Gandhi Upanishad, Vedanta are the greatest source of Indian philosophy and religion and spiritualism. He says that if all the great books are destroyed in some kind of an accident like in a fire or so but even then if one single sloka of Isopanishad survives then everything is survived. He was impressed by Mohammed, Buddha, Jaina, and also by the heritage of Christianity, Jesus, and universal brotherhood and message of love of Koran.

But G. Grant comes to Spiritualism through intellectual connection. He was very articulated by philosophy of 17th and 18th century.

Gandhi realized the human questions by confronting himself. He was totally unhappy with Hinduism with untouchability. Hence ultimately he was killed by not a Muslim or Christian but by a Hindu fanatic. Grant also liked his Christianity different from the dominant Christianity.

Still there is a parallel interest in them; point of convergence and that is spirituality-

Two important converging points between the two, which brings M. K. Gandhi and George Grant together are – spiritualism and suspension of technological modern civilization. Grant came to spiritualism though intellectual connection and Gandhi came through religion.

Grant talks about the disenchantment of modernity. Europe died in giving birth to this 'baby of modernism', which gave birth to two wars. The idea of good is rooted in controlling our instinct and Gandhi was convinced of the power of non-violence/ *ahimsa*. In respect of instinct we are close to animals but to reach divinity is to go through spirituality, by non-violence. The same point is emphasized by Grant also. The present human is destined to have holocaust of which the rehearsal was done in 2nd World War.

Both believed in the revival of this spirituality.

Both of them accepted the success story of the German tradition of thought. They appreciated the German culture as best example which was successful in its revival of their culture and tradition at the same time without being aggressive to the culture and tradition of others.

They believed that explanations from the ancient should not be rejected as they are not from experience but of powerful past. Science and technology make M. K. Gandhi to believe in re-birth. In fact both Gandhi and G. Grant believe in faith and re-birth.

Relevance of M. K. Gandhi and George Grant

Gandhi is always adored by everyone. But if we want to compare his position amongst the present day intellectuals can we say the same thing? According to thinkers like S. Gopal, Gandhi is still relevant in a contemporary global crisis. For others like D.R. Nagaraj, it is necessary to re-evaluating Gandhi in the present context so that a greater number of people can be removed from the evils of industrialization. According to Mira S. Bhattacaryaya "the root cause of present day problem lay in the industrial, technological civilization that impelled Gandhi to write *Hind Swaraj* almost a century ago". For environmentalists like R. C. Guha, the problem of environmental decay faced by the present generation could be sorted out by the experiments in village reconstruction conducted by Gandhi and his followers like J. C. Kumarappa and Mira Ben "do constitute an eminent usable" example for environmentalists.

Ramashray Roy says that Gandhian solution was found by many to be either too radical or too drastic, too obscurantist, too much against the grain of historical situation and tends to be taken seriously: "And yet it is perhaps the only solution which many others feel as it is like a beacon in the troubled ship of humanity to the safety of a hospitable sore". (from a Report- R A Padmanabhan) [38].

Conclusion

In a video taped interview George Grant said that the central assumption of today is that the man's essence is his freedom, freedom without limit, to receive the world as he or she wants it, to reduce everything as raw materials for knowing and making. What use is of knowledge if we cannot apply it? Is it to master by machines and to free people from work and labor or to master disease and prolong our lives or to master nature and human nature or to master chance?

But is it good to do so to control our genes, to make ourselves whatever we think we want to be, to master the universe to make it ours? Control of the world is seen as what is essentially moral, but it appears to him that technology is now been pursued not to free human beings from labor and work or disease but for the investigation of nature and human nature for its own sake.

Modern society is committed as an end in itself. If it can be done it should be done, change for its own sake. Where does it lead the people, the individual with a rather less desire to dominate on the part of the manager? An endless search for private consolation among the powerless majority? I fear this was tyranny and in this smooth tyranny of consumerism would we be anything more than consumers?

What is about becoming freedom, freedom from what? Public invaders and private ecstasy?

ETERNAL and JUSTICE

It is true that there might be some similarity between Grant and Gandhi regarding the relationship between the eternal and the temporal. For example Grant writes in the conclusion of the *Lament for a Nation* "changes in the world ...take place within an eternal order that is not affected by their taking place". This clearly expresses Grant's love, faith and respect for the eternal order, which he believes to be unchangeable. For Gandhi also Truth is God and non-violence or *Ahimsa* was the only path to perceive the ultimate Truth.

Notes

1. *Lament for a Nation: the defeat of Canadian Nationalism*: 40th anniversary edition: McGill Queen's University Press, 2005 (with a new introduction by Andrew Potter).
    Gandhiji is commonly known around the world as Mahatma Gandhi (mahâtmâ or "Great Soul", an honorific first applied to him by Rabindranath Tagore) and in India also as Bapu (Gujarati: bâpu or "Father"). He is officially honoured in India as the Father of the Nation; his birthday, 2 October, is commemorated there as Gandhi Jayanti, a national holiday, and world-wide as the International Day of Non-Violence
2. Through Prof. Christian in a personal letter to me.
    Also see my other article "Grant and Gandhi: a live interview with Mrs. Sheila Grant" in this book.
3. In a review by George Elliott Clarke.
4. Grant affirmed the role of philosophy in teaching and helping people understand the discipline of philosophy, Margaret Boyd, review, *George Grant books*.
5. *Gandhi's life in his own words*, p 3. Navajivan Trust, 1983. *AMG* or *An Autobiography*, p 3, Navajivan Trust, 1927.
6. *Ibid*, p 5.
7. The first and most powerful force in his life was his mother Maude-p 21, *George Grant: Redefining Canada*. T.F. Rigelhof. Montreal, PQ: XYZ Publishing, 2001.
8. "*The Story of My experiments with Truth*", M K Gandhi.
9. *Kitchener-Waterloo Record Column*, William Christian .
10. I had an intense discussion on this with Prof John G Arapura in Mc Master University.
11. Review by Alexander Gregor, of *George Grant: Redefining Canada*. (The Quest Library, 15). T.F. Rigelhof. Montreal, PQ: XYZ Publishing, 2001.,179 pp.,) in CM-(*Canadian Review of Materials*)vol. VIII, no 18, May 10, 2002. Also: Regarding Gandhi's *Hind Swaraj* it is said, — " Gandhi's *Hind Swaraj* is surely a foundational text for any understanding of the man and his mission. In dialogue with the text in its context, with the author and among ourselves, we hope to locate the

text within it's own horizon of meaning and then interrogate it from within our own contemporary. For Gandhi's text is 'a proclamation of ideological independence' (Dalton1993: 61) he never compromised, his 'confession of the faith' (Nanda 1974: 66) he never abandoned, 'a rather incendiary manifest' (Erikson 1969: 217) to enkindle his revolution. No wonder it was banned by the colonial government in 1910 for fear of sedition." *Rudolf C. Heredita.

12. *The Philosophy of Mahatma Gandhi*, Dr. D. M. Dutta. 1953, U of Wisconsin Press.
13. *Ibid*.
14. 'When David asks him about the things that have formed and informed in his belief in Christianity, George Says, "I just remember going off to work one morning and I remember walking through a gate; I got off my bicycle and walked through a gate, and I believed in God. I can't tell you more, I just knew that it was for me. And that came to me very suddenly. I don't mean that in a very dramatic sense; I just mean it as the case, because I'd come from a world where God had not been taken seriously. Religion was something that was good for a society and kept people in order, but really, if you explore it intellectually, it was b.s., it was nonsense. This was prodigious moment for me. I think it was a kind of affirmation that beyond time and space there is order"'.
George Grant: Redefining Canada. (The Quest Library, 15). T.F. Rigelhof. Montreal, PQ: XYZ Publishing, 2001., p.55.
15. *Gandhi's life in his own words.* p10
16. B.N.Ray, *Indian Political Thought*, p.341. Ajanta Books, 1997.
17. *Ibid*, p 341.
18. *Ibid*, p 342.
19. William Christian on George Grant.
20. *Hind Swaraj*, P 31.
21. *Ibid*, p 32.
Also: P 31 *Hind Swaraj*,
"To fly through the air in trains at the rate of four hundred and more miles per day.. is considered the height of civilization .." (p 32) . Gandhi says that " Everything will be done by machinery "(p32). Formerly men were made slave under physical compulsion . Now they are enslaved by temptation of money and of the luxuries that money can

buy". (P33)."There are now diseases of which people never dreamt before and an army of doctors is engaged in finding out their cures, and so hospitals have increased. This is a test of civilization". (P33).

Further he writes: " This civilization takes note neither of morality nor of religion .... immorality is often taught in the name of morality". (P33).

22. Ibid, P 33.
23. Dr. D M Dutta., *The Philosophy of Mahatma Gandhi*, 1953, U of Wisconsin Press. p 115, Gandhi, M K, *Hindu Dharma*, p 67.Navajivan Pub House, Ahmedabad, 1949.
24. William Christian, in Kitchener -Waterloo Record Column
25. Ibid.
26. Ibid.
27. Ibid.
28. *Technology and Empire*, G G.
29. Kitchener -Waterloo Record Column, William Christian.
30. G. Grant , *Technology and Justice*, p 19.

Grant's views on modern life as given in his essay "Thinking about technology" becomes clear in the following statement: " In the novelties of our hourly existing, it is easy enough to recognize how much we have encompassed ourselves within tech. We sweep along superhighways to work in factories, or in the bureaucracy of some corporation; our needs are tended to in supermarkets and health complexes. We can cook, light, heat, refrigerate, be entertained at home through energy, which has been produced and stored in quite new ways. If we have even a slight knowledge of the past we are aware that we can make happen what has never before been possible". (Thesis, Jim Gerrie-78, in *Technology and Justice* pp. 14-15).

31. *George Grant Reader,* Ed., W. Christian and Sheila Grant, 1998, p78.
32. Robert Oppenheimer, a nuclear scientist,
33. *Technology and Justice*, G. Grant, 1986, p 60, William Christian – on GG paper
34. *G. Grant A biography*, pp. 184-85, W Christian and Shelia Grant, Toronto, 1994, Toronto University Press.

35. He is commonly known as Mahatma Gandhi in Sanskrit, 'mahâtmâ' or "Great Soul", an honorific first applied to him by Rabindranath Tagore.
36. *Biography*, p 304-5,
37. Kitchener -Waterloo Record Column, William Christian.
38. R A Padmanabhan, A Report.

ಃ ಅ

16

GANDHI'S IDEA OF NATION IN *HIND SWARAJ*

Anthony J. Parel

HIND SWARAJ is recognized by all as being Gandhi's most fundamental work. In this article I propose to argue that a proper understating of the idea of "nation" propounded therein is a necessary condition for a proper understanding of the teaching of that book taken as a whole. That teaching concerns, in the immediate instance, the nature of *swaraj* and the ways and means of attaining it. But the nature of *swaraj* cannot be fully understood unless it is also understood that the subjects enjoying it or going to enjoy it are the nation and the self, i.e., each Indian considered as a member of that nation are the two subjects of *swaraj*. The originality of Gandhi's teaching in this book consists in arguing that there is a connection between the process by which the nation attains its independence and the process by which the self attains control over itself. The attainment of self-control, in Gandhi's view, ought not to be considered as a solipsist affair. Gandhi's most important contribution to Indian thought is that self-control and self-realization ought to lead simultaneously to the well-being of the nation as a whole. This is also Gandhi's distinct contribution to political theory. At the time of the writing of *Hind Swaraj*, Gandhi was painfully aware that those who cared for the nation, such as the apostles of violence, did not care for the soul; and that those who cared for the soul, did not care for the nation. Gandhi, wanted to bridge the gap between these two forms of human striving. That is to say, he sought to purge modern Indian nationalism of its reliance on brute force, and to instill in the minds of those who cared for the soul, the need to become civic minded as well as peace minded. Such is the complex meaning of *swaraj* in *Hind Swaraj*.

But that meaning can be fully appreciated only if we understand what Gandhi means by "nation" and the concepts associated with it, such as "nationalism", "nationality" and "national". And it is towards clarifying that meaning that this article is dedicated.

That in writing *Hind Swaraj* the idea of nation was uppermost in Gandhi's mind can be inferred from several sources. First, there is an important letter which he wrote to Lord Ampthill on the eve of writing the book. The letter in question gives a preview of what he was going to argue in the work. It would contain, he wrote, "the result of my observations... on the nationalist movement among my countrymen.... . An awakening of the national consciousness is unmistakable. But among the majority it is in a crude shape and there is not a corresponding spirit of self-sacrifice".[1] The Indian nationalists he met in London in 1909 relied, he felt, on the presumed efficacy of violence. This was the chief defect of their nationalism. And the position that he would adopt in the book seeks to remove this defect. As he said: "I share the national sprit but I totally dissent from the methods whether of the extremists or of the moderates. For either party ultimately relies on violence."[2] Given these views one is not surprised at what one finds in the Preface to the original Gujarati version of the book : "The only motive", in writing the book, it states, "Was to serve my country, to find Truth and to follow it".³ For him serving the country and finding and following the Truth were connected, inseparable processes. The Preface to the English version of the book also underlines the nationalist intent of the book: "Had I not been called upon by hundreds of my countrymen, and not a few English friends, to express my opinion on the Nationalist movement in India, I would even have refrained... from reducing my views in writing".⁴

How important the idea of nation is for the argument of *Hind Swaraj* may be gauged from the number of times the word "nation" and its cognates occur in the book: they occur 75 times; not an insignificant fact, considering that the text of the book is only 56 pages long in the *Collected Works of Mahatma Gandhi*. The frequency is eleven in each of chapters 1 and 9, and ten in each of chapters 10, 17 and 20.

An equally significant phenomenon is the Gujarati word he uses to express the idea of nation: the word is *praja*. One can only speculate as to what prompted Gandhi to think of nation in terms of *praja* rather than in those of *rashtra*. The Hindi translation of *Hind Swaraj* consistently renders *praja* as *rashtra*. The common usage in other Indian languages also seems to have been *rasthra*. Thus, for example, Aurobindo Ghose refers to the "Nationalist Committee" set up by the Extremist party at the Surat Congress as *Rashtriya Mandali*.⁵ It could be that for Gandhi *Praja* underlined the idea of "people" or "community", whereas *rashtra* underlined that of power. Whatever the reasons, for Gandhi Indians are in the first instance a *praja*, and only secondarily are they the speakers of this or that language, or the followers of this or that religion, or the inhabitants of this or that region. Also, the term *praja* helps to bring out the notion that Indians taken as a whole constitute one democratic entity.

An analysis of the idea of nation in *Hind Swaraj* raises four major issues. First, against those who assert that India is not a nation, the book argues that India is indeed a nation. Secondly, there is the issue of the relationship of religion and language to the concept of nation. Thirdly, the book assesses the contributions that the Indian National Congress made to the evolution of Indian nationalism upto 1909 and evaluates the merits and demerits of its Extremist and Moderate factions. Finally, the book focuses its special attention on the national elite- the lawyers, the doctors and the rest of the newly educated Indian intelligentsia. It exposes their deficiencies as a national elite and suggest ways and means of correcting them. I shall take up these points by turn.

India is a Nation

Gandhi meets head-on the opinion that India is not a nation, that there is nothing in India's history or traditions that presages nationalism, and that India is an artificial country put together by the British for administrative convenience. And if Indians now talk of India as being a nation, it is due to the introduction of Western ideas and to the changes brought about by modern means of communication such as the railways and the telegraph. He recognizes that such ideas are widespread and that they are sometimes held by even some Indians. The source of such opinions, however, in his view, is the British interpretation of Indian history. "They (the British) have a habit of writing history. They pretend to study the manners and customs of all peoples. God has given us a limited mental capacity but they usurp the function of the Godhead and indulge in novel experiments. They write about their own researches in most laudatory terms and hypnotize us into believing them. We, in our ignorance, then fall at their feet".[6] The concept of orientialism had not yet been invented. But Gandhi here seems to anticipate the essence of that later theory.[7] The discussion of whether or not India is a nation is introduced by the Reader as a casual aside to the discussion of the railways. One of the hidden benefits of the introduction of railways into India, the Reader claims, is that "we see in India the new sprit of nationalism". The Editor's response quick and sharp: "I hold this to be a mistake, the English have taught us that we were not one nation before and that it will require centuries before we became one nation. This is without foundations. We were one nation before they came to India".[8]

Gandhi's argument in support of the proposition that India is a nation rests on two bold assumptions. The first is that ancient Indian civilization had an accommodating capacity and the second is that in ancient India the *acharyas*, in founding certain places of pilgrimage, laid the basis for the evolution of an all-India consciousness.

Though the ancient civilization of India was basically Hindu in character, it was nevertheless a civilization that was potentiality open to non-Hindu ideas and values. The Gujarati word that Gandhi uses to express his idea of accommodation is *samas*. According to the grammar of most Indian language, this term refers to the capacity of these languages to coin new complex words out of existing simple words. To take an example: the word *mahatma* is a new word composed of two already existing words *maha* and *atma*, words which have originally their own identity. Yet when they combine, they produce a new but more complex word which then acquires its own unique identity. Similarly, though originally the Indian word *praja* was composed of simpler identities, in course of time, under certain historical conditions, it became capable of forming a more complex but unified *praja*. Indeed, it may be said that Gandhi's concept of *samas* as applied to Indian sub national communities is not far removed from Renan's notion of "fusion". It may be remembered that Ernest Renan, in his well-known essay *Qu'est- ce qu'une Nation?*, spoke of the "fusion of the populations" as being one of the conditions for the formation of the various nations of Europe.[9] Gandhi is in effect saying that India also is the result of a process of *samas* taking place for over several centuries.

There is a corollary implicit in the idea of *samas*. It is that each of the uniting elements should be actually capable and willing to unite and form a more complex population unit. Where many sub-nationalities are involved, national unification cannot be a one-way process. This means that in India the late-comers, whoever they might be —whether Muslims, or Christians, or Parsis, or Sikhs, —should each in their own way be able to adopt the accommodating spirit of Indian civilization. Of course they can and must retain their own individual identity. But, in so far as they are Indians, they must do so within the framework of an all-embracing Indian civilization. "A country is one nation only when such a condition (which enables new-comers to merge with the original group) obtains in it. That country must have a faculty for assimilation. India has ever been such a country".[10] Gandhi's point is that whatever else one may identify as characteristic of ancient Indian civilization, none can be considered as crucial to India's future as its accommodating, open characteristics. And whatever may be the specific identity of the late-comers, nothing should be allowed to stand in their way of accommodating themselves to the temper of Indian civilization.

Gandhi's second assumption concerns the activities of those whom he calls "our leading men" or the "foreseeing ancestors of ours". He is no doubt referring to the acharyas of ancient Indian civilization. These individuals, he points out, travelled the length and breadth of India "either on foot or on bullock-carts", and their activities had the effect of creating a common consciousness. The slowness of their locomotion was the very source of their strength. It enabled them to come to know the people among whom they moved and to establish among them a sense of community. According to Gandhi, their greatest achievement, as far as future national identity was concerned, was the establishment of centres of pilgrimage in key places in India. He mentions, for example, Hardwar in the North, Rameshwaram in the South and Jagannath in the East. "What do you think could have been the intention of those far-seeing ancestors of ours?", the Editor asks, "You will admit they were no fools". They did not establish these places of pilgrimage merely for religious benefits. Religious benefits, he points out, could have been procured in ways other than by pilgrimage to faraway places. "They knew that worship of God could have been performed just as well at home. They taught us that those whose hearts were aglow with righteousness had the Ganges in their own homes". Yet they instituted these holy places and they had an ulterior motive in doing so. If spiritual benefits were the only or even the chief purpose, travel to North and South, East and West would not have been necessary. No, the reason why the ancient *acharyas* established these places of pilgrimage had a deeper significance: it was to create and sustain a sense of common identity among Indians scattered over an immense territory. For, "they saw that India was one undivided land so made by nature. They, therefore, argued that it must be one nation. Arguing thus, they established holy places in various parts of India, and fired the people with an idea of nationality in a manner unknown in other parts of the world".[11]

Recent scholars have noted that in ancient India, pilgrimages were powerful means of reinforcing a sense of common identity. Thus David G. Mandelbaum remarks that pilgrimage "helps to continually confirm a sense of identification of people with entire India", and M.N. Srinivas opines that "the concept of the unity of India is essentially a religious one".[12] But Gandhi anticipated these scholarly discoveries by at least half a century. He is the first major figure in modern India to recognize the significance of the places of pilgrimage for the evolution of a national identity. And it is a sign of his genius that he should single out the ancient *acharyas* rather than the Maharajas or emperors of the past as the creators of a sense of common identity. It is as if by reading the lives of a Sankara or a Ramanuja, one can learn as much about what India means as by reading the exploits of this king or that or of this dynasty or that.

Also, there is subtle irony in the contrast he draws between railways and bullock-carts. To the Reader who thinks that the sense of nationality came only with the railways, he points out that the bullock-carts do better in this regard. There is no doubt in Gandhi's mind that slow travel is still a very powerful way of reinforcing national sentiment. Throughout his life he maintained that *padayatra* or slow motion by foot was an effective means of nation-building and consciousness-raising. One need only think of the Salt March or of his walks through the riot-ridden Noakhali region. But it is clear from *Hind Swaraj* that, as early as 1909, he had become keenly aware of the communicative value of travel on foot. To get the best out of pilgrimages one had to do them on foot. The use of high-speed travel for the purpose of pilgrimage, he felt, tended to turn holy places into mere tourist centres, unholy and "abominable". Writing to Henry Polak a month before *Hind Swaraj* was completed, he observed: "When there was no rapid locomotion, traders and preachers went on foot, from one end of the country to the other, braving all the dangers, not for pleasure, not for recreating their health (though all that followed from their tramp), but for the sake of humanity. Then Benares and other places of pilgrimage were holy cities, whereas today they are an abomination".[13]

The argument that the slow mode of travel of the ancient acharyas contributed much to the development of a common consciousness in India did not remain a mere *academic* tool for him. Throughout his life, whenever possible, he tried to implement the insight contained in it. He often referred to his political tours as "pilgrimages", fully realizing that the *padayatra* solidified the sense of awakening and enriched his own experience of community. He claimed that his "best work" was done in places which he could reach by foot. As he wrote in the *Harijan*: "it is never a pleasure to me to travel by motor or rail or even a cart. It is always a pleasure to walk. Nor would I mind in the least if every rail was removed and men, except the sick and the maimed, had to walk to their businesses. I can only imagine, but I am working for a civilization in which possession of a car will be considered no merit and railways will find no place".[14] No doubt, for practical reasons, Gandhi made full use of travel by train or car: "being a highly practical man", he said, "I do not avoid railway traveling or motoring for the mere sake of looking foolishly consistent".[15] But his personal predilection was for the traditional mode of travel. He once recounted an incident in which he had to prevail upon Thakkar Bappa, the "manager" of the tour, to let him travel by foot. "So I put my foot down and insisted on performing the remaining pilgrimage on foot". The "pilgrimage" in question was one of the *Harijan* tours of the 1930s. He could cover only eight or ten miles per day. But he considered the section he covered on foot as "the most effective part of our tour. The awakening was solid. Our experiences were rich".[16] Travel by foot was an important part of Gandhi's way of nation-building: he was doing nothing extraordinary, he would have claimed; he would have protested that he was doing in the present only what the *acharyas* were doing in the past.

Religion and Language

The argument that Indian civilization supplies the basis for nationhood runs into a major difficulty. The Reader poses it bluntly: "Has the introduction of Mahomedanism not unmade the nation?"[17] Indian civilization may have supplied a basis for a common identity in the pre-Islamic period; "but now we have Mahomedans, Parsis and Christians. Our very proverbs prove it". The Muslims turn to the West for worship and the Hindus to the East; the Muslims kill cows, the Hindus worship them. The Muslims do not believe in *ahimsa*, while the Hindus adhere to it. "We thus meet with differences at every stop. How can India be one nation?"[18]

In approaching, Gandhi's position on the relationship between nationalism, religion and language, it is important to bear in mind that his approach is normative, not positivistic. Certainly, he takes into account historical facts. At the same time he realizes that norms have shaped and will always shape historical facts and that in moral and political sciences there are no such things as pure facts.

What are sometimes referred to as pure historical facts have themselves been moulded by their component norms. And if certain facts of Indian history show the existence of animosities between Hindus and Muslims, as undoubtedly they do, it is no reason to conclude that such animosities are inevitable and that they should continue for ever. New norms can and should be developed which in turn can create new historical facts conducive to the growth of India as a *praja*. Thus, though Gandhi recognizes the factual differences between Hindus and Muslims, his normative approach to them disposes him to consider them to be not serious enough to prevent the growth of a composite nationalism. For him the presence of Muslims, and for that matter that of Christians, Sikhs, and Parsis, constitute not so much a challenge to Indian civilization as an opportunity to manifest its accommodating potential. Furthermore, he takes as norm that religion as sect ought not to be the basis of nationality. That being the case, he reasons: "India cannot cease to be one nation because people belonging to different religions live in it. The introduction of foreigners does not necessarily destroy the nation".[19]

Gandhi's conception of the relationship between nationality and religion deserves close attention. We have to understand first his meaning of religion itself. In religion, according to him, one has to distinguish between the core and the periphery, the ultimate goal and the different paths leading to it. The core and the ultimate goal of religions are compatible with multi-religious nationalism. Put differently, one has to distinguish between (i) religion as social organization, as sect and (ii) religion as the source of ethical beliefs. Religion in the first sense is a social phenomenon, while in the second sense, it is a personal matter. And Gandhi's norm is that the claims of religion in the first sense should be subordinated to the demands of Indian nationalism. If this can be brought about, there would be no unmanageable difficulties between Indian nationalism and religion in the second sense. Gandhi's nationalism, accordingly, is neither fundamentalist nor secular. It is not fundamentalist because it does not identify the nation with the sociological formation that religion as sect creates. It is not secular because it recognizes the autonomy of religion as ethics and the harmony between such ethics and Indian nationalism. He writes: "In reality there are as many religions as there are individuals; but those who are conscious of the spirit of nationality do not interfere with one another's religion. If they do they are not fit to be considered a nation".[20] "If everyone will try to understand the core of his own religion and adhere to it, and will not allow false teachers to dictate to them, there will be no room left for quarrelling".[21]

Gandhi is quite aware that the fundamentalists think of religion and nationality as identical. The above reference to "false teachers" implies such awareness on his part. We need not take too much space here to determine who these "false teachers" might have been. It is enough to recall that certain schools of *ulemas* and *swamies* were preaching the uncompromising fundamentalist stand of "one religion, one nation". Gandhi totally rejects such theories. "If the Hindus believe that India should be peopled only by Hindus, they are living in dreamland. *If Muslims believe that only Muslims live here, they are living in dreamland too.* The Hindus, the Mahomedans, the Parsis and the Christians who have made India their country, are fellow countrymen and they will have to live in unity, if only for their own self-interest. In no part of the world are one nationality and one religion synonymous terms; nor has it ever been so in India".[22]

Given Gandhi's normative position on religion and nationalism, it is not difficult for him to suggest ways and means of reducing the animosities between Hindus and Muslims. If there have been "deadly" proverbs applicable to *mahadevs* and *mians*, so there have been equally vicious proverbs applicable to Vishnavites and Sivites: "Yet nobody suggests that these (last two) do not belong to the same nation".[23] Similarly sectarian differences need not necessarily spell national differences. Thus the Jains and Vedic Hindus differ as sects, yet "the followers of the respective faiths are not different nations". [24] What the Hindus and Muslims therefore ought to seek now is "true knowledge" regarding religion and nationalism. "The more we advance in true knowledge, the better we shall understand that we need not be at war with those whose religion we may not follow".[25]

The argument now shifts to the question of race. There are no racial differences, Gandhi points out, between Indian Hindus and Indian Muslims: "many Hindus and Mahomedans own the same ancestors and the same blood runs through their veins..... Do people become enemies because they change their religion? Is the God of the Mahomedans different fro the God of the Hindus?"[26] To fight for separate nations, therefore, has no religious justification. Using the metaphor that should be very familiar to students of Gandhi, *Hind Swaraj* suggests that religions, understood as social formations, are different roads converging to the same point and it did not matter what road one takes, "so long as we reach the same goal".[27] That is to say, Indian nationalism may legitimately demand that religion as sect accommodate its demands to the needs of the Indian *praja*.

The sincerity of Gandhi's position on religion and nationalism cannot be better expressed than by the stand he takes on the vexed issues of cow protection and cow sacrifice. For his part, in the final analysis, he is willing to accommodate cow protection to the demands of a composite Indian nationalism. Assuming cow protection belongs to the periphery, not the core of Hindu religion, one should be able to treat it within the dictates of a composite nationalism. If the choice was between a unified nation and cow protection, he was prepared to opt for the former. He would no doubt attempt to persuade the Muslims to respect Hindu feelings in the matter. But he was not prepared to go beyond persuasion. "I myself respect the cow, that is, I look upon her with affectionate reverence". "But just as I respect the cow, so do I respect my fellowmen".[28] Moreover, the Muslim is the "blood-brother" of the Hindu. That being the case, "the only method I know of protecting the cow is that I approach my Mahomedan brother and urge him *for the sake of the country* to join me in protecting her. If he would not listen to me, *I should let the cow go* for the simple reason that the matter is beyond my ability. If I were over full of pity for the cow, I should sacrifice my life to save her, but not take my brother's. This, I hold, is the law of our religion."[29]

At this point, the Editor reminds the Reader that there have been and there still are meat-eaters among Hindus and that Hindus mistreat the cow, etc. Yet the cow protection societies do nothing against these Hindus, least of all do they think of them as being anti-Hindus and anti-national. "Who protects the cow from destruction by Hindus when they cruelly ill-treat her? Whoever reasons with the Hindus when they mercilessly belabor the progeny of the cow with their stick? But this has not prevented us from remaining one nation".[30]

In *Hind Swaraj* Gandhi's attitude towards Muslims is marked by both self-confidence and generosity. He felt that a self-confident majority can afford to be generous towards minorities and that the majority community should take the first initiative to build confidence in their national minorities. "That man who has inspired confidence has never lost anything in this world".[31] The obverse of this principle is that there is nothing more intolerant and more inhumane than a national majority community that feels threatened by its national minorities. One needs only to think of Germans and Jews in Nazi Germany. In the India of 1909 Gandhi felt that the Hindus were "superior in number", "more educated" and therefore, "better able to shield themselves from attack on their amicable relations with the Mahomedans".[32] And especially because of this secure position, *Hind Swaraj* is supportive of the separate electorate (what it calls "certain concessions") that the Minto-Morley reforms had made available to the Muslims. He wondered why anyone interested in national unity should oppose them. "There is mutual distrust between the two communities. The Mahomedans, therefore, ask for certain concessions from Lord Morley. Why should the Hindus oppose this?"[33]

Turning now to the language question, Gandhi's approach was guided by three general norms: the need to reject the Macaulayan concept of the role of the English language in India, the primacy of the mother tongue, (or what *Hind Swaraj* calls "the provincial language"), and the desirability of having an Indian language as the common language of India.

In his letter to Lord Ampthill, referred to above, Gandhi had already declared the following: "I no longer believe as I used to in Lord Macaulay as a benefactor through his Minute on education".[34] *Hind Swaraj* reverts to the same idea: "The foundation that Macaulay laid of education has enslaved us".[35] However, the present problem as he sees it, is not so much with the Minutes of Macaulay, as with the uncritical acceptance of its spirit by some Indians: "by receiving English education, we have enslaved the nation... It is we, the English knowing Indians, that have enslaved India. The curse of the nation will rest not upon the English but upon us".[36]

What is the "foundation" and what is the "slavery" that Gandhi is alluding to here? He is not alluding to the practical knowledge of the English language as such, which he recognizes as being necessary for improving the quality of the "provincial" languages of India, and for disseminating knowledge of modern science.[37] The "foundation" he objects to is the cultural assumptions underlying Macaulay's thesis, namely that Sanskrit and Persian have no foundational value for the Indian civilization of the future, and that English should replace them as the new foundational language of modern India. To give English language this cultural role, Gandhi recognized, was tantamount to committing national suicide. Those Indians who looked upon English as the foundation of a new Indian culture were enslaving, not liberating, India. Profound as Gandhi's insight here is, it is important nevertheless to understand the distinction that Gandhi makes between English as a means of national slavery and English as a means of national development. His rejection of English is neither total nor mindless. "Do I then understand that you do not consider English education necessary for obtaining Home rule?" The Reader asks. The Editor's response is guarded indeed: "My answer is yes and no".[38] It is "no", as far as the Macaulay thesis is concerned. It is "yes", as far as the practical needs of the nation are concerned. Such needs include, the needs of scientific education, and inter-provincial communication- "our dealings with our own people, when we can only correspond with them through that language". Ever the practical man, Gandhi realized in the cultural conditions prevailing in India at the turn of the century, knowledge of the English language was practically necessary. "We are so much beset by the disease of civilization, that we cannot altogether do without English education".[39] It is clear, then, that what Gandhi was objecting to was the wrong kind of use that the new English educated Indian elite was making of their English education. They were looking upon English education as a means of gaining power and prestige and of getting better jobs in relation to their non-English educated fellow nations. It was setting English-knowing Indians apart from Indians who did not know English. "The object of making money"[40] had become the decisive object of English education in the minds of the vast majority. It had become the means whereby one could become a "doctor" or a "lawyer", or a member of the ruling bureaucracy such as the Indian Civil Service. It was becoming a means of acquiring status in society and control over fellow Indians. It was creating an ambitious, selfish and unscrupulous Indian elite, with little sense of civic responsibility and national solidarity. "English-knowing Indians have not hesitated to cheat and strike terror into the people".[41] It is this evil tendency among the new Indian elite and not the knowledge of the English language as such, that *Hind Swaraj* is attacking. On the contrary, it endorses the tactical use of English to bring about national benefits in the areas of communication and scientific progress. But such use of English must be consciously placed within the framework of a robust Indian nationalism.

As for the mother tongue, it had to be the primary basis of the cultural life of each "province". At the same time, Gandhi clearly recognized that English had to be used to bring about the further growth of the mother tongue. *Hind Swaraj* unequivocally states: "We have to improve all our languages. What subjects we should learn through them need not be elaborated here. Those English books which are valuable we should translate into the various Indian languages."[42] Perhaps what is most insightful is his observation that whereas English should be for the time being the language of scientific education, the mother tongue should remain the language of ethical education: "Those who have studied English will have to teach morality to their progeny through their mother tongue".[43] By assigning to the mother tongue the fundamental role in ethical education, Gandhi attempted to show that English education need not have a denationalizing effect on Indians.

As for a common language for India, *Hind Swaraj* reflects Gandhi's thinking in 1909: he opts for Hindi "with the option of writing it in Persian or Nagari characters".[44] No doubt Gandhi is conscious of the fact that his positon on the mother tongue is not entirely in sync with his position on the need for a common language. The accent in *Hind Swaraj* is on voluntary, not legal and coercive, methods of brining about a working harmony between the mother tongue and the common language. It is therefore accommodating to the feelings of linguistic minorities. It proposes a rather elaborate scheme of making the language issue consistent with the demands of Indian nationalism. Thus Gandhi said: "Every cultured Indian will know in addition to his own provincial language, if a Hindu, Sanskrit, if a Mahomedan, Arabic; if a Parsee, Persian, all Hindi. Some Hindus should know Arabic and Persian, some Mahomedans and Parsees, Sanskrit. Several Northerners and Westerners should learn Tamil".[45]

Assessment of the Indian National Congress

We have already seen that one of the aims of *Hind Swaraj* was to give an interpretation of the Indian nationalist movement. This meant that Gandhi had to give his own assessment of the achievements of the Indian National Congress up to 1909. Chapters 1-3 and part of chapter 20 address this specific issue. The issue is treated polemically: the Reader taking the offensive and the Editor offering the defence. In the Reader's view, "Young India seems to ignore the Congress. It is considered to be an instrument for perpetuating British rule".[46] The involvement of such Britons as Allan Octavian Hume and Sir William Wedderburn is "beyond my comprehension", says the Reader.[47] The leaders of the Moderate faction-Dadabhai Naoroji, Gopal Krishna Gokhale and Badruddin Tyebji- are dismissed unceremoniously for being "subservient" to the British. The Reader wants Indian nationalism to abandon its constitutional approach, the approach of petition and prayer, and to adopt a deliberately violent approach, which would legitimize the use of brute force (*darugolo*). In the Reader's view, split between the Moderates and the Extremists was most salutary, and the latter should be prepared to adopt the methods even of terrorism. Briefly, there was a danger of Indian nationalism becoming by the turnoff the century more and more like the violent nationalism of the West. The Reader wanted it to become fully "modern", i.e., "Western" violent, selfish, closed, and exclusive.

Gandhi's response was that the Congress, for all its inadequacies, was the first institution which had "enthused us with the idea of nationality" - it brought together Indians from different parts of India, for that very reason, it was looked upon with suspicion by the colonial government; it had "always insisted that the Nation should control revenue and expenditure"; and it "had always desired self-government after the Canadian model"; and it gave us a "foretaste of Home Rule". To deprive it of "honour" would not only be not proper, it would "retard the fulfillment" of the final object of obtaining true *swaraj*. "To treat the Congress as an instrument inimical to our growth as a nation would disable us from using that instrument".[48]

It is significant that *Hind Swaraj* identifies only three Congress nationalists by name, Naoroji, Gokhale, and Tyebji- a Parsi, a Hindu, and a Muslim respectively. India's claim to being a *praja* could not have been better substantiated than by such a list. Naoroji is "the Father of the Nation" and "the author of nationalism".[49] He is the model of service to the nation, had he not "prepared the soil", even the Reader could not have spoken of *swaraj;* his drain theory taught us "that the English had sucked our life-blood". In short, "we have learned what we know from him".[50] The case of Gokhale is no less compelling. "Professor Gokhale, in order to prepare the nation, embraced poverty and gave twenty years of his life. Even now he is living in poverty". He "occupies the place of a parent.... His devotion for the Motherland is so great that he would give his life for it". Tyebji is also one of those who "through the Congress, sowed the seed of Home Rule".[51] The conclusion is clear enough: "A nation that is desirous of securing Home Rule cannot afford to despise its ancestors".[52]

Gandhi's unequivocal endorsement of the role that Hume and Wedderburn played in the rise and development of Congress nationalism is equally worthy of attention. It gives evidence not only of his respect for historical facts but also of his normative position on the nature of nationalism as such. He did not see anything inconsistent in the fact that Indians and Britons could work together and nourish Indian nationalism. His nationalism is not ethnocentric, *Hinduttva* as a criterion of Indian nationality is not one of his inventions. He would not support such invention on philosophical and historical grounds. "Many Englishmen desire Home Rule for India". Some have gone beyond and made India their adopted home. These deserve fair treatment which the extremists and the terrorists were not willing to accord. "We who seek justice will have to do justice to others". The Editor insists: "How can we forget what Mr. Hume has written, how he had lashed us into action, and with what effort he has awakened us, in order to achieve the objects of the congress?"⁵³ As for Wedderburn, he has "given us his body mind and money to the same cause. His writings are worthy of perusal to this day".⁵⁴

Recognition of the historic role that the moderate wing of the Congress has played does not make Gandhi blind to its defects. He is fully aware that if India is to become free, it would have to go beyond constitutionalism and embrace the principles of *satyagraha*. He found their strategy of petitioning and prayer "derogatory". Neither does he accept their providentialist theory of colonialism, which he believes "is almost a denial of the Godhead".⁵⁵ He would rather adopt the dictum of an English divine "that anarchy under Home Rule were better than orderly foreign rule".⁵⁶

As for the extremists, their ideology is more objectionable than that of the moderates. Their misunderstanding of the true nature of *Swaraj* is more profound than that of their adversaries. They foolishly believe that *swaraj* can be obtained by the use of political violence and the forceful expulsion of the British.⁵⁷ They identify *swaraj* with the establishment of the modern, coercive, nation-state or "English rule without the Englishman". They want "the tiger's nature, but not the tiger", they want to make "India English. And when it becomes English, it will be called not Hindustan but Englistan. This is not the *swaraj* that I want".⁵⁸ He is highly critical of their infatuation with the Italian mode of achieving national independence. Chapter 15 of the book is devoted to the analysis of Italian nationalism. If Italy has any valuable lesson for India, it is to show how India ought not to proceed. According to Gandhi, the Extremists were more impressed by Garibaldi and Cavour than they were by Mazzini. Mazzini's vision of freedom has yet to be realized, but Italians think that "the whole of Italian people" have become free simply because Garibaldi and his associates have managed to expel the Austrians by force of arms. "I am sure you do not wish to reproduce such a condition (as that of modern Italy) in India", the Editor observes. "I belive that you want the millions of

India to be happy, not that you want the reins of Government in your hands".[59]

The Nation and the National Elite

The contours of Gandhi's conception of nationalism can now be better identified. Indian nationalism should produce a form of self-rule in which (i) the whole community, not just the elite, is free and active (ii) soul force, not brute force, should form the basis of public order; and (iii) "the national interests" (*prajana swarth*) is not the ultimate ethical criterion of state action.[60] To state this point differently, he rejects the notion that government by the national elite is beneficial simply because it is government by the national elite. The point is powerfully made by his scathing criticism of tyranny of Indian nawabs and maharajas, which he thinks is worse than the tyranny of the British. "You will admit", he reminds the Reader, "that the people under several Indian princes are being ground down. The latter mercilessly crush them. Their tyranny is greater than that of the English."[61]

It is no wonder that Gandhi is unambiguous in his criticism of Madan Lal Dhingra, "Do you not tremble to think of freeing India by assassination?... It is a cowardly thought, that of killing others. Whom do you suppose to free by assassination? The millions of India (*praja*) do not desire it. Those who are intoxicated by the wretched modern civilization think these things. Those who will rise to power by murder will certainly not make the nation happy".[62]

Gandhi's interpretation of Indian nationalism reaches its high-water mark in chapter 17, the most important chapter in the whole book. It starts with the question whether there is any historical evidence of "any nation having risen through soul force".[63] Gandhi concedes that historians have paid far too much attention to the violent doings of kings and princes. On the surface, it may appear that brute force is effective and that soul force is ineffective. But Gandhi is not prepared to make his case for nationalism solely on the basis of the behaviour of princes. He would rather base the first premise of his nationalist thought on love and compassion (*daya*) rather than the force. Tulsidas for him is a better guide here than are the princes–the Tulsidas, who teaches that *daya* is the turning basis of *dharma* and therefore also of the *dharma*, that should the *praja*. However, widespread the use of brute force may have history, it is no reason to doubt the validity of the counterpart namely that soul force is the valid basis of the political community the story of the universe had commenced with wars, and not a man would have been found alive today[64]... Therefore, the greatest and the most unimpeachable evidence of the success of this forces is to be found in the fact that, in spite of the wars of the world, it still lives on... Hundred of nations live in peace... History is really a record of every interruption of the even working of the force of love or of the soul". And it is Gandhi's belief that Indian nationalism has a golden opportunity to give something new to the world, namely the model of functioning multilingual and multireligious nation. Indian civilization has the potential to bring such a nation into being. But if India is to succeed in producing something new, it should unambiguously reject the political philosophy of both the Extremists and of the Terrorists. It should instead adopt something genuinely —Indian for example, the principles of *Satyagraha* and *Sarvodaya*. The Dhingras and the Savarkars he met in London in 1909 were misled by the nationalist philosophies of the West —of Spencer and Mill. There is delicious irony in Gandhi's use of G.K. Chesterton's analysis of the nationalist ideas propagated by such organs of the Indian terrorist groups as *The Indian Sociologist* published from London. Chesterton readily grants that "Indians have a right to be and to live as Indians". But he is wondering what the philosophies of Spencer and others like him have to do with it. "What is the good of the Indian national spirit if they (Indians) cannot protect themselves from Herbert Spencer?... Do the Indian youths want to pollute their ancient villages and poison their kindly homes by introducing Spencer's philosophy into them?"[65] "But Herbert

Spencer is not Indian, his philosophy is not Indian philosophy; all this clatter about the science of education and other things is not Indian. I often wish it were not English either. But this is our first difficulty, that the Indian nationalist is not national".[66] Gandhi thoroughly enjoyed Chesterton's wit. "Indians must reflect over these views of Mr Chesterton", he concluded. The misguided terrorist groups in his view were "endeavouring to destroy what the Indian people have carefully nurtured through thousands of years".[67]

Hind Swaraj does not suggest that state violence can be entirely eliminated. What it suggests is that whatever violence the state may have to exercise must be exercised in the interest of the people as a whole, not just in that of the national elite, and that too, strictly within the bounds of the principle of compassion (*daya*). The metaphor that Gandhi uses here is that of a child rushing into fire. Is he justified in using force to restrain the child? Gandhi's opinion is that he/she is justified in doing, so provided it is done from pure motives, namely the motive of securing the child's welfare. Not otherwise. [68]

What emerges from Gandhi's analysis of nationalism is the stress he laces on the need to develop the right relationship between the principle of *daya* and national interest. The error of modern nationalism has been to take for granted that national interest divorced from *daya* is the ultimate principle of national conduct. There is the insidious tendency in modern nationalism to urge the national elite to invoke national interest without any reference to *daya* and to use it (national interest) for its own narrow gains. Gandhi is certain that the interest of the national elite do not necessarily coincide with those of the *praja*. He sees the distinct possibility of the national elite,— the "doctors", the "lawyers", and the modern professional class taken as a whole- acting in their own interest and exploiting, deceiving, and oppressing the people at large in the name of the nation. The national elite is certain to act in this way so long as they remain under the influence of modern nationalism. On the other hand, they would be able to act in the interests of the *praja* only if their nationalism is founded on the principle of *daya*. But to be able to found in this way, they have to undergo a process of inner liberation (*Chhutkaro*). How the emerging Indian elite may achieve this inner liberation is the burden of the final argument of *Hind Swaraj*.

The argument is introduced with great artistic finesse. "what will you say to the nation?" The Reader asks. The Editor responds with a question of his own: "Who is the nation?" It is as if Gandhi wants to emphasize the point that the elite is the nation in a special sense. If up to now Gandhi had been talking of nation in a general sense, as *praja* now, in the concluding chapter, he is talking of it in a narrower sense. Thus through the mouth of the Reader he conveys this narrower meaning: "For our purpose it is the nation that you and I have been thinking of, that is those of us who are affected by (modern) European civilization, and who are eager to have Home Rue." *Hind Swaraj* is addressed to them in a special way.

What Gandhi says in this connection deserves close scrutiny as it outlines the national task lying before the national elite. It anticipates what later would come to be known as "constructive programme". First of all, the elite have to undergo a genuine moral transformation. The transformation in question has to do with their adoption of modern nationalism. They have to free themselves from it and adopt instead a different nationalism, one that is in tune with the spirit of Indian traditions as Gandhi interprets them. That is to say, they have to be "imbued with real love", and must have "experienced the force of the soul within themselves." Only those who are so imbued and who have undergone such an experience can "speak to the English" without fear or hatred. Only such transformed Indian nationals can really understand the threat posed by modern civilization and the promise held by Indian civilization. They would have to grasp the true meanings of *swaraj*. In the first place, *swaraj* is a mental condition (i) of inner liberation from the temptations of greed and power offered by modern civilization , (ii) freedom from hatred towards the national "enemy", the British and (iii) of active love for the Indian *praja*, a love that can conquer the temptations of greed and power. Secondly, *swaraj* is an external condition (i) of political independence from alien domination and (ii) of life-long dedication to the task of improving the material conditions of poverty and caste oppression of the Indian *praja*. In concrete, terms, *swaraj* requires one to take a stand on brute force and soul force. "If there be only one such Indian", the Editor affirms, "the English will have to listen to him".[69] Between such transformed Indians and the morally sensitive Britons there can ensure a genuine dialogue. There would then be no need to resort to the arts of violence and terror as means of achieving national liberation.

It should be clear by now that the task of attaining national liberation is not so much one of getting rid of the British as getting rid of the fascination for modern civilization which teaches the Indian elite to oppress the Indian *praja*. Once Indians liberate themselves from the evils of modern civilization, they would have become morally fit to deal both with the British and with the Indian people. Gandhi's real purpose is as much to find fault with the behaviour of "modern" Britons as it is to cure "modern" Indians from the disease of modern civilization. If Indians must find fault with the British, they themselves should not be guilty of the fault which they find in the British. Moral integrity requires at least that much.

It is to bring about the above mentioned mental transformation of the Indian elite that the last chapter of *Hind Swaraj* proposes its nineteen points. They are addressed to the national elite on whom the fate of the nation depends. Gandhi thinks that only such moral transformation can give them "the requisite strength" to make the national effort. There is nothing sacrosanct about number nineteen. Their specific injunctions will have to be understood in the context of the needs and conditions of the year 1909. But their spirit has to be adapted to the changing needs of the nation.

Of the 19 points, three are addressed to doctors, four to lawyers and the rest to what Gandhi calls the "wealthy".

That is to say, Gandhi's target is the modern professional classes of the nation, whether they be doctors or lawyers, scientists or administrators, politicians or business executives. Modern professions must become means of service to the nation first and means of making money or attaining status only second. That is to say, the pursuit of *artha* must be conducted within the framework of *dharma*. And *dharma* under modern conditions would require that the "machinery" that is adopted for national development be conducive to the health of body and soul and the well-being of the weak and the poor, not just the powerful and the wealthy. Gandhi's recommendation of the "handloom" and "hand-made goods" is symbolic of the requirement. Likewise, the mention of "repentance, expiation, and mourning", "goal", "banishment" and "deportation for life to the Andamans" makes sense only in the context of the particular strategy adopted by the terrorists in 1909. In short, the task before the national elite has to do with love, soul force, and the use of appropriate technology. In other words, self-reform, constitutional reforms, and economic reforms are all activities linked to the pursuit of *swaraj*. That is the national message of *Hind Swaraj*.

Conclusion

If the preceding analysis is correct, it follows that *Hind Swaraj* propounds the thesis that India is a nation, a *praja* and that everything that one wishes to do for the well being of India must proceed from this fact. But it does not propound the *modern* concept of nation in so far as the latter is based on the notions of brute force, the priority of national interests, and a principle of exclusiveness based either on religion, or language, or race.

India is a *swadesh* for Indians and for foreigners who wish to adopt India as their adopted *swadesh*. For Gandhi, the idea of *swadesh* is consistent with the idea of an open society, shaped as it is by the legacy of Indian civilization, with its stress on soul force, and its capacity to make *samas* out of diverse ethnic, linguistic and religious elements.

It follows that Gandhi's concept of the nation imposed certain obligations on the majority community as well as on minority communities. On the majority community- whether the majority is based on religion or language or race- it imposes the norms of openness, accommodation and tolerance. On the minorities- whether the minority status is based on religion or language or race- it imposes the norm of adaptation to the ethos of Indian civilization.

The Gandhian concept of national *samas* had, and still has, I think a special reference to Indian Muslims. Accepting the Gandhian concept of *praja* would mean making a creative adaptation of Islam to the ethos of Indian civilization. Above, all it would mean the legitimization of the principle that Muslims could become the members of the Indian *praja* legally as well as emotionally. For, in the final analysis, the question that faced and still faces Indian Muslims is whether a good Muslim can be an Indian citizen, legally as well as emotionally, but especially emotionally of a non-Muslim country. Would the Islamic principle of legitimacy legitimize Gandhi's concept of praja? The fact that the course of Indian nationalism did not follow the path marked out by Gandhi does not prove the Gandhi's concept was invalid nor that this analysis of Indian civilization was flawed. Partition meant that India was not ready to meet the challenge posed by Gandhi to both the majority and the minority communities.

Perhaps, the most important corollary to the Gandhian theorem is that the fate of India as *praja* depends on the moral character of the Indian professional classes- the character of its "lawyers", "doctors", and the "wealthy", —to use the language of *Hind Swaraj*. Gandhi realized with great acuity that India's problems lay not so much with its colonial experience as with her professional classes who have been transfixed by greed, reinforced by caste. He realized that unless these professional classes could be converted to the ideal of nationalism that *Hind Swaraj* proposes, India would not have a bright future. Gandhi's thought here is not dissimilar to that of Plato. There is a link between the health of the soul and the health of the city, and the maintenance of the health of the city depends in practical terms on the moral character of the "guardian class". It is the "guardians" who had to undergo a moral transformation first. Gandhi was equally conscious of the fact that the "guardians" could hijack nationalism and use it for satisfying their own greed and power. Briefly, Gandhi's concept of *swaraj* links the nation (*praja*), the self, the professional classes, soul force and public service. And the final test of India's nationalism is whether the Indian professional classes will actually dedicate their lives to the attainment of *swaraj* in the dual sense- as personal self -improvement and as the material improvement of the least member of the nation.

Notes

1. *The Collected Works of Mahatma Gandhi* (hereafter referred to as CWMG) New Delhi: The Publication Division, Ministry of Information and Broadcasting, Govt. of India, 1958-1984), vol.9, pp. 508-09.
2. *Ibid*, p.509.
3. *Ibid*, vol.10, p.7.
4. *Ibid*, p.190.
5. Sri Aurobindo, *Bande Mataram: Early Political Works* I, (Pondicheery: Centenary Edition, 1972), pp.571,585.
6. *Hind Swaraj*, (hereafter referred to as HS) C.X, pp.47-8. The references to HS throughout this article is to the 1989 reprint of second edition published by Navajivan Publishing House, Ahmedabad.
7. Perhaps the following situation might serve as an example of the sort of orient list British scholarship of the day: "This is the first and most essential thing to learn about India- that there is not and never was an Indian or even any country of India, possessing, according to European ideas, any sort of unity, physical, political, social, or religious... that men of the Punjab, Bengal, the North Western Provinces, and Madras should ever feel they belong to one great nation is impossible". John Strachey, writing in 1888; cited by Ainslie Embree, *India's Search for National Identity*. (Revised Edition), Delhi: Chankya Publications, 1988),p.1.

8. *HS*, Ch. ix, p.42.
9. For the text of Renan, see Hans Kohn, *Nationalism: Its Meaning and History* (Princeton, N J:Van Nostrand,1955), p.136.
10. *HS*, Ch. X, p.45.
11. *Ibid*, p.48.
12. See Surinder Mohan Bharadwaj, *Hindu Places of Pilgrimage in India: A Study of Cultural Geography* (Berkeley and Los Angeles: University of California Press, 1973), p.217.
13. Letter of 14 October 1909, *CWMG*, Vol.9, p.481.
14. *Harijan*, 14 October 1939, p.303.
15. *Ibid*.
16. *Ibid*.
17. *HS*, Ch. X, p.44
18. *Ibid*, Ch. IX, p.43.
19. *HS*, Ch. X, p.45.
20. *Ibid*, Ch. X ,p.45.
21. *Ibid*, p.48.
22. *Ibid*, p.45. The underlined portion is in the Gujarati version, but not in the English version of *Hind Swaraj*.
23. *Ibid*, p.46.
24. *Ibid*.
25. *Ibid*, p.46.
26. *Ibid*, p.45.
27. *Ibid*, pp.445-46.
28. *Ibid.*, p.46.
29. *Ibid*, p .46; emphasis mine.
30. *Ibid*, p.47.
31. *Ibid*, p.49.
32. *Ibid* ,p.48.
33. *Ibid*, p.48.
34. *CWMG*, Vol.9, p.509.
35. *HS*,Ch.19, p.79.
36. *Ibid*, p.80.
37. *Ibid*, p.81.
38. *Ibid*, p.79.
39. *Ibid*, pp.80-81.
40. *Ibid*, p.81.

Gandhi's Idea of Nation in Hind Swaraj | 285

41. *Ibid*, p.80.
42. *Ibid*, p.81.
43. *Ibid*, p.81.
44. *Ibid*, p.81.
45. *Ibid*, p.81.
46. *HS*, Ch.1, p.18.
47. *Ibid*, p.21.
48. *Ibid*, p.22.
49. *Ibid*, pp., 19-20.
50. *Ibid*, p.19.
51. *Ibid*, p.19.
52. *Ibid*, p.20.
53. *Ibid*, p.21.
54. *Ibid*, p.18.
55. *HS*, Ch.20, p.86.
56. *Ibid*, p.87.
57. *Ibid*, p.86.
58. *HS*, Ch.4, p.27.
59. *Ibid*, Ch.15, p.61.
60. *Ibid*, Ch.16, p.68.
61. *Ibid*, Ch.15, p.61.
62. *HS*, Ch.16, p.62. Dhingra, a Punjabi student studying in London, committed a notable assassination, that of Sir William H. Curzon-Wyllie, the Aide-de-camp to the secretary of State for India, on 1 July 1909, a few days before Gandhi's arrival in London from South Africa.
63. *HS*, Ch.17, p.69.
64. *Ibid*, pp.69-70.
65. *CWMG*, Vol.9, p.425.
66. *Ibid*, p.427.
67. *Ibid*, p.427.
68. *HS*, Ch.16, p.68.
69. *Ibid*. p.89.

ಬಿ ಲ

17

GANDHI'S ECONOMIC PHILOSOPHY

Joseph Prabhu

Gandhi's economic thought has long been an academic orphan. While his moral, political, philosophical ideas have received considerable attention, his economic ideas have been largely ignored. Only a handful of his scores of commentators take interest in them, and those who do, tend to be embarrassed by them, and dismiss them as confused, ill thought out, or archaic.

[***Bhikhu Parekh***] [1]

I

This essay has two main aims: 1. to rescue Gandhian economic philosophy from the oblivion to which it is largely consigned, and 2. by so doing, to provide a challenge to the contemporary discipline of economics.

"Gandhian economics" –is there such a thing asks the modern professional economist? True, Gandhi made a lot of pronouncements on production, distribution, consumption, and other economic matters, but they are no more to be regarded as constituting "economics" than my remarks on my digestion are to be regarded as constituting "biology." His economic ideas do not fit easily within the received opinions about economics. They certainly do not have the same status as Keynesian or Marxian economics, i.e., of a strict science. Furthermore, one may concede that Gandhi regarded himself more a man of action than an intellectual in the conventional sense. And to the extent to which he can be regarded as an original thinker, his contribution lies more in the moral and political fields; his economic thought consists of the application to the economic realm of his moral and spiritual ideas. But these concessions do not necessarily work to the disadvantage of Gandhi. On the contrary, to the extent to which he has a clear moral vision, something which few contemporary economists possess, and precisely because his economic pronouncements emerge from a certain moral perspective, they ought, I contend, to be taken seriously.

What is at stake here is a methodological point, namely, what in our day should count as "economics." There is a purely theoretical part of the subject that is developed at such a high level of abstraction that it renders itself relatively free of institutional assumptions, e.g., Walras's general equilibrium theory. But large areas of economics are not like this and have their *raison d'etre* solely in their applicability to social reality. It is with economics in this sense that I am concerned. Karl Polanyi has convincingly shown how exceptional the modern industrial world is in human history with regard to the separation of the economic from other aspects of life and its emphasis on the unique predominance of the market and its ethos from the late eighteenth century to the present. The history of economics reveals that until then, even when the scope of economic concerns was limited to material well-being, the latter was itself seen as part of a wider context of happiness or human flourishing [2]. In its self-understanding, economics, together with politics and ethics, was until the early part of the twentieth century considered one of the moral sciences, not just in the sense of having moral dimensions or implications, but more importantly as issuing from moral premises and being assessed in terms of moral criteria like value or utility.

Indeed, the very word "economics" comes from two Greek words, *oikos* (household) and *nomos* (law or rule). Aristotle relates the law and running of the household to a hierarchy of goods, those sought for their own sake, and those sought as means to other goods. The "master science" for Aristotle is politics, "for it is the one which uses the other sciences concerned with action and moreover legislates what must be done and what avoided." It follows for Aristotle that the good which politics seeks is the highest social good, "for while it is satisfactory to acquire and preserve the good, even for an individual, it is finer and more divine to acquire and preserve it for a people and for cities." The science of economics having the production and distribution of wealth as its immediate end is linked up with other sciences involving more basic goods. "The money-maker's life is in a way forced on him [not chosen for itself]: and clearly wealth is not the good we are seeking, since it is [merely] useful for some other end" [3]. Economics for Aristotle relates closely to the study of ethics and politics, and is concerned with the good which is both instrumental and, axiologically, at the lower end of the hierarchy of goods culminating in what he considers the highest good.

To the extent to which economics in recent times has wished to shore up its scientific status, it has done so by attempting to disavow its moral and political elements and by modeling itself on the natural sciences with an increased emphasis on mathematical and quantitative methods. At the same time, the scope of economics is reduced to those aspects of behavior that are quantifiable. Confining myself for the moment to Western societies, it is easy to see how the stress on quantification has gone along with the acceptance of the marketplace:

> In the marketplace, for practical reasons, innumerable qualitative distinctions which are of vital importance to man and society are suppressed.... Thus the reign of quantity celebrates its greatest triumphs in 'The Market.' Everything is equated with everything else. To equate things means to give them a price and thus to make them exchangeable. To the extent that economic thinking is based on the market, it takes the sacredness out of life, because there can be nothing sacred in something that has a price. Not surprisingly, therefore, if economic thinking pervades the whole of society, even simple non-economic values like beauty, health or cleanliness can survive only if they prove to be 'economic.' [4]

Gandhian economics shares the same insight. If the criterion of what counts as economics is a purely quantitative one, then Gandhian economics cannot gain admission to the fold. Alternatively, however, it is possible that Gandhian economics, like that of Aristotle, could challenge the norms of such an economics and put in their place an alternative standard: the maximization not of wealth but of human well-being. And, indeed, I believe that one of its most important potential contributions is precisely such a challenge, not just to the self-understanding of modern economics but also to the overall context in which it is at home. One of my main contentions is that economics today is not just an academic science, but an ideology whose theoretical mode is an increasingly instrumental conception of reason and whose practical mode is technocracy. What I mean by an instrumental conception is a means-ends model of rationality, where ends in the final analysis are considered beyond the pale of reason, and where rational debate is therefore confined to discussion about means to fulfill what turn out to be ultimately arbitrary ends. It is only a positivistic lack of self-reflection that makes modern economists pursue the goal of making their science as precise as physics—the syndrome known as "physics envy"—thereby overlooking the difference between human behavior and that of mindless atoms. The irony, however, is that precisely to the extent that this difference is eliminated, a view has been taken about the metaphysical status of human beings. This view is not explained or supported by the propositions of the science itself, but is brought to the science from the outside. In a word, modern economics stands convicted of the very charge it most dreads: that of being methodologically value-laden.

If modern economics is inevitably value-laden, the question then arises what values are chiefly espoused. The answer is simple: money and utility measured in quantitative terms. It is money that is made the highest of values. Marx, who saw clearly the subordination of human relationships to the relation between human beings and things made possible by the money economy, quoted Shakespeare in *Timon of Athens*:

> Gold? Yellow, glittering precious Gold? No gods,
> I am no idle voterist. Roots, you clear heavens!
> Thus much of this will make black white, foul fair,
> Wrong right, base noble, old young, coward valiant. [5]

Compare this with Lord Keynes, perhaps the most famous economist of our times. Writing in 1930 during the Great Depression, he was led to speculate on the economic future of the world and thought that the day might come when everybody would be rich and we would once more value ends above means and prefer the good to the useful. But beware . . . the time for all this is not yet. For at least another 100 years, we must pretend to ourselves that fair is foul and foul is fair: for foul is useful and fair is not. Avarice and usury and precaution must be our gods for a little longer still. For only they can lead us out of the tunnel of economic necessity into daylight. [6].

Whether such dubious means and values as Keynes here advocates has led us into "daylight" is debatable, especially at a time [this essay is written in February 2009] when avarice does not seem to have led to precaution and when economists say we are headed for the greatest global recession since the Great Depression.

I have started with these somber comments not to be alarmist but to present the background against which I shall view Gandhian economics. I wish to consider some of the theoretical and practical issues raised by his economic thinking. In doing so I shall concentrate more on the spirit of Gandhian economics, its philosophy of economics as it were, rather than on its technical details and see what challenge it provides to our contemporary situation. I trust I have made it clear that philosophical assumptions about human beings and their natural and social environment shape the self-understanding of economics and its aims, methods, and prescriptions.

II

Let me now present a broad overview of Gandhi's economic philosophy:

1) First of all it is clear that Gandhi is not a system builder nor a thinker who thinks through the relationships of economic variables. If economics consists of metaphysics, morals both positive and negative, and science, Gandhi concentrates on the metaphysics and the positive morals, but seems to want to ignore the negative morals and the scientific aspect of the subject. Economics has been called the science of Mammon. If this definition strikes us as unduly negative in tone, insofar as it appears to sanction self-interest, calculation, and acquisitiveness, the proper response would seem to be to accept these aspects of human character and provide constructive channels for them rather than to underestimate or, even worse, ignore or simply wish them away. Nevertheless, insofar as Gandhi does emphasize the moral and metaphysical aspects of the subject by reintegrating economic purposes within the wider context of human well-being, his thought can be used to provide a corrective to a discipline that under the illusion that it is a value-free science actually, in its present form, caters to human greed and envy.

2) That contribution, however important and urgent in our time as it is, is still only one aspect of a comprehensive reshaping of economics. Good moral intentions have still to be combined with proper scientific methods for progressive social change. Moral exhortation is no substitute for theoretical analysis. Rather, as Kenneth Boulding, a morally

sensitive economist and an authority on conflict theory, remarked in an article entitled "Why Did Gandhi Fail?"*

> The modern world is so complex that the truth about it cannot be perceived by common sense or by mystical insight, important as these things are. We must have more delicate and quantitative sampling and processing of information by the methods of the social sciences if we are really to test the truth of our images of social and political systems. [7]

3) Consonant with my view that economics is situated within an institutional context, it is no disparagement of Gandhi's economics to say that its chief practical contribution is to Indian and to the "developing" countries, and perhaps secondarily to "developed" countries. Its relevance as economics to the industrialized world is more as a moral corrective and pointer, a prophetic reminder that values of simplicity, directness, harmony, and wholeness are ones that it ignores as its peril in its relentless pursuit of material wealth and comfort. There is something clearly irrational and inadequate about an existence that makes money the supreme value and ignores the overall quality of life, including the anxiety, alienation and stress required to sustain such an existence. To this end some of the most important ideas of Gandhi are those of decentralization, regional development, the creation of a technology that is adapted to the needs and resources of a particular area and to the creative urges of people, and finally economic growth that allows for harmony with nature and between human beings, even if such growth is slower and more gradual. Ecological awareness, a matter of great concern to the world in the wake of a development that has systematically plundered its natural base and is, in fact, consuming the very basis on which it is built, is something that Gandhi brought to the forefront of his thinking as early as in *Hind Swaraj*, written in 1909.

4) Gandhi was also remarkably perceptive in seeing how a technological mode of existence is essentially an alienated mode of existence insofar as it brings about great disruptions in the social relations of human beings with one another and the relations of human beings vis-à-vis

nature. As far as social relations are concerned, he discerned that technological society not only fails to tap the moral resources of people but in fact tends to destroy them to the extent that human beings are reduced to the status of things. He was also alive to some of the nuances of social power and to the inevitable tendency of a technological system to foster a managerial society characterized by bureaucracies and elites. To counteract the elitism of technocrats and so-called experts, Gandhi was strongly in support of mass movements and the mobilization of the power of the poor.

Gandhi's views on technology did, however, change over his lifetime. In *Hind Swaraj*, Gandhi comes out with a long list of evils spawned by the modern industrial system familiar to readers of Ruskin, Tolstoy, and Thoreau, by all of whom he was deeply influenced. He ties together his critique of the economic system with that of its technological underpinning, the larger phenomenon of industrialism, a self-propelling process of creating larger and larger industries to satisfy the insatiable demand for cheap consumer goods and profits. Since it has a built-in momentum of its own, it renders people largely powerless and passive and hence represents a modern and invidious form of slavery. It mistakes material comfort for progress, restless and constant movement made possible by modern forms of transport for dynamism and vitality, locomotion for purposeful movement, speed for efficiency, and consumerism for an improved quality of life. One passage from *Hind Swaraj* will be sufficient to indicate his fervid, unnuanced and extremist tone: "Machinery has begun to desolate Europe. Ruination is now knocking at the English gates. Machinery is the chief symbol of modern civilization; it represents a great sin" [8]. Later on, he moderated his position somewhat to allow for what we would today call "appropriate technology." Although it might be objected that the notion of "appropriate technology" is question-begging, Gandhi felt that there was a significant difference between machines that enhanced a worker's skill and machines that replaced and ultimately enslave human labor. This development of large-scale technology for Gandhi was even worse in a country like India with millions of unemployed people.

> *Machinery has its place . . . it has come to stay. But it must not be allowed to displace the necessary human labor . . . I would welcome every improvement in the cottage machine . . . what I object to is the craze for machinery. Men go on "saving labour" till thousands are without work and thrown on the streets to die of starvation. I want to save time and labour, not for a fraction of mankind, but for all. I want the concentration of wealth not in the hands of a few, but in the hands of all. Today machinery helps us to ride on the back of millions. The impetus behind it is not the philanthropy to save labour, but greed. It is against this constitution of things that I am fighting with all my might. [9]*

Gandhi's best known scheme to employ and feed the unemployed millions was through homespun cloth (*khadi*) produced by the spinning wheel, which Gandhi wanted to make the foundation of village, and by extension, national economic life. He described it as a symbol of self-help, freedom from domination, and non-violent economic self-sufficiency. He was quite aware that from one set of criteria commonly adopted in economic calculation, *khadi* was both "inefficient," insofar as power-driven spindles could do the work more quickly, and more costly in terms of the amount of labor that had to be employed relative to labor-and-time-saving machines. But in talking of his "socialism of the spinning wheel," Gandhi responded to these criticisms thus: "*Khadi* serves the masses, mill cloth is intended to serve the classes. *Khadi* serves labour, mill cloth exploits it." Its main purpose, he said, was to harness every single idle minute of our millions for common productive work [10]. Appropriate technology and economics required that one see what resources were in abundance and what in relative scarcity, and within those parameters that one maximize the social good. While from a narrowly economic point of view textile mills might prove cheaper, from a broader social perspective Gandhi believed that the social costs of unemployment in terms of dehumanization and the loss of self-respect should figure more prominently.

5) Within this framework, Gandhi's general philosophy of work becomes clearer:

   a) Everyone has a right to work, and society has the obligation to provide work, even if it means a reduction in Gross National Product (GNP) or some other quantitative measure of economic performance. Gandhi was more concerned with "production by the masses than mass production," more interested in improving the life of ordinary people than in enriching a select few.

   b) All work enjoys equal dignity, be it a lawyer's or a barber's; each person has the duty to contribute to the commonweal according to his or her capacities.

   c) The good of the individual is contained in the good of all, given his organic view of the self.

   d) Manual labor should be an essential component of each person's work. The purported superiority of intellectual to physical work is a false one. Each individual should strive for self-sufficiency and self-reliance by taking care of his manual chores. For this reason he recommended that the Congress Party, which was leading India's national struggle against the British, should make the wearing of *khadi* a condition of membership and should also advocate the practice of spinning for all as a symbol of political self-determination and of spiritual protest against the depredations of industrial civilization.

   e) There is a special grace to the work of the peasant and handicraftsman, both because they provide essential food and clothing and also because they stay close to the land and to the rhythms of nature.

All these principles, Gandhi adopted from his reading of Tolstoy, Ruskin, and Thoreau, but he added to them another one which he took from the *Bhagavad Gita*, the single most important scripture for him, namely the principle of *naiskarmyakarma* or detachment in, but not from, work: "To action alone hast thou a right, but not to the fruits thereof"

[11]. No work is good unless it is purged of attachment for extrinsic gain or advantage. By contrast, that action is right that is done for its own sake and not as a means to some further end.

The Indian philosopher and economist, J.C. Kumarappa, in his important book, *The Economy of Permanence*, sums up the Gandhian philosophy of work:

> *If the nature of the work is properly appreciated and applied, it will stand in the same relation to the higher faculties as food is to the physical body.*
>
> *It nourishes and enlivens the higher man and urges him to produce the best he is capable of. It directs his free will along the proper course and disciplines the animal in him into progressive channels. It furnishes an excellent background for man to display his scale of values and develop his personality. [12]*

Gandhi's attitude toward work is therefore quite opposed to modern economic ideology. From the standpoint of the individual employer, work figures as an item of cost in the wage bill and should therefore be reduced to a minimum, if not altogether eliminated by automation. From the standpoint of a professional economist looking at employment in macro-economic terms, the chief criteria are inflation on the one hand, and the GNP on the other, the volume of goods produced in a given span of time. Gandhi's economics, to adopt Schumacher's famous phrase, was an "economics as if people mattered." Unemployment does not just deprive a person of an income or reduce her contribution to GNP; it does something far more serious from Gandhi's perspective; it dehumanizes and degrades a person by depriving her of the opportunity to discipline herself in creative and self-affirming work.

6) In short, Gandhi's economic and industrial policy strongly rejected the imitation of Western models so beloved not only by so-called experts from the West, but also by Indian educated elites, models stressing development from "on top:" frantic urbanization, heavily capital-intensive industrialization, mass productions, centralized development planning or unregulated market capitalism, and finally,

sophisticated technology. By contrast, Gandhi's scheme was one of a grass-roots development strategy "from below" village economic self-sufficiency, stabilization, and enhancement of a traditional peasant way of life by way of labor-intensive manufacture and handicrafts, decentralized decision-making, even if this drastically reduced the pace of urban and industrial growth.

As far as India is concerned, the single most valuable idea of Gandhi was village reconstruction and his stress on a self-sufficient, relatively non-industrialized, "natural" rural life characterized by compulsory bread labor for all, handicrafts and simple market and distribution structures. Gandhi saw this as the best answer to the steep unemployment and the illiteracy and the powerlessness of the village poor, exploited both from within by rural landlords and from without by urban interests plundering their natural resources. Given the existence of 700,000 backward villages, the village was for him the obvious place to start. Gandhi's Constructive Program, his most fully worked out social blueprint presented in 1941 in his booklet entitled *Constructive Program: Its Meaning and Place*, envisages a society where mutual voluntary aid between members of the village community would gradually replace the social control exercised by the state to harmonize conflicting interests. Decentralization and weakening the power of a centralized state are possible for Gandhi only on the basis of village self-reliance.

7) While his insights and his objectives are commendable, it is at least questionable whether Gandhi fully understood the operational dynamics of power and whether his strategy of moral exhortation was sufficient to counteract it. Indian society was and remains one of the most elitist societies in the world with the disparities between the few rich and the many poor, if anything, steadily increasing and where the rich have exploited to their advantage the very schemes that Gandhi thought would neutralize their power.

It was not that Gandhi wanted to revert to what Marx once called "the idiocy of the village." He knew very well that the Indian village of the past was characterized by severe social inequalities; in fact, it was there that untouchability originated and it was from there that it spread. In the situation of his day, international and national, Gandhi was convinced that the only viable development was development "from below." This required freeing oneself from the hegemony of the world market controlled by the industrialized powers, who, motivated solely by considerations of profit would never grant fair prices to the products of under-developed countries [13]. On the contrary, the logic of the international market imposed the classic economic condition on colonies: that of supplying cheap raw materials to the rich nations and of being a dumping ground for foreign goods. Escaping the imprisonment of the international market meant being independent and relying on local resources which had to be distributed equitably or else the same pattern of inequality would be reproduced on the local level. Given the under-developed nature of the village economy, this perforce implied an equal sharing of poverty, but it is important to see this not just as an exercise in asceticism as it is usually presented, but as shrewd economic realism. There was no hope whatsoever for the poor if they depended on the rich; their only hope was to shake off such dependence and to regain control over their lives and destiny. Once that was achieved they could think of entering into voluntary cooperation to build larger economic structures, but such cooperation presupposed the economic freedom of the constituent units.

8) Gandhi's notion of *swaraj* (self-government, both political and personal) was, therefore, in the first place a protest against imperialism. True, the nineteenth century nationalists, and the Bengal militants in particular, had already introduced the idea of *swadeshi* or patriotism into the political currency of the day, but Gandhi understood more deeply the pathology of imperialism—that colonialism is

possible only if victims accept and allow their colonization. And so instead of directing his fire solely at the victimizers, as the nationalists had done, he emphasized the need for the victims to shake off their servile attitude and to find their own voice and to fashion the institutions where they could express it. The self-rule that Gandhi was propounding therefore embraced both negative and positive freedom, both freedom from external exploitation and freedom for voluntary cooperation. Gandhi took this radical idea to the limit and insisted that each individual achieve self-sufficiency.

The premises behind village *swaraj* were an idea of civilization that emphasized not the multiplication of wants, but their voluntary restriction, and in fact the radical ideal of non-possession. Given this assumption of austere consumption, Gandhi could consistently call for small-scale production, simple technology and village self-sufficiency. Once again there is valuable insight that consumption ought not be made an end in itself as it is in modern materialistic economics, but as a means to an end namely the maximization of human well-being. The emphasis then shifts to simplicity and the overall quality of life rather than just to material comfort and prosperity.

At the same time there is something unrealistic about proposing non-possession and severe austerity as a universal goal, just as there is something romantic about the idealization of the village. It is not possessions themselves that are bad, surely, but the craving for and the attachment to them, and to propose the ideal of non-possession is to deprive human beings of one of the most powerful incentives for effort and advancement. After all, it is not enjoyment of pleasurable things that is reprehensible but the craving for them. Again, while the revitalized village communities based on work and moral autonomy could well be the energizing principle for a grass roots democracy, Gandhi underestimated the despotic content of actual village life, the tyranny often exercised by the community over the individual in the form of casteism, class-based oppression, superstition and rigid custom. For all his charisma and influence, Gandhi was able to make little impact on these reactionary forces. That too is not surprising. Just as moral exhortation is no substitute for theoretical analysis, it is also no substitute for political struggles that seek to shift the alignment of organized class and caste power and the dynamics of property distribution dependent on it.

III

This exposition of Gandhi's economic philosophy has gone some way, I hope, to fulfilling the two objectives set out at the beginning of this essay: first, rescuing it from the neglect it has suffered and second, arguing that as a moral vision it has much to offer both to the theoretical science of economics and to modern economic life.

Regarding the first goal, I trust I have made it clear that his economic ideas are a crucial part of his broader moral and political ideas, just as they were for Aristotle. They draw out the practical implications of these ideals and give them substance. It is clear, therefore, that we cannot fully understand the nature and scope of his moral vision without taking his economic ideas into account. One may, as I do, disagree with many of his concrete economic proposals without repudiating some of the deeper philosophical ideas underlying them, because the former are not rigidly necessitated by the latter. It is possible and perhaps more fruitful to distinguish the vision underlying Gandhian economics from his specific policies because that vision allows for embodiments different from his own.

As far as the critique of modern economics is concerned, I have argued that economic behavior is shaped by an agent's moral and spiritual beliefs, cultural conditioning and historical context, and to abstract from them as modern economics often does in the interests of a "value-free" science is seriously mistaken. Gandhi's philosophical anthropology sees human beings as primarily moral and spiritual agents. Given this picture, his economic philosophy critiques modern economics at three interrelated points.

First, it has an exclusively materialistic character in that it equates material satisfaction with human welfare. Seeing human beings primarily as consumers, the modern economic system operates through encouraging an endless multiplication of wants, well in excess of need. In doing so, it encourages greed and envy, which in turn breed competitiveness, dishonesty and violence. Gandhi's economic prescriptions go in the opposite direction. "There is enough in the world for everyone's need, but not for everyone's greed." With his *dharmic* notion of mutual responsibility, Gandhi emphasizes not the multiplication of wants but their voluntary restriction, frugality in lifestyle and economy in our use of resources. Granted that some material comfort is a condition of spiritual welfare, it nonetheless ought to be seen as a means to an end and not an end in itself.

> *Economics that hurts the moral well-being of an individual or nation is immoral and, therefore, sinful... True economics never militates against the highest ethical standard; just all true ethics to be worth its name must at the same time be also good economics. [14]*

Second, self-interest is both the cause and the consequence of the economic individualism of market capitalism. Indeed, the notions of preference, choice and maximization which are the core concepts of modern microeconomics all operate on the unquestioned assumption that what should be maximized is the set of preferences of the individual economic actor. If materialism deals with the anthropological side of the economic system, self-interest concerns its ethical aspect, although it is obvious that the two are closely related. Gandhi's notion of *dharma* and soul-force again point in a radically different direction toward mutual care and concern. It is axiomatic for Gandhi that we are out brother's (and sister's) keeper. If that is so, then what has to be maximized is not individual satisfaction, but the common good and it is via the common good that individuals ought to seek their well-being. Instead of the atomistic idea of the self that exists prior to and independently of social relations, Gandhi as a communitarian holds an organic conception of the self, where parts and the whole are essentially connected.

Third, as far as the social organization of production is concerned, Gandhi is critical of both unregulated market capitalism and bureaucratic socialism. The first he feels inevitably leads to a social Darwinism in the economic sphere with cutthroat competition and a Hobbesian war of all against all. The "fittest" that survive do not necessarily go in for socially useful production or promote the social good. Furthermore, such laissez-faire capitalism ineluctably results in gross inequalities of income, wealth and power, so that any kind of democratic accountability is circumvented and abuses of various sorts flourish unchecked. As far as bureaucratic socialism is concerned, in Gandhi's judgment, that leads to a different kind of harm, with the concentration of power now in the hands of state bureaucrats. In addition, centralized planning is notoriously insensitive to the needs and condition of the people, especially those residing in villages. Gandhi's own ideas here go in the direction of decentralization, with each village trying as far as possible to achieve self-sufficiency and then organizing regional markets and cooperatives. These ideas have been in the vanguard of contemporary movements in localized and regional production from "local exchange and trading systems" (LETS) to "community supported agriculture" (CSA).

John Ruskin in *Unto This Last*, a book that deeply influenced Gandhi [to the extent that he paraphrased the whole book and published it first in 1908 in a nine-part series in *Indian Opinion* (Durban) and then as a book with the title of *Sarvodaya*], proclaimed famously, "There is no wealth but life." By that he meant that the real wealth of a nation lies not so much in its material resources or its commodities as in it human capital, the capacities and self-cultivation of its people. Some eighty years later, Amartya Sen would develop that idea, though admittedly from a different starting point, to argue that the wealth of a country should not be measured by quantitative measures like Gross Domestic Product (GDP), or Gross National Product (GNP), but by the more qualitative measures of "capabilities" and "freedoms" [15]. A good deal of Sen's work, while being quite "materialist," has tried to show the mutual links between ethics and economics, and has attempted to rehabilitate economics as a moral science. It is beyond the scope of this essay to go into the details of Sen's extensive work, but it is not an accident that Sen got a large part of his economic training in the 1950s in the Cambridge (England) of Joan Robinson and Maurice Dobb, two of the stalwarts of the Cambridge School of political economy [16]. And Sen, like Gandhi, has also demonstrated in his work on famines, democratic freedom and on development generally, that the visioning of economics has a great impact on practical life [17]. In spite of the Nobel Prize in economics that Sen won in 1998, it would be too much to say that he has had much of an influence on mainstream economics, but at least a start has been made [18].

Notes

1. Bhikhu Parekh, "Foreword" to B.N. Ghosh, *Gandhian Political Economy: Principles, Practice and Policy,* Ashgate, Aldershot, England, 2007.
2. Karl Polanyi, *The Great Tranformation,* 2nd Ed., Beacon Press, Boston, 2001.
3. Aristotle, *Nichomachean Ethics,* Trans. by Terence Irwin, Hackett Publishing Company, Indianpolis, 1985, Sections 1.2-1.43.
4. E.F. Schumacher, *Small is Beautiful,* Harper and Row, New York, 1973, p.43.
5. William Shakespeare, *Timon of Athens,* Act IV, Scene 3.
6. J.M. Keynes, *Treatise on Money,* Routledge and Kegan Paul, London, 1930, quoted in Schumacher op. cit, p 24.
7. K. Boulding, "Why Did Gandhi Fail?" in *Gandhi Marg,* Delhi, Oct. 1964, p. 83.

8. Anthony Parel, *Gandhi: Hind Swaraj and Other Writings*, Cambridge University Press, Cambridge, 1997, p. 107.
9. B.N. Ganguli, *Gandhi's Social Philosophy: Perspectives and Relevance*, John Wiley and Sons, New York, 1973, p. 314. Chapter XV, "Challenges of an Industrial Civilization" contains a detailed account of the evolution of Gandhi's views on industrialization and technology.
10. Quoted in Glyn Richards, *The Philosophy of Gandhi*, Barnes and Noble, New Jersey, 1982, p. 119.
11. *Bhagavad Gita*, iii, 4; iv, 20; xviii, 49.
12. J.C. Kumarappa, *The Economy of Permanence*, Sarva-Seve Sangh Publications, Rajghat, Kashi, 4th Ed., 1958, p. 32.
13. For the inequities of the global trading system, see David Korten, "The Failures of Bretton Woods in Jerry Mander and Ed Goldsmith (Eds.) *The Case Against the Global Economy*, Sierra Club Books, San Francisco, 1996. See also Susan George, *A Fate Worse than Debt*, Penguin, London, 1986.
14. Gandhi, *Selected Works*, Ed. by S. Narayan, Volume 6, Navjivan Press, Ahmedabad, 1968, p. 321-322.
15. Amartya Sen, *On Ethics and Economics*, Basil Blackwell Ltd., Oxford, 1987, and *Development as Freedom*, Alfred A. Knopf, New York, 1999.
16. See, as representative works, Joan Robinson, *Econoomic Philosophy*, Watts, London, 1962, and Maurice Dobb, *Political Economy and Capitalism: Some Essays in Economic Tradition*, Allen and Unwin, London, 1937.
17. Among Sen's many books, see *Poverty and Famines: An Essay on Entitlement and Deprivation*, Clarendon Press, Oxford, 1981; *Rationality and Freedom*, Belknap Press, Cambridge, MA, 2004; and *Choice, Welfare, and Measurement*, Harvard University Press, Cambridge, MA, 1997.
18. This essay represents a substantial reworking of two previous articles of mine: "Gandhi's Economics of Peace" in *Peace Review*, Spring 1995, Vol. 7, No. 1, and "Gandhi's Philosophy of Work and Its Contemporary Relevance" in *Concepts and Transformation*, Sweden, Winter 1997, Vol. 2, No. 1.

৪০ ০৪

18

A Tribute to Dr. George Grant

John G. Arapura

Under the caption "tribute" I here make some remarks about my honoured and dear friend of cherished memory, Dr. George P. Grant who passed away in 1988, many years ago that is, though I feel as though he just left my house after one of our frequent, personal meetings for talks and discussions. We used to meet in our department (not our favourite place for thinking and talking) or in either of our homes, but he particularly preferred my house because of its exceptional quietness, in contrast to his busy household, destracted by many phone calls and visitors for the reason that he was a much sought after man and many wanted to talk to him, politicians, scholars, journalists and so on. Between him and myself we had a deep philosophical rapport. The things he brought for discussion were not matters merely of academic interest but matters of deep concern about the world, which had consequences, spiritual moral and material the approach whereto is necessarily philosophical. He had a peculiar, gift for binding the eternal and the present, which led him to care for things at hand in today's society, investing them with importance, brought down from the transcendent realm of reality which was his perennial focus to the present affairs of the world, both immediate and distant, near and remote, cared for with an earnestness truly Socratic.

My own knowledge of Dr. Grant is something that developed over the years but with an intellectual friendship that started from our first meetings. Before I joined his department at McMaster University, of which he was then head, I had heard of him mainly because of a reputation he had based on a very provocative book then recently published and much talked about by the name, *Lament for a Nation*. It was not by any means of jeremiad but as I understood it a profound historical analysis of things in his beloved Canada, combined with a reel challenge to thought. But like everything he wrote or spoke about, it had bearing on the entire western civilization. And by the way, he did not think only about the West, for he thought about the world, and *for* the world as any true thinker should.

Modern academia requires every thinker or scholar to be put into this or that pigeon-hole and that not without some justification in view of the diversity of modern intellectual enterprise. Accordingly grant would be readily assigned to political philosophy and he was a political philosopher (more correctly a political thinker) *par excellence*, but he was that in a much deeper sense than is gatehrally understood. In this respect he would be close enough to Plato and the Greeks while deeply engaged with modern thinking. In the thinking of the Greeks something that is above all things permeated the entire fabric of life and reality held it all together transactionally by what was called politeia. The name that comes closest to expressing what that something is despite all the problems appertaining, is "religion" that is speaking in our language today. Grant became convinced of the importance of religion as result of his own contemplation, in fact a very focused contemplation on politics, held in proper perspective by his reflections on Plato's teachings.

Now one can see how he chose to work in a department of religious studies for a big part of his teaching career.

Dr. Grant worked with religion in the sense that it stood for wholeness of things that philosophy tries to unravel. He was a religious thinker within the parameters of this statement, implying that religion is not an academic subject he wanted to think about of or inquire as professional scholars in the discipline of religious studies do. Yet he was comfortable working within a department of such studies, as comfortable as he felt working within departments of political science. Yet it was easy to see that essentially his view of reality was defined by *Res publica* the "Republic" and that his approach to religion was moulded by it. Religion, which is at least as much unseen as seen held all things in the republic together, focused on wholeness of the republic and itself held as whole. He held, rightly, that the approach to religion from this angle is different in respect of what is sought from the approach laid for example in the famous definition of religion given by William James "as what a person did with his solitude". Grant was concerned about religion as what belonged in the public realm the *res publica*. Grant's approach to the issue of "religion and reality" has this public character, i.e., public in the truly platonic sense. It has a very powerful, platonic implication when looked at in the light of modern day approaches to the issue of "religion and reality", so then for Grant religion is a *public good*, in direct contrast to Karl Marx's declared opinion that religion is a public evil, the so-called "narcotic of the people". Let it be marked that Grant's approach is a radical break-through, one with great consequences for thought and for social organization.

Grant viewed religions, as the historical realities that they evidently are not so much, in terms of the parochial expressions as in terms of the traditions they in truth represent. "Tradition" was a big concept for him. He saw much in common among the great traditions of religion, which were implicitly philosophical. He often spoke of the three greatest figures of history, Jesus, Socrates and

Buddha, particularly, as a Plato was the felt a special kinship with Vedanta, much before he know me, myself being one deeply immersed in it in respect of thought. I too reciprocated with my interest in the things that held him, especially Platonism— and the thought of the modern west, and talking with him was always immensely profitable to me. And only rarely would one come to know a person who almost always lived what he thought, Grant indeed was one who did, so he had always struck me.

Grant was a university professor by calling, although he was an educator in a larger sense in as much the world in which he lived was a class-room for him that in the view of that world rather than in his won view, for I honestly think he was not imbued with any such feeling about himself. For I do not believe that he was not in any degree narcissistic person. His dominant interest was thinking about great issues, namely issues of intrinsic significance that confronted modern humans. He called such thinking "asking the great questions". He himself always asked them both in his privacy and in company especially of these who on the slightest cue he knew would join him in asking them. As for his students, which is a constituency much wider than those in the class or seminar room he performed a double task with them, first to summon them and enable them to confront issues of immense significance and then to ask "the great questions" pertaining to them. He did not have to make any effort to perform it, for all that he had to do was to be himself in a manner modulated to the situations. He indeed was a charismatic teacher by all accounts. He always expressed his views on education. For him education must have for its goal reaching, especially teaching students to think by confronting the world, which taking on the trends set by the technological outlook of today, required all learners to follow them as if they are sacrosanct. He philosophically opposed the prevailing approach to education as an activity devoted to imparting information to passive students whose role is to absorb it and if possible increase on it if and when they graduate into being researchers. He questioned the ideology of progress for its own sake like an unquestioned public good, a substitute religion which defined modern civilization, or rather civilization *ipso facto* defined as modernity. Whilst he no doubt, was willing to let progress be and allow education geared to it within the inevitable framework of "fate", *fatum,* as the ancients who had thought about it called it he felt that there was no excuse for giving up the profoundly vital role of thought to exercise criticism. One of the most original aspects of Grant's thought lay here.

Grant often spoke of the darkness that has unveiled the modern world. He did not complain about technology than is the centre of it, but of the mentality that goes with it, which makes modern man unable to look at it from a standpoint freedom of thought. He saw the darkness of the modern world here. To resort to a standard dichotomy, I have felt that his response entailed distinguishing between the objectives and the subjective aspects of the fatefulness that it spelled, although he never used those terms. For objectively as it was the fatefulness could be accepted as there is no other alternative. The subjective aspect of not only accepting it but accepting it as "good" is where the darkness law. His real response to the situation was what he called "an animating vision" that he held for himself and offered to others. This is something that came out of the depth of his thinking, a product of his constant wrestling. It was far from just academic but "an urgent experience of every lived movement". Now he never said these things directly to me, for between friends or in a situation of personal discussion such things are never said, but I put my own words to what I think he did experience intellectually, and I did see them in his published writings in his own words too (see for example in *Time as History* p.9).

Grant registered a radical reaction to what went on in the world of modernity closest to him, in fact his home-base, namely the English speaking world community, with its roots in England. One of the things that struck me was the deep significance he attached to what humans do with themselves in their world in the sense that they are not just transient things for they have bearing on transcendent meaning that impinges upon humans. In that respect he looked upon what transpires in the realm of history with utmost seriousness. Accordingly, he viewed history as something weighed with heavy responsibly and history for him was not something parochial. I have felt that such connection between the transcendent (in other words called "the eternal") and what transpired in the world of history owing to human contrivance and deliberation, either observing or ignoring responsibility, has for him profoundly to do with "justice". It has appeared to me that such a view of history is Plato extended. His concern with technology lay here and it was marked by no ordinary angst. He always turned to thought as that which should be able to deal with this issue. But he felt nothing but deep disappointment with the way technology-oriented philosophy of the modern world viewed thought, always electing my most hearty agreement. Here I give a remark of his from his printed pages. "Analytical logistics plus historical scholarship plus rigorous since do no when added up equal philosophy". But considering the low esteem in which he held contemporary philosophy as practiced in departments of philosophy what he had in mind as true philosophy is thought, which he extolled as do I and some others. He felt that what is called philosophy today is "not capable of producing that thought which (to advert to what I have just discussed above) is required if justice is to be taken out of the darkness which surrounds it", (*English Speaking Justice*, pp.95-96). As for the word "darkness", he did not us it merely rhetorically for it expressed a deep feeling in him.

Technology indeed has been subjected to profound reflection before- by Nietzsche, by Heidegger, most prominently. However, Grant reflected on it in reference to a Plat and religion–oriented concept of justice. The way technology tends to cast the eternal into the shadows was something that greatly concerned Grant. He felt that the oblivion of the eternal made the realization of justice to any degree impossible and would throw the door open to a more contractualist approach to great human issues - justice being number one. He knew that technology as the engine that drives history and with unprecedent's power too in the modern world has been brought to thought by modern world's great thinkers I referred to, such as Nietzsche and Heidegger. But he felt that the justice aspect illumined by Plato and the great religious traditions has become murky in their approach. He felt the need to establish the absolute importance of justice by the only way in which that can be done, which is by affirming the eternal. He felt that within the framework of modernity and technology there is still a glimmer of hope of actualizing meaning despite the contrarians, deterring flow of history. He seemed to look out into the future by combining fatefulness and freedom, by paying heed to the eternal. Such meaning, I believe is what he ultimately meant by justice. It does appear to me that this insight lay at the root of his rather intricate theory of time. In his own words "time is a developing history of meaning which we make" (See *Time as History*, p.17). I believe that the words "we make" are very central to his thinking. What we have is a blend of freedom and fatelandness, which seems basic to his thought.

He seems to have been deeply convinced of the possibility embedded in our freedom of bringing to pass actual meaning despite its being not present now. He seems to have been grappling in this connection with the issue of the eternal in its two-foldness, i.e., as beyond time and as endless time. Whilst I cannot say what resolution he arrived at, it is clear that he repudiated Nietzsche doctrine of eternal recurrence. In as much as modernity tended to cast justice into the shadows and so throw meaning into jeopardy, he focused much of his thinking on the fate of humans in this world. To bring the eternal to bear on the present. The humans and the natural world in which humans live became very important for him. Ht attitude that responds to such importance he couched in a traditionally beautiful word, "reverence" whilst in no way minimizing the importance and sanctity of all natural life, he did recognized human life as absolute paradigm. In this connection he emphasized "will". For him human life meant both humanity as a whole as well as individual human beings, the latter conceived definitely in terms of persons. He believed person hood begins at the stage the fetus. Hence he took a stand against instinctive. To take such a stand too called for will and he maintained that upon our will he been placed the whole burden of meaning. He opposed all modern genetic engineering as it amounted to wanton destruction of meaning.

For him the affirmation of meaning by will have to do with "knowing", a concept that became extremely important for him. Knowing now implicitly combined with wiling became cardinal in comporting with humans, and in the world where in time stood as the guarantor as it were. However, even without this implicit presence of will, knowing in the sagely sense of wisdom pertaining to the humans seemed to dominate his thinking in a rather contemplative ambience towards the end. I had a meeting with him a few years before his demise (untimely indeed) when we met at the World Philosophy congress in Montreal, where he was a plenary speaker, at a leisurely lunch at his instance. I could see his turn towards contemplative approach to being human and being *as* human in our world, time still a dominant concept with him- and by no means in the sense of eternal recurrence, and not once and for all in an absolutist sense either, but in a way that radiates hope in the midst of seeming hopelessness. He thus found a new meaning to the word "know". In context he brought up the subject of Shakespeare, with whose works he seemed to be delighted. We never discussed Shakespeare before. He held that Shakespeare "knew". Having not read Shakespeare at any depth, I only listened and nodded, wanting to hear more. Later I happened to read Harold Bloom's works on Shakespeare, characterizing him as "the inventor of the human". Allowing enough of a margin for a literary scholar's tendency to be hyperbolic, I too delved a little into some of the works of the great playwright and gained some sense of what Grant was talking about. With Dr. Grant's statement ringing in my mind I too get the feeling that Shakespeare must have shown that humans are both creators and creatures of the play called history and that history whilst it is the totality of purposes both expressed and unexpressed is the wholeness whose essence, i.e., meaning lies beyond it. And that way Shakespeare' own playful words", "all the world is a stage and men and women are merely players" hide a deeper meaning, which I am sure Grant saw with great clarity and he had clarity of vision.

It is encouraging to know that he lives in the memory of friends and of the public, to whom he had a message for the times. Friendship (phileia) was an important concept for him. He did not apply the concepts friendship upon people rather he found it in friends. That characteristic was true all around, for him persons came first. I can characterize him as an empiricist of morality of justice, in as much as moral truth and justice were, for him what individual persons and public were all about. For him a most important aspect of thought was acting out this belief through will. A vision that embodied this will not wane with the passage of time.

༅ ༄

APPENDIX: NOTES OF GANDHI AND GRANT

NOTES OF GANDHI

Ahimsa:

Non-violence is the greatest force at the disposal of mankind. It is mightier than the mightiest weapon of destruction devised by the ingenuity of man. Destruction is not the law of the humans. Man lives freely by his readiness to die, if need be, at the hands of his brother, never by killing him. Every murder or injury, no mater for what cause, committed or inflicted on another is a crime against humanity. (*Harijan*, 20-7-'35.)

Identification with everything that lives is impossible without self-purification; without self-purification the observance of the law of Ahimsa must remain an empty dream; god can never be realized by one who is not pure of heart. Self-purification, therefore, must mean purification in all the walks of life. And purification being highly infectious, purification of oneself necessarily leads to the purification of one's surroundings. (*Autobiography*, 1948, p 615.)

A votary of Ahimsa cannot subscribe to the utilitarian formula (of the greatest good of the greatest number). He will strive for the greatest good of all and die in the attempt to realize the ideal. He will, therefore, be willing to die, so that the others may live. He will serve himself with the rest, by himself dying. The greatest good of all inevitably includes the good of the greatest number and therefore, he and the utilitarian will converge in many points in their career but there does come a time when they must part company, and even work in opposite directions. The utilitarian to be logical will never sacrifice himself. (*Young India*, 9-12-26.)

Faith and Reason:

This belief in god has to be based on faith which transcends reason. Indeed; even the so-called realization has at bottom an element of faith without which it cannot be sustained. In the very nature of things it must be so. Who can transgress the limitations of his being? I hold that complete realization is imposable in this embodied life. Nor is it necessary. A living immovable faith is all that is required for reaching the full spiritual height attainable by human beings. God is not outside this earthly case of ours. Therefore, exterior proof is not of much avail, if any at all. We must ever fail to perceive Him through the senses, because he is beyond them. We can feel him, if we will but withdraw ourselves from the senses. The divine music is incessantly going on within ourselves, but the loud senses drown the delicate music, which is unlike an infinitely superior to anything we can perceive or hear with our senses. (*Harijan*, 13-6-'36.)

Man's ultimate aim is the realization of God, and all his activities, social, political, religious, have to be guided by the ultimate aim of the vision of God. The immediate service of all human beings becomes a necessary part of the endeavor simply because the only way to find God is to see him in his creation and be one with it. This can only be done by service of all. I am a part and parcel of the whole and I cannot find Him apart from the rest of humanity. My countrymen are my nearest neighbours. They have become so helpless, so resource less, so inert that I must concentrate myself on serving them. If I could persuade myself that I could find him in a Himalayan cave I would proceed there immediately. But I know that I can not find him apart from humanity.(*Harijan*, 29.8.36.)

The impenetrable darkness that surrounds us is not a curse but a blessing. He has given us power to see only the step in front of us, and it should be enough if heavenly light revels that step to us. We can then sing with Newman, 'One step enough for me'. And we may be sure from our past experience that the next step will laws may be in view. In other words, the impenetrable darkness is nothing so impenetrable as we imagine. But it seems impenetrable when in our impatience, we want to look beyond that one step. (*Harijan*, 20-4-'34.)

The harmony of artha, dharma and moksha—Gandhi's unique contribution:

> *To see the universal and all-pervading spirit of truth face to face one must be able to love the meanest of creation as oneself. And a man who aspires after that cannot afford to keep out of any field of life. That is why my devotion to truth has drawn me into the field of politics; and I can say without the slightest hesitation, and yet in all humility, that those who say that religion [dharma] has nothing to do with politics do not know what religion [dharma] means.*

(*Autobiography*, 1948, p615.)

Sources:

Book: *Truth is God* (Gleanings from the writings of Mahatma Gandhi bearing on God, God –Realization and Godly way) by M K Gandhi,

Compiled by R K Prabhu, Navajivan Publishing House, Ahmedabad-380014.

(With due permission from the publisher).

Notes of Grant

Foreword to 'Neo-Vedanta and Modernity' by Bithika Mukerji 1983

To a Westerner such as myself, uneducated in the truth of the Vedanta but with knowledge of what has happened to

Christianity in the face of the modern, Dr Mukerji's (book is) of the greatest interest. I am not qualified to speak with authority on Indian thought, but having read these chapters with close attention I can affirm that Dr Mukerji's argument is beautifully expounded. The thesis of that argument is that the impact of westernization on Indian thought has resulted in obscuring what was meant by 'bliss' in the Vedanta, and therefore distorting that philosophy... Above all, what is particularly wonderful in Dr Mukerji's book is her enucleation of the ontology of Ananda. This is breathtaking for any western listener. How right it is that the word Ananda be translated as bliss. The word 'joy' would be too subjective and miss the knowledge that what is spoken of here concerns Being. What has come to be in the dynamic civilization of North America - indeed in all these societies which express in themselves the thoughts of Locke and Marx, Rousseau or Darwin or Hume - is the restless search for bliss, which escapes one because it cannot be known as being itself. Modern life has become the joyless pursuit of joy. One of the truly great stories of the English-speaking world is called Bliss. (It is also written by a woman, Katherine Mansfield.) The story recognizes beautifully the crying need that bliss be more than the subjectivity of feeling but rooted in the Being of beings. What is more pressing for us westerners than the understanding that there is an ontology of bliss? That this should be unthinkable is perhaps the greatest price that we have paid for modernity. For those of us who are Christians, it is the elimination of the understanding of the Trinity as bliss, which leaves Christianity floundering in the midst of the modernity it so much made. What is sad in the western world is the deep desire to participate in bliss, for instance through the detached pursuit of the orgasm, which because it is outside any ontological understanding of bliss results in the good of the pursuit often being blackly negated.

George Grant, 'Foreword to *Neo-Vedanta and Modernity*' by Bithika Mukerji, iii-vi. Varanasi: Ashutosh Prakashan Sansthan, 1983.

Good Friday 1952

Oh dearest word, the very word indeed, Breathes on our striving, for the cross is done; All fate forgotten, and from judgement freed, Call Him then less - Who shows us this - Your Son? Look it is here at death, not three days later, The love that binds the granite into being, Here the sea's blueness finds its true creator, His glance on Golgotha our sun for seeing. Nor say the choice is ours, what choice is left? Forgiveness shows God's Will most fully done, There on the cross the myth of hell is cleft And the black garden blazes with the sun. Hold close the crown of thorns, the scourge, the rod, For in his sweat, full front, the face of God.

Torture 1977

Torture is obviously the central crime against justice. Justice is rendering others their due. The shattering of the moral will by the systematic infliction of pain is the most complete denial that anything is due to human beings. Indeed justice is affirmed in the fact that all of us, when we suffer injustice, cry from the centre of our souls that this is not our due. And this cry must never ring more terribly than from those who endure sustained torture. When I have met people who have so endured there is always a grim distance in their eyes which is the recognition that they have suffered the inexcusable. Clearly torture is most unjust when it is employed by the state. Yet it is a useful means for any government. Therefore as torture is at the same time both useful and a crime against justice, its control is a continuing problem. As its limitation must always be difficult of achievement, the proper means towards that limitation is one of the key questions of political philosophy. The present volume is an account of the trial in 1975 of 32 Greek military police officers and soldiers on charges of acts of torture, carried out under the rule of Greece by the junta of colonels from 1967-1974. It is an appalling account. As torture is the temptation of all governments, it is well to read this record as to what takes place when a government overtly throws away limitations upon what it is permitted to do. The record of this trial is of particular significance, because it is rare in our era for regimes which have indulged in massive torture to have then been brought down, so that their record could be exposed to the light of day.

Most torture in the modern world takes place under regimes which are not likely to be brought down. In this case the regime fell because of its folly towards Archbishop Makarios, and therefore its crimes have been exposed.

Decent people owe Amnesty International a debt for presenting an English record of this trial about what happens when a regime finds it useful to put aside limitations upon torture. It is an exemplary document which should be read by students and teachers in our law faculties and police academies, as an example of what above all needs to be politically avoided, and as a preparation for thought as to how such avoidance is achieved.

Who were responsible? As torture should be forbidden against anybody, whether they be 'Fascists' or 'Communists' or whatever, this is a much more important question than who were the victims. At the top were the leaders of the junta who were faced by problems of the greatest political difficulty. They lived in a society on the edge of the east-west conflict; they were nationalists who envisaged their opponents as betraying their country to a foreign empire. They believed that a high level of public order was necessary if they were to modernize their country quickly without it losing its national traditions. From this they were lead into the belief, so prevalent in all the varying forms of modern thought, namely that if one's ends are good, one has the right to achieve them by any means.

Underneath the leaders were the officers who were actually responsible for these abominations. From this report one gets the sense that when `political necessities' unleash torture, there is a natural tendency for those who get pleasure from the infliction of pain to gravitate to where these methods of investigation and prosecution are taking place. The attempt to limit this terrible tendency is therefore one of the key responsibilities of those who are the final guardians of law and order in any society. At the lowest level were the soldiers who carried out orders from their officers; this was for me the greatest point of tragedy in the report. Young conscripts were trained to be torturers by having been themselves tortured, in their training. Always the plea in court was that those responsible were just carrying out orders, and indeed, blame is a quite inadequate response to such a report. Blame is generally the language of self-righteousness when it comes from people in our easier situation. The essential lesson of this report cannot be blame, but rather the necessity that those responsible for investigation and prosecution and punishment in any society should be educated as to what actions are impermissible, and why they are impermissible, and should be aware that they are open to prosecution when they pass beyond the limits of the permissible.

In Canada, which may be moving towards more stringent necessities, care about such education has become a priority. In highly advanced societies, public decency depends above all on the medical, legal and police professions. Their religious education is the central core of the control of torture. One cannot be optimistic about that core, because of the weakness of such education in these professions. This education is the sustaining force behind formal constitutional guarantees.

In the twentieth century, discussion of torture has been too often carried on within the framework of ideology. People of the 'left' affirm that torture is a phenomenon of the 'right,' concentrate on the extremities of the Communists, and gloss over their own extremities. In the 'democratic' world it is often implied that we have passed beyond torture, and that it is only a phenomenon of non-democratic regimes. Such ideological talk makes people forget that torture is a political problem at all times and places. In the modern era it is returning not only in its old form but in new forms.

The quick changes and expansions consequent on technology make the maintenance of public order difficult, and torture is invitingly useful instrument. At a subtler level, the central driving force of our society is the science which puts nature 'to the question,' and why should that 'putting to the question' stop with non-human nature, when it is useful or convenient to control human beings? Despite the advantages of our English-speaking constitutional systems, all kinds of new forms of social control are arising which verge on torture or are directly torture. The growth of deprogramming in North America is a simple example. Our torture of non-human species grows and is taken for granted.

Beyond the pressing needs of practice, thoughtful human beings are ceaselessly torn by the contradiction between the perfection of God and the misery of man. Torture is the height of that misery. The fact that the central symbol of Christianity is an instrument of torture has made that religion the supreme way of contemplating that contradiction. But one must think about it in the realities of injustice which are going on now. Amnesty International does a notable service in opposing torture in whatever regime it arises. One aspect of that opposition is bringing out books such as this which keep the reality before us.

SIMONE WEIL (1909-1943)
Introduction to Simone Weil 1970

First, let me sketch the outward going of her existence. Simone Weil was born in Paris in 1909. Her parents were prosperous French who had come from the tradition of European Judaism. She had one older brother who is today a famous mathematician. She was brought up by her parents and brother in that civilized humanist agnosticism of the enlightenment, which so characterized middle-class European culture before 1914. But it was that culture in its finest form. Whatever else she was to become, it must be remembered that she partook of two remarkable traditions; both her Frenchness and her secularized Jewishness gave her that intense love of learning and cultivation of the intellect, which may not of themselves be enough, but are the seed-ground from which even higher activities can proceed, and without which society and individuals are likely to become mediocre or even base. French education for the very clever is prodigiously difficult and highly competitive.... It is therefore necessary for me to say something of those events between 1936 and 1943 whereby God's perfection became immediate to her. (And I use the word 'immediate' in the sense that we see each other right now.) But let me say that in doing so I have very great hesitation - and would like to cover my head with a cloth as Socrates did when he spoke with Phaedrus about most difficult matters. Let me begin by quoting her words which set the context of the problem: I may say that never at any moment in my life have I sought for God - I do not like this expression and it strikes me as false. As soon as I reached adolescence I saw the problem of God as a problem of which the data could not be obtained here below, and I decided that the only way of being sure not to reach a wrong solution, which seemed to me the greatest possible evil, was to leave it alone. So I left it alone. I neither affirmed nor denied anything. It seemed to me useless to solve the problem, for I thought that being in this world, our business was to adopt the best attitude with regard to the problems of this world. Let me read you one extract about these events. In doing so one must remember it is part of an account written to an intimate friend which she never thought would pass beyond him. In 1937 I had two marvelous days at Assisi. There, alone in the little twelfth-century Romanesque chapel of Santa Maria degli Angeli, an incomparable marvel of purity where Saint Francis often used to pray, something stronger than I was compelled me for the first time in my life to go down on my knees. In 1938 I spent ten days at Solesmes, from Palm Sunday to Easter Tuesday, following all the liturgical services. I was suffering from splitting headaches; each sound hurt me like a blow; by an extreme effort of attention I was able to rise above this wretched flesh, and leave it to suffer by itself, heaped up in a corner, and to find a pure and perfect joy in the unimaginable beauty of the chanting and the words. This experience enabled me by analogy to get a better understanding of the possibility of loving divine love in the midst of affliction. It goes without saying that in the course of these services the thought of the Passion of Christ entered into my being once and for all.

There was a young English Catholic there from whom I gained my first idea of the supernatural power of the Sacraments because of the truly angelic radiance with which he seemed to be clothed after going to communion. Chance - for I always prefer saying chance rather than Providence - made of him a messenger to me. For he told me of the existence of those English poets of the seventeenth century who are named metaphysical. In reading them later on, I discovered the poem of which I read you what is unfortunately a very inadequate translation. It is called Love. I learnt it by heart. Often, at the culminating point of a violent headache, I make myself say it over, concentrating all my attention upon it and clinging with all my soul to the tenderness it enshrines. I used to think I was merely reciting it as a beautiful poem, but without my knowing it the recitation had the virtue of a prayer. It was during one of these recitations that, as I told you, Christ himself came down and took possession of me. In my arguments about the insolubility of the problem of God I had never foreseen the possibility of that, of a real contact, person to person, here below, between a human being and God. I had vaguely heard tell of things of this kind, but I had never believed in them. In the Fioretti the accounts of apparitions rather put me off if anything, like the miracles in the Gospel. Moreover, in this sudden possession of me by Christ, neither my senses nor my imagination had any part; I only felt in the midst of my suffering the presence of a love, like that which one can read in the smile on a beloved face.

I had never read any mystical works because I had never felt any call to read them. In reading as in other things I have always striven to practise obedience. There is nothing more favourable to intellectual progress, for as far as possible I only read what I am hungry for, at the moment when I have the appetite for it, and then I do not read, I eat. God in his mercy had prevented me from reading the mystics, so that it should be evident to me that I had not invented this absolutely unexpected contact. Yet I still half refused, not my love but my intelligence. For it seemed to me certain, and I still think so to-day, that one can never wrestle enough with God if one does so out of pure regard for the truth. Christ likes us to prefer truth to him because, before being Christ, he is truth. If one turns aside from him to go towards the truth, one will not go far before falling into his arms. Such events cannot, of course, be spoke of simply. For instance, her involvement in the twentieth-century through becoming a member of the industrial proletariat and through experience of war, shows that there was in her something beyond intellectual brilliance, namely what in the West is called attention of the will or better love and which has always been considered necessary to the highest knowledge. This already present attention was what led her to the afflictions of the century, even before she knew what she was doing, and in turn the afflictions are the condition of her amazing attention. Moreover the afflictions of modern civilization taught her to question the philosophic principles on which modern civilization is based, and so enabled her to read and participate directly in what the Greeks and Indians have said about alternative principles, in a way that is quite impossible for most of us. Yet in saying that her involvement in the afflictions of the world is central to the understanding of her sanctity, we must avoid being led to that anti-intellectual position which sees possession by deity as an happening which has little to do with intellectual life. (This I may say is a position very popular in many circles these days.) For it is perfectly clear from her own testimony that her reading of the Bhagavadgita, the Iliad, and above all Plato and the Gospels, were the very means of her receptivity. What I am saying is, in its most general form, the following: in the tradition and I can only speak of the western, there has been much controversy about the respective places of the way of love and the way of knowledge, and indeed some followers of the way of love have been so presumptuous as to ridicule thought. This is not true of Simone Weil. In her the ways of love and of knowledge are inextricably bound together. It is particularly necessary to say this in our present society in which knowledge and love are so disastrously bifurcated that each falls into its own particular errors and perversions. What is one to make of such a sentence as: 'It was during one of these recitations that, as I told you, Christ himself came down and took possession of me.' I of course, believe that what happened is exactly what she says happened. And yet this seems to me highly surprising; for I do not like or trust the writings of most mystics and am full of suspicion of their claims. Also as a twentieth-century person, I am inclined to a certain image of the relation of sexuality to religion and therefore such language as Christ taking possession of people is highly suspect - particularly from women. Yet I am sure it happened for the reason that what she knows and writes about elsewhere is, I am sure true, and whatever her faults I cannot think they were those of self-delusion. This comment is of course in no sense a proof because I could not prove it unless someone would sit down and read in detail and discuss with me in detail what she has said about affliction and the beauty of the world in her notebooks. Let me also say that I think that official, institutional Christianity has been quite right in being so firmly suspicious of those claims to direct contact which we call mysticism, because of the obvious and manifold abuses to which they may lead. But when it happens, I am sure it happens, and I am convinced it happened here.... She remained, she has told us, at the intersection of Christianity and everything that is not Christianity: all the ancient wisdom of mankind what we hypostatize that the Church had repudiated and excluded, the traditions banned as heretical, even the limited goods that resulted from what we hypostatize of the Renaissance. 'I remain beside them all the more' she wrote to Father Perrin, 'because my own intelligence is numbered among them.' In her eyes the Church fails as a perfect incarnation of Christianity mainly because it is not truly Catholic. 'So many things are outside it, - so many things that God loves - Christianity being

Catholic by right but not in fact, I regard it as legitimate on my part to be a member of the Church by right but not in fact, not only for a time but for my whole life if need be.' This may sound as if she were advocating a foolish syncretism or asserting the Church should embrace falsehood as well as truth. But of course politically she was in no sense a liberal (that is, and optimist about the results of falsehood) and so she recognizes the Church's duty to guard the truth and warn the public against error. But this guarding has been done in the wrong way by the use of force and anathema. This rejection of the Church meant of course that she excluded herself from the Eucharist which she knew to be a priceless treasure. Now clearly it is difficult (I do not know whether it be possible) for a Roman Catholic to accept at its face value Simone Weil's position that it is Christ who demands for her the obedience of remaining outside the Church. It would be folly to say impossible considering the river of divine charity which in the last years, has flowed from the Roman Catholic Church, which must make the rest of us humble. The alternative is to say that at the centre of her existence she has been in some way mistaken, she confused obedience with spiritual pride and Cardinal Danelon has said that. It is quite honest to interpret her this way and in the last years there have been many books by Roman Catholic theologians explaining the sources of her errors. My point about her writings is it is quite evident that the extracts published by Thibon were affected by the contradiction on the one hand of his friendship and admiration for her, on the other the desire to play down her total thought. Obedience to their Church meant that M. Thibon and Father Perrin could not be expected to edit her manifold manuscripts properly. There were too many passages to which they were entirely unsympathetic. Nevertheless the effect of their early editing on her public image still remains. Thibon's Gravity and Grace was the chief was her writings became known in English, and it is a very one-sided set of extracts. Father Perrin's book, Waiting on God, is fairer, and is indeed a good first volume to read, (also cheaply available in English.)

However, it must be noted that Father Perrin's introduction to that books has been withdrawn, and he has published elsewhere a more cautious and less enthusiastic account of her. Now that her manuscripts are edited, not as extracts, but more in the way she left them, the central difficulty remains however of seeing her thought in unity, because her main writings were not intended for publication. This unification of her thought is further complicated by the fact that for a person who died at thirty-three, and spent most of her adult life as a labourer, her writings are voluminous. Since the end of the war this immense mass of material has been brought out by the French presses. Let me say that many of the theologians who have written books or articles about her have singled out certain aspects of her thought at the expense of others and therefore have interpreted her totality in a very limited way. Some of the descriptions of her in American journals could only have been written by people whose reading had been to say the least partial. There is such a desire on the part of scholars these days to get into print that they sometimes write about that of which they do not know enough. For the sake of clarity I will divide her writings into two main classes: her political and social writings and her philosophical, scientific and religious writings. Obviously this division is arbitrary because each depends on the other. There are three main books about politics and society. First L'Enracinement (The Need for Roots.) (In giving an English title, I am not implying any lack of French in my audience, but simply stating that there is an English translation of the work. Where there is no translation I will give only one title.) This is the only book that she wrote for a public purpose - indeed her only book which is not a collection of pieces. It was written as a report for the Free French government in London as to the principles on which French society should be based after the war. It is divided into three sections: (a) the needs of the soul in any society, (b) the cause of modern uprooted ness, and (c) the possibility of enrooted ness in advanced industrial society. By 'uprooted ness' she means what Marx means by alienation, but uses it in a wider context because she has a fuller understanding than him of the demonic aspects of bureaucracy. This is the least absolute of her books because it was written as a report to practical men, who knew they would soon have responsibility for the reconstruction of a conquered society. Second, Oppression et Liberté (Oppression and Liberty.) This group of essays is in my opinion her most remarkable writing about politics, and is a good place to start the study of her thought. Albert Camus, also thought it was one of the masterpieces of European political philosophy. At its centre is a long essay called 'Reflections on the causes of liberty and social oppression,' which is at base an understanding not only of the causes of social oppression in general, but of the particular forms of oppression which arise in societies which are oriented to the future, that is, which are progressive. This volume also contains her amazing critique of Marxism. I must emphasize that this criticism of Marx is not of the order of those we have got used to in North America since 1945 - criticisms which miss the point because they distort Marx and therefore do not come to grips with his thought. Simone Weil has a profound understanding of Marx's greatness and therefore what she says is truly a critique, not the passing wind of propaganda. Third, La Condition Ouvrière. At the centre of this volume is her diary while she worked for the Renault factory. This is however no personal affair but comments about the relations between men and machines and men and bureaucracy. It also contains an essay on the conditions necessary if industrial work is not to be servile. Besides these three mains works there are two volumes of miscellaneous essays on social and political subject, ranging from several analyses of French colonial policy to essays on the Cathar religion and the civilization of Languedoc that is, the Albigensians. Two of these essays I would particularly single out. A long essay called 'Reflections on the origins of Hitlerism' turns out to be a sustained and detailed criticism of the civilization of Rome. I single this out not only because it helps us escape some of the more comfortable platitudes about Roman history, but because in it is expressed her central theme about history in general - namely that the nobler and better does not necessarily survive, indeed because of the ultimate rule of force over the world, truth and beauty can only be tenuously held in the being of any society. She agrees with Plato that society is always and everywhere the Great Beast or the Cave. The other essay I would single out is 'The Person and the Sacred' in which she maintains that what is sacred in man is not what is individual or personal but what is impersonal. Seen negatively, this essay is an attack on so much popular modern writing, both inside and outside Christianity, which is based on a sentimentalizing of personality and mankind. These essays have been published in English by the Oxford Press under the editorship of Sir Richard Rees, who is the leading English exponent of her work. The core of her philosophical and religious writing - indeed the core of all her work is found in her Notebooks. The first batch of these which cover her life in France have been published in English in two volumes under the title Notebooks. Her later Notebooks written in the US and England have been published in French under the title La Connaissance Surnaturelle (new translation in English under the title First and Last Notebooks. As to me the greatest modern European language is always French and she is a marvellous explorer of that language, try and read some of her in French.) This I think is the most remarkable but the most difficult of all her writings. What are all these notebooks about, taken as a whole? They are a sustained commentary on what she has been thinking, reading and experiencing. She continually returns to such themes as the history of philosophy, the nature of ethics and religion, the Indian writings and Christian scriptures, northern and ancient mythology, French literature, the worship of the future, mathematics, physics, art, war, work, industrialism and sexuality. Perhaps if one were to single out one subject that more than any other binds the whole together one could put it in her own words; 'I am ceaselessly and increasingly torn both in my intelligence and in the depth of my heart through my inability to conceive simultaneously and in truth, the affliction of men, the perfection of God and the link between the two.' Or, in other of her words: 'As Plato said, an infinite distance separates the good from necessity — the essential contradiction in human life is that man, with a straining after the good constituting his very being, is at the same time subject in his entire being, both in mind and in flesh, to a blind force, to a necessity completely indifferent to the good.' This contradiction above any other is for her the means by which the mind is led to truth. I quote again: 'There is a legitimate and an illegitimate use of contradiction. The illegitimate use lies in coupling together incompatible thoughts as if they were compatible. The legitimate use lies, first of all, when two incompatible thoughts present themselves to the mind, in exhausting all the powers of the intellect in an attempt to eliminate at least one of them. If this is impossible, if both must be accepted, the contradiction must then be recognized as a fact. It must then be used as a two-limbed tool, like a pair of pincers, so that through it direct contact may be made with the transcendent sphere of truth beyond the range of the human faculties. The contact is direct, though made through an intermediary, in the same way as the sense of touch is directly affected by the uneven surface of a table over which you pass, not your hand, but your pencil. The contact is real, though belonging to the number of things that by nature are impossible, for it is a case of a contact between the mind and that which is not thinkable. There is an equivalent, an image as it were, very frequent in mathematics, of this legitimate use of contradiction as a means of reaching the transcendent. It plays an essential role in Christian dogma, as one can perceive with reference to the Trinity.' Her Notebooks are indeed a sustained exercise in this legitimate use of contradiction, that is, is making as clear as can be the factual nature of the contradiction that human existence presents, and then in using those contradictions as pincers. One point I must make in passing is about the word I have translated as 'affliction.' This word, which is central to her thought, is in the French 'malheur.' There is no word in English with the complete connotation of that French word. I use affliction, but if anyone can think of a better word I will be deeply grateful. For any of you who may be interested in the history of philosophy, I single out her continuous commentary on the dialogues of Plato, which runs like a thread through all her notebooks. As well as her comments in her notebooks there is a group of essays on the same subject which has been published in English with the inapposite title of Imitations of Christianity. In these essays about Greece she writes not only on Plato, but on the Illiad, the Electra, the Antigone, Pythagoras and Greek mathematicians. As I have more right to speak about Plato than the others, I would say that her comments on his writings go to the heart of the matter in a way that much modern scholarship does not. Most modern students of the philosopher start with the presupposition that since they come later than Plato in time they must be able to judge that thinker from a superior height. The result of such a standpoint is that instead of seeing what Plato thought, they say that he was really saying what he ought to have said if he was a modern intellectual. It is because the assumptions of modernity had been smashed in Simone Weil that her commentary on Plato is illuminating.

I must finally mention three books of hers that do not fit into my division. The first is Sur la Science (remember her brother.) The second is Lettre à un Religieux (Letter to a Priest.) This is a long letter she wrote to an American Roman Catholic priest, putting down in detail why she did not become a member of the Christian Church. The third volume is a play she worked at for many years but never finished called Venise Sauvée.

Let me now attempt to place Simone Weil within the tradition. In doing so, however, I in no way imply that such historical placing has anything to do with the question of whether what she says is true. I am not an historicist, and do not think that truth of the philosophical or religious order can be reached by historical analysis. To say that Simone Weil belongs to the extreme wing of Greek Christianity is not to imply that this tradition incorporates the truth more fully than western Christianity. The statement of historical fact simply leads forward to the fuller and more difficult question of truth. This evening my paper has been with a description of the life and writings of a person and I intend to leave aside for this occasion the incomparably more difficult question of the truth of what she says. The inference, however, must be made explicit that since I spend a great part of my life reading and thinking about this woman, it must be that I think I am there drinking at a fountain of the divine truth. To place Simone Weil squarely within Greek Christianity is, however, to make one fact apparent. What she says will appear extremely alien and unlikely to western Europeans or to North Americans because this form of Christianity has not played a significant role in our world for many centuries. To be a western person is to think within western Christianity - Catholic or Protestant - or within one of Christianity's secular offshoots - Marxism or Liberalism. Indeed so powerful has been the west that it is possible almost to say that to be a man at all is to think in a western way. But of course Christianity was more than western from the beginning, and eastern or Greek Christianity included in itself things that have been lost in the west. But in saying that Simone Weil belongs to this Greek Christianity, I am not saying that she was near to the institutionalized form, namely the Greek Orthodox Church - because I am taking Greek Christianity to be something much wider than this - I include in it much that has disappeared from the world. Its last appearance in the western world as more than an individual phenomenon was according to her in the civilization of Languedoc and the religion of the Cathars - the civilization which was extirpated by the Dominican order and the feudal knights of norther France, in what is known euphemistically as the Albigensian crusade. (History is indeed written by the victorious.) This Greek Christianity is nearest of any of the forms of our religion to Indian religion. While of course to take Hegel's dictum 'en pleine conscience de cause' that progress moves from east to west, North American Christianity is farthest from them. Indeed she saw Europe in its mediterranean form as a halfway house between America and India. It is not accidental then that Simone Weil should have written of the civilization of Languedoc as the highest that Europe has known; nor is it accidental that she should have learned sanskrit and considered the Bhagavadgita as a work of revelation to be accepted at a level of authority only just lower than the Gospel according to St. John. Indeed, to state the matter in a trite historical way, Simone Weil's value as an object of study could be put thus: She was a person who as much as anyone I know experienced the twentieth-century - knowing its wars and its intellectual assumptions, its hopes and its factories. In the full sense of the word she was incarnate in the twentieth-century - that is, she knew it not only as an observer, but its afflictions became her flesh. It was because all that the twentieth-century has been was immediately and mediately know, that she was able to transcend it and rediscover certain treasure which our world had lost for many centuries. Her pierced and piercing apprehension of our immediate world enabled her to overcome that loss in ourselves, so that the ancient religion can appear to us as more than an academic curiosity. I end by singling out two aspects of her doctrine that clearly illustrate what I mean by placing her in the tradition of Greek Christianity. In stating her doctrine, I will compare what she says with the more usual western view on the same matter.

First she stands unequivocally on the side of saying that the affirmation of the being of God is a matter of knowing and not of willing - that is, that belief or unbelief is never a matter of choice or commitment, but of intellect and attention. As the West has been without faith, faith has often been interpreted by men of faith who wished to get on with understanding as if it finally came down to an act of committal by the will. For instance, my experience of the clergy has often been that one raises difficult intellectual questions, their answer is likely to be 'Have Faith,' and when one asks them why one should have faith they are likely to say 'Commit yourself to it,' as if truth were not a gift, but a free act. More and more, religion is talked about in the west as if it were some kind of choice or opting, despite or even against the evidence. In present-day Christianity, it is now leading to the pitiful grabbing at existentialist philosophy as a buttress to faith, as Rahner and Heidegger. For existentialism is after all the dead end of voluntarism in philosophy. Against this praise of commitment, Simone Weil makes clear that belief cannot ultimately be based on choice. In her own words: 'The consent of the intellect is never owed to anything whatsoever. For it is never in the slightest degree a question of choice. Only attention is voluntary and thus is the only matter of obligation. If one wishes to provoke in oneself a voluntary consent of the intellect, what is produced is not consent to truth but autosuggestion. Nothing more contributes to the degrading and enfeebling of faith and leads to the spread of unbelief than the conception that one ought to believe in anything.' In other words, one cannot force faith on oneself. The intellect should be entirely free to go where the necessity of the argument leads it. This approach to the divine is of course essentially Greek. Second and more difficult, she rejects the language of personality and individuality as the final truth about human beings. This language is of course basic to the way that western people talk of the human condition. Today in our present world we see the consequences of such talking in the belief that religion is in essence warmth of feeling to other people. This worship of warmth, coated with the more comfortable parts of the Gospel or Judaism, takes a myriad of forms in the superstructure of talk which justifies our society, but its philosophical and religious basis is in western philosophy and religion, which asserts that the individual qua individual is an ultimate irreducible in reality. So deep does this go in our culture that thinking outside personality language is very hard for us. Yet this is what we must do if we are to read Simone Weil. The concrete, the personal, the particular has some preliminary meaning in talking about human beings, but it is according to her not ultimate. In as much as we partake in the universal we partake in the divine. In this sense Plato is her master and she takes him seriously in a way that nobody can who makes the language of personality final. Let me read you some words of hers which show clearly where the denial of personality language leads - words which could not be written by anyone who saw the wester tradition as sufficient. God created; that is not to say that he produced something external to himself, but that he withdrew, allowing a part of being to be other than God. To this divine renunciation answers the renunciation of the created, namely, obedience. The whole universe is nothing but a compact mass of obedience studded with luminous points. Each of these points is the supernatural part of the soul of a rational creature who loves God and who consents to obey. The rest of the soul is part of the compact mass. The rational creatures who do not love God are only fragments of the compact and dense mass. They also are fully obedient, but only in the manner of a stone which is falling. Their souls are matter, psychic matter, subject to a mechanism as inexorable as gravity. Even their belief in their own free will, the illusions of their pride, their defiances, their rebellions, are, simply, phenomena as strictly determined as the refraction of life. Considered in this way, as inert matter, the worst criminals are part of the order of the world, and for that reason, part of the beauty of the world. Everything obeys God; everything is therefore, perfectly beautiful.

This universal love belongs only to the contemplative faculty of the soul. He who truly loves God leaves to each part of his soul its proper function. Below the faculty of supernatural contemplation is found the part of the soul that responds to obligation, and for which the opposition of good and evil must have as much meaning as possible. Below this, is the animal part of the soul, which must be carefully instructed by a skilful combination of whip-lashes and lumps of sugar. Such a statement helps us to understand why according to her affliction is the lot of all human beings. It always includes in itself physical pain, but is more than this. It is the pounding in upon men that they are really nothing, by the blind force of necessity and of social and personal degradation. The final affliction to which all comes is death. The only difference between people is whether they consent or do not consent to necessity. What most supports the possibility of this consent is our attention to the beauty of the world. For that beauty is our one image of the divine. And of its very nature it is not known as purposeful, but only lovable, in the sense that a great work of art has no purpose outside its own being. In her language, the beauty of the world is caused by the divine son because it is the mediator between blind obedience and God.

In terms of this very difficult language she would see the human condition in the following way: 'The portion of space around us, limited by the curve of the horizon, and the portion of time between birth and death, in which we live, second after second, and which is the tissue of out life, are together a fragment of that infinite distance crossed by divine love. The being and life of each of us are a small segment of that lie whose ends are two persons but one God; and back and forth on this line moves love who is also the same God. Each of us is but a place through which the divine love of God for himself passes.'

Sources

1) The works of Dr Grant would be the primary sources
2) The source of the first passage is given at the end of it
3) 'Good Friday' was an unpublished poem.
4) 'Torture was a book review that appeared in the newspaper Globe and Mail 11 June 1977, p 41.
5) The article on Simone Weil was an unpublished talk.

Used with the kind permission of Sheila V. Grant through William Christian.

ঔ ༄

Contributors

1. Bhikhu Parekh is emeritus professor of political philosophy at the universities of Hull and Westminster. He was until recently Centennial Professor at the London School of Economics, and has been a visiting professor at the universities of McGill, Harvard, Paris and Barcelona. He is the author of several widely acclaimed books in political philosophy including *Rethinking Multiculturalism*, published by Harvard University Press (2000), and *A New Politics of Identity,* published by Macmillan, London (2008).

He is the recipient of many honours in India and Britain. He has received BBC's Special Lifetime Achievement Award for Asians, and Sir Isaiah Berlin Prize for Lifetime Contribution to Political Philosophy. He has also received Pravasi Bhratiya Saman and Padma Bhusan, two of India's highest honours, from the President of India. He is a Fellow of the British Academy and was until recently President of the Academy of Social Sciences.

2. Ramjee Singh, Ph, D., D Litt. (Philosophy & Political Science) Emeritus Fellow. Ex Member of Parliament; Former Vice Chancellor, Jain Viswa Bharati; Former Director, Gandhian Institute of Studies, Varanasi; Ex President , Indian Society of Gandhian Studies; Secretary Afro Asian Philosophical Association, (Asia); National Convenor- Shanti Sena, President- Bihar Sarvodaya Mandal.

3. John Arapura, was a Professor (Eastern Philosophy) at McMaster University, Hamilton, Canada, where he and

Dr. Grant were colleagues for a number of years. He is now retired and is Professor Emeritus, still living in the vicinity of McMaster University. Dr. Arapura is the author of several books and many articles on Vedanta and Eastern as well as Comparative Philosophy. Among his books are *Religion as Anxiety* and *Tranquility and Gnosis* and the *Question of Thought in Vedanta*.

4. William Christian is Professor of Political Science at the University of Guelph in Ontario, Canada. He holds a BA and MA from the University of Toronto and a PhD from the London School of Economics. He is the author or editor of eleven books, including *George Grant: a Biography*, *George Grant: Selected Letters*, and *The George Grant Reader*. He has also written several articles and book chapters on different aspects of Grant's thought. His most recent book is a *biography of Sir George Parkin*, George Grant's maternal grandfather. William Christian was a personal friend of Dr Grant, and knew him for the last fifteen years of his life.

5. Johannes ("Hans") Iemke Bakker (Ph.D. Toronto, 1979) was born in Friesland, the Netherlands (1949) and is a Full Professor of Sociology and Anthropology at the University of Guelph in Ontario, Canada. His main interest is in sociological theory, particularly the application of philosophical insights concerning epistemology to Meta-Paradigmatic aspects of theory in the social sciences and physical or life sciences. He is currently pursuing the relevance of Charles Sanders Peirce's Pragmatist Semiotics for "consilience" (E. O. Wilson's term) in the sciences. His interest in Gandhi was developed as a result of one year spent working with the Gandhi Peace Foundation in ten different states in India. He has done practical rural development work in Indonesia. He has a diploma in hatha yoga from Kripalu Center in Massachusetts and taught yoga in Guelph for a decade (1995-2005).

6. S. R. Bhatt is an eminent philosopher, Sankritist and profound thinker. He retired as Professor and head of the department of Philosophy and Coordinator of UGC's Special Assistance Programme in Philosophy in the

University of Delhi. He is an internationally known authority on Ancient Indian Philosophy and Culture, having specialization in Nyaya, Buddhism, Jainism and Vedanta. He has been the general President of Indian philosophical Congress and All India Philosophy association (Akhil Bharatiya Darshan Parishad). He has authored and edited several books and research papers on themes pertaining to philosophy, culture, values and society.

7. R. Raj Singh, Professor and Chair of Philosophy, Brock University, Canada. Books: *"Death, Contemplation and Philosophy"* (Ashgate, 2007), and *"Bhakti and Philosophy"* (Rowman and Littlefield, 2006). Published several articles on Contemporary Continental Philosophy, Heidegger, Schopenhauer, History of Western Philosophy, Vedanta, Buddhism, Gandhi and the Bhakti movement. Delivered many lectures in academic events in India, China, Japan, Australia, USA, Germany, France, Italy, Trinidad and many other countries.

8. Ron Dart has taught in the Department of Political Science, Philosophy, Religious Studies at University of the Fraser Valley in British Columbia (Canada) since 1990.

He was on staff with Amnesty International in the 1980s, and he has published twenty books and many articles. Ron has written extensively on the Canadian Red/High Tory Tradition, and he recently edited a book on George Grant called, *Athens and Jerusalem: George Grant's Theology, Philosophy, and Politics* (University of Toronto Press: 2006). Ron is on the National Board of the Thomas Merton Society of Canada, and he is the political science advisor to the Stephen Leacock Home/Museum.

9. Peter C. Emberley is Professor of Political Science at Carleton University. He received his B.A. at the University of British Columbia (1978), his M.A. at the University of Toronto (1979), and his Ph.D. at the London School of Economics (1983). His publications include *Divine Hunger: Canadians on Spiritual Walk About* (Toronto: HarperCollins, 2002), *Zero Tolerance: Hot Button Politics in Canada's Universities* (Penguin, 1996), *Values Education and Technology:*

The Ideology of Dispossession (University of Toronto Press, 1995), *Bankrupt Education: The Decline of Liberal Education in Canada* (University of Toronto Press, 1994), and *Faith and Political Philosophy: The Correspondence Between Leo Strauss and Eric Voegelin* (Pennsylvania State University Press, 1993). He has published articles in political philosophy in Interpretation, Social Research, and the Canadian Journal of Political Science, and contributed chapters to edited books. In 1994 he was asked by Carleton University to design a core curriculum in the humanities and the result was a new school, the College of the Humanities, of which he was the Founding Director. He is currently working on a study of globalization and tradition, with a focus on folk art communities in West Bengal and Rajasthan.

10. Joseph Prabhu is Professor of Philosophy and Religion at California State University, Los Angeles (CSULA). He is active as both a scholar and a peace activist. He has edited, *The Intercultural Challenge of Raimon Panikkar* (Orbis Books, 1996) and co-edited the two-volume *Indian Ethics: Classical Traditions and Contemporary Challenges* (Ashgate Publishing Co, 2007 and Oxford University Press, India). He has two books in process, *"Liberating Gandhi: Community, Empire and a Culture of Peace,"* and *"Hegel, India and the Dark Face of Modernity."* He has been a Senior Fellow of the Center for the Study of World Religions at Harvard University and of the Martin Marty Center at the University of Chicago and a Visiting Professor there. He has also been co-editor of *Re-Vision* and a contributing editor of *Zygon*. He is the incoming President of the international Society for Asian and Comparative Philosophy, 2008-2010, and the Program Chair for the Melbourne Parliament of the World's Religions. Among his many awards are the Outstanding Professor Award of CSULA for 2004-2005.

He serves on the Board of Trustees and the Executive Committee of the Council of a Parliament of the World's Religions. He serves also on the Advisory Board of the Toda Institute for Peace Research associated with Soka Gakkai International. He is also the Chair of the Southern

California Committee of a Parliament of the World's Religions and is an active member of Interfaith Communities United for Justice and Peace.

He has lectured at more than fifty universities either as visiting professor or as guest lecturer in Asia, Africa, Australia, Europe and the United States.

11. Anthony J. Parel, Born in Kerala in 1926, naturalized citizen of Canada since 1973. Educated in India and the US, Ph. D. in Political Science from Harvard University (1963).

Emeritus Professor of Political Science at the University of Calgary, Canada, where he taught Political Philosophy from 1966 to 1994.

Among his publications are *Gandhi: Hind Swaraj and Other Writings* (ed.), Cambridge University Press, 1997; into 10th printing, 2008; Indian edition, into 4th printing;

Gandhi, Freedom and Self-Rule (ed.), Lexington Books, USA, 2000; Indian edition, Vistar Publications, New Delhi, 2002; *Gandhi's Philosophy and the Quest for Harmony*, Cambridge University Press, 2006, reprinted, 2007; paperback edition, 2007; Indian edition with a New Preface, 2008; *The Political Calculus: Essays on Machiavelli's Philosophy* (ed. and co-author), University of Toronto Press, 1972; and *The Machiavellian Cosmos*, Yale University Press, 1992; and *Calgary Aquinas Studies* (ed. and co-author), The Pontifical Institute of Medieval Studies, Toronto, 1978, reprinted in 2006.

12. George Melnyk is an Associate Professor in the Faculty of Communication and Culture at the University of Calgary. He is the author and editor of almost 20 books on political, social and cultural issues. He is a cultural historian specializing the in the study of Canadian film and literature. From 2005 to 2008 he served as the co-chair of the Consortium for Peace Studies at the University of Calgary during which time he wrote on Gandhi and Grant. Among the titles he has published that are relevant to the topic of Grant and Gandhi are / *Canada and the New American Empire:*

War and Anti-War/ (2004) and */ The Poetics of Naming/* (2003). He is also the Series Editor for Global Peace Studies, a new series of books on peace issues in a global context published by Athabasca University Press.

13. James B. Gerrie, James Gerrie was born in Burlington Ontario Canada in 1967 to Gordon and Marnie Gerrie. With their generous support his older sister Jo-Ellen and he were able to pursue their educational aspirations beyond the secondary level. With the help of his thesis advisor, Dr. Jay Newman, James received his Ph.D. in Philosophy in 1999 from the University of Guelph. His doctoral dissertation was entitled "Some Ethical and Public Policy Implications of Technological Dependency with Reference to the Works of Harold Innis, Marshall McLuhan and George Grant. <http://www.collectionscanada.ca/obj/s4/f2/dsk1/tape9/PQDD_0002/NQ40370.pdf>". James has published articles and book chapters in the fields of the Philosophy of Technology and the Philosophy of Religion. He is currently an assistant professor at Cape Breton University in Sydney Nova Scotia, where he teaches courses in Philosophy and Religious Studies. James is husband to Patricia Gerrie (they celebrated 14 happy years of marriage in (2008) and proud father of Madeleine (11) and Charlie (9).

14. Geeta Mehta, retired as head of the Dept. of Philosophy from Maharshri Dayanand College. At present Director, K.J. Somaiya centre for Studies in Jainism. President, Bharatiya Mahila Darshanik Parishad. Recognized Research Guide for Ph.D. at Mumbai University. books (i) *Philosophy of Vinoba Bhave: A new perspective in Gandhian Thought,*(ii)*A Study Material for Moral philosophy* (iii) *Ahimsa:From Mahavir to Mahatma* (iv) *Aba* (Shivaji Bhave) Apne Sabdonme. 32 Research Articles Published in International Journal , 105 other articles published in News Papers and Magazines . An inmate of Vinobaji's Padayatra from 1960-1965. Visited and delivered lectures to peace Group workers and students in 32 countries. Participated and presented Papers in 82 National and International conferences. Woman of the year- 2006 and leading intellectual of the world 2002-03, American Biographical Centre .Plato Award, International year of Education 2006, International Biographical Centre. Included in Asian/American who's who.

15. Arati Barua is an Associate Professor and Head of the Department of Philosophy, Deshbandhu College, University of Delhi. She is the Founder Director of the Indian Division of the Schopenhauer Society (IDSS). Besides being a member of various academic Societies such as *Schopenhauer Gesellschaft*, Germany, *North American division of Schopenhauer Society*, USA, *Indian Association for Canadian Study*, India, she is a member of the *Scientific advisory board* of the *Schopenhauer Jahrbuch*, Germany.

Her main research interests are in the areas of philosophy of Schopenhauer in relation to Indian Philosophy (particularly to Sankara), philosophy of Interpretation (particularly with reference to Michael Krausz) and study of George Grant in comparison to Gandhi.

She was awarded a *DFG fellowship* by the *German Research Foundation*, Germany for her collaborative research on 'Schopenhauer and Sankara' at the *Schopenhauer Research Center*, University of Mainz, Germany in 2006 and earlier a *Faculty Research fellowship* of SICI (Shastri Indo-Canadian Institute) in 2003 for her project on 'Grant and Gandhi' at the University of Guelph, Canada.

Book: *'The Philosophy of Arthur Schopenhauer'* (Intellectual publishing, New Delhi, 1992). Her Edited volume *"Schopenhauer and Indian Philosophy: A Dialogue between India and Germany"* got published from Northern book Center, New Delhi, 2008. Published research articles in reputed journals (national and international) of philosophy, particularly on Schopenhauer, Michael Krausz, George Grant and Gandhi. She has also participated in various national and International Conferences.

16. Andrew Kaethler wrote his MA on George Grant at Trinity Western University in Langley, British Columbia (Canada). The thesis was called 'The Synthesis of Athens and Jerusalem: George Grant's Defence Against Modernity' (2006). Ron Dart was Andrew's MA Thesis Advisor, and William Christian was Andrew's External Examiner. Andrew taught at Lithuania Christian College in 2007-2008, and he will be teaching again at LCC in 2008-2009.

☙ ❧

BIBLIOGRAPHY

Primary Sources

A) Books: By George Grant—

1. *The Empire, Yes or No?* Ryerson Press, (1945).

2. *Philosophy in the Mass Age.* CBC, (1959)

3. *Lament for a Nation : the Defeat of Canadian Nationalism.* Mc Clelland & Stewart, (1965).

4. *Time as History.* CBC, (1969).

5. *Technology and Empire : Perspectives on North America.* House of Anansi, (1969)

6. *English-speaking Justice.* Mount Allison University, (1974).

7. Grant, G.P. (1976). The computer does not impose on us the ways it should be used. In W. Christian & S. Grant (Eds.), *The George Grant reader.* Toronto, Canada: University of Toronto Press.

8. *Technology and Justice.* House of Anansi, (1986).

9. *George Grant : selected letters* edited, with an introduction by William Christian. University of Toronto Press, (1996).

10. *The George Grant Reader.* William Christian and Sheila Grant (editors). University of Toronto Press, (1998)

Selected Secondary Literature

B) Books: On George Grant—

1) *The Greek East and the Latin West: A Study in The Christian Tradition.* Sherrard, Philip, London: Oxford University Press, 1959.

2) *Canada's First Century*, Creighton, Donald, Toronto: Macmillan of Canada, 1970.

3) *George Grant in Process: Essays and Conversations.* Edited by Larry Schmidt. Toronto: Anansi Press, 1978

4) *The idea of Canada and the crisis of Community*, Armour, Leslie, Ottawa: Steel Rail Publishing, 1981.

5) *Modernity and Responsibility: Essays for George Grant.* Edited by Eugene Combs. Toronto: University of Toronto Press, 1983

6) *Technology and the Canadian Mind*, Kroker, Arthur, Montreal: New World Perspective, 1984.

7) *George Grant and the Twilight of Justice.* Joan O'Donovan. Toronto: University of Toronto Press, 1984.

8) *The Moving Image of Eternity.* David Cayley. Toronto: CBC, 1986

9) *George Grant's Platonic Rejoinder to Heidegger*, Angus, Ian Lewiston and Queenston: Edwin Mellon Press, 1987.

10) *Two Theological Languages by George Grant and other Essays in Honour of His Work.* Edited by Wayne Whillier Lewiston: The Edwin Mellen Press. 1990.

11) *By Loving Our Own: George Grant and the Legacy of Lament for a Nation.* Edited by Peter Emberley. Ottawa: Carleton University Press, 1990.

12) *George Grant & the Future of Canada.* Edited by Yusuf K. Umar. Calgary: University of Calgary Press, 1992.

13) *George Grant: A Biography.* William Christian. Toronto: University of Toronto Press, 1993.

14) *George Grant in Conversation.* David Cayley. Toronto: Ananasi, 1995.

15) *George Grant and the Subversion of Modernity: Art, Philosophy, Politics, Religion and Education.* Edited by Art Davis. Toronto: University of Toronto Press, 1996.

16) *George Grant: Selected Letters.* Edited with an Introduction by William Christian. Toronto: University of Toronto Press, 1996.

17) a). *Collected Works of George Grant:* Volume I: 1933-1950. Edited by Arthur Davis and Peter Emberley. Toronto: University of Toronto Press, 2000.

b). *Collected Works of George Grant:* Volume 2: 1951-1959. Edited by Arthur Davis. Toronto: University of Toronto Press, 2002.

c). *Collected Works of George Grant:* Volume 3: 1960-1969. Edited by Arthur David and Henry Roper. Toronto: University of Toronto Press, 2005.

d). The 4th and final volume of *The Collected Works of George Grant* should be out in 2008. It will be published by University of Toronto Press. Art Davis has done most of the work on the 4 volumes.

18) *George Grant: Redefining Canada.* T.F. Rigelhof. Lantzville: XYZ Publishing, 2001.

19) *George Grant and the Theology of the Cross: The Christian Foundations of His Thought.* Harris Athanasiadis. Toronto: University of Toronto Press, 2001.

20) *George Grant's Betrayal of Canada.* Robin Mathews. Vancouver: Northland Publications, 2004.

21) *Athens and Jerusalem: George Grant's Theology, Philosophy, and Politics.* Edited by Ian Angus, Ron Dart, and Randy Peg Peters. Toronto: University of Toronto Press, 2006.

22) *George Grant: A Guide To His Thought.* Hugh Donald Forbes. Toronto: University of Toronto Press, 2007.

23) *A Border Within: National Identity, Cultural Plurality and Wilderness,* Andrew, E. Montreal and Kingston: McGill-Queen's University Press, 1997.

24) *The idea of Canada and the crisis of Community*, Armour, Leslie, Ottawa: Steel Rail Publishing, 1981.

25) "George Grant and the Theology of the Cross: The Christian Foundations of His Thought" Athanasiadis, Harris, Ph. D. dissertation McGill University, 1997.

26) *George Grant and the Theology of the Cross*. Athanasiadis, Harris, Toronto: University of Toronto Press, 2001.

27) *The Maple Leaf Forever: Essays on Nationalism and Politics in Canada*, Cook, Ramsay, 2nd ed. Toronto : Macmillan of Canada, 1977.

28) *Canada's First Century*, Creighton, Donald, Toronto: Macmillan of Canada, 1970.

29) *The technological society* (John Wilkerson, Trans.). Ellul, J. New York: Vintage. (1965).

30) George Grant's critique of technological liberalism. Doctoral thesis, Flinn, F. St. Michael's College, University of Toronto. 1981.

C) Articles: On G Grant:

Adria, M. (2003). Arms to communications: Idealist and pragmatist strains of Canadian thought on technology and nationalism in *Canadian Journal of Communication*, 28(2), 167-84.

Andrew, E. (1988). George Grant on technological imperatives. In R. Beiner, R. Day, & J. Masciulli (Eds.), *Democratic theory and technological society*. Armonk, NY: Sharpe.

— "George Grant on the political economy of technology" in *Bulletin of Science, Technology and Society*, 23,no.6 (December 2003):479-85.

—"For a Canadian Philosophy: George Grant " in *Canadian Journal of Political and Social Theory*, 13, no.1 (1989):140-3.

Badertscher, John "The Prophesy of George Grant", in Canadian Journal of Political and Social Theory 4, no.1, (1980):183-9.

Badertscher, J. (1978). George P. Grant and Jacques Ellul on freedom in technological society. In L. Schmidt (Ed.), George Grant in process: Essays and conversations. Toronto, Canada: Anansi.

Blodgett E.D., "George Grant, the Uncertain Nation and Diversity of Being" in Canadian Literature 152-3 (Spring-Summer 1997):107-23.

Box, Ian, "George Grant and the Embrace of Technology", in Canadian Journal of Political Science 15, no.3 (1982):503-15.

Cayley, David, "The Moving Image of Eternity" transcript of interview with George Grant, *Ideas*, Toronto: Canadian Broadcasting Corporation, 1986.

Christian, William, "George Grant and the Twilight of Our Justice", in *Queen's Quarterly* 85 (1978):485-91.

—" George Grant and Love: A Comment on Ian Box's 'George Grant and the Embrace of Technology' with Box's Reply: Thinking Through Technology'" in Canadian Journal of Political Science 16, no.2 (June 1983):347-59.

—" George Grant and Religion: A Conversation Prepared and Edited by William Christian". In *Journal of Canadian Studies* 26, no.1 (1991): 42-6.

—"Religion, Faith and Love" in Studies in Political Theory 1, no.1 (1992):61-73.

—"Canada's Fate: Principal Grant, Sir George Parkin and George Grant in Journal of Canadian Studies, 34, no.4 (1999/2000):88-104.

—"Was George Grant a Red Tory?" in *Athens and Jerusalem: George Grant's Theology Philosophy and politics*, edited by Ian Angus, Ron Dart and Randy Peg Peters, 39-61, Toronto: University of Toronto Press, 2006.

Cook, Ramsay . "Loyalism, Technology and Canada's fate", in Journal of Canadian Studies 5 (1970):50-60.

Crook, R.W., "Modernization and Nostalgia: A Note on the Sociology of Pesimism" Queen's Quarterly 73 (Summer 1966):269-83.

Duffy, Dennis, "The Ancestral Journey: Travels with George Grant. in *Journal of Canadian Studies* 22, no.3, (1987):90-103.

Emberley, Peter, "Values and Technology: George Grant and Our Present Possibilities", in Canadian Journal of Political Science 11, No 3, 1988, 165-94.

Forbes, H D, "The political thought of George Grant". in *Journal of Canadian Studies*, 26, no.1 (1991):46-68.

Lee, Dennis, "Cadence, Country, Silence: Writing in Colonial Space" *Boundary* 2-3, no.1, (1974):151-68.

Lee, D. (1990). Grant's impasse. In P. C. Emberley (Ed.), By loving our own: George Grant and the legacy of "Lament for a Nation." Ottawa, Canada: Carleton University Press.

Macdonald, R.D., "The persuasiveness of Grant's Lament for a nation", in Studies in Canadian Literature2 (Summer 1977):239-51.

Mandel, F. H., " George Grant, language, Nation, the Silence of God" in *Canadian Literature* 83 (1979) : 163-75.

Martin, Geoffrey, "Justice in the Thought of George Grant", in *Canadian Journal of political and social theory* 13, no.1-2 (1989):144-61.

Mathie, W. (1978). The technological regime: George Grant's analysis of modernity. In L. Schmidt (Ed.), *George Grant in process: Essays and conversations*. Toronto, Canada: Anansi.

Noel, S.J.R. "Domination and Myth in the Works of George Grant and C.B. Macpherson". In *Dalhousie Review* 59 (1978):534-51.

O'Donovan, Joan, ed, "George Grant Special Edition". In *Chesterton Review* 11, no.2 (1985).

Thomas, Tim, "George Grant, the Free Trade Agreement and Contemporary Quebec", in Journal of Canadian Studies, 27, no.4 (1992-93):180-95.

Select Bibliography: (M K Gandhi)

Primary Sources

The Collected Works of Mahatma Gandhi 100 volumes, New Delhi: Publication Division, Ministry of Information and Broadcasting, 1958-94.

BOOKS BY GANDHI

1. *Hind Swaraj*, Ahmedabad: Navajivan, 1938.

2. *Satyagraha in South Africa* (translated by V. G. Desai), Ahmedabad: Navajivan, 1928.

3. *The Story of My Experiments With Truth* (translated by Mahadev Desai), Ahmedabad: Navajivan; Volume I, 1927; Volume II, 1929.

4. *The Constructive Programme: Its Meaning and Place*, Ahmedabad: Navajivan, 1941.

5. *Ashram Observances in Action*, Ahmedabad: Navajivan, 1955.

6. *Discourses on the Gita*, Ahmedabad: Navajivan, 1960.

7. *A Guide to Health*, Madras: S. Ganesan, 1921. Ahmedabad: Navajivan, 1967.

JOURNALS EDITED BY GANDHI

1. *Indian Opinion*, Natal, South Africa (1903-14).
2. *Young India*, Ahmedabad, India (1919-32).
3. *Navajivan*, Ahmedabad, India (1919-31).
4. *Harijan*, Ahmedabad, India (1933-48).

COLLECTIONS OF WRITINGS BY GANDHI

1. *Bapu's Letters to Mira* (1928-48), Ahmedabad: Navajivan, 1949.

2. *Cent Per Cent Swadeshi*, Madras; G. A. Natesan, 1933.

3. *Conversations of Gandhiji* (edited by Chandrashankar Shukla), Bombay: Vora & Co., 1949.

4. *More Conversations of Gandhiji* (edited by Chandrashankar Shukla), Bombay: Vora & Co., 1950,

5. *Delhi Diary*, Ahmedabad: Navajivan, 1948.

6. *The Economics of Khadi*, Ahmedabad: Navajivan, 1941.

7. *Ethical Religion*, Madras: S. Ganesan, 1922.

8. *For Pacifists*, Ahmedabad: Navajivan, 1949.

9. *From Yeravda Mandir*: Ashram Observances (translated by V. G. Desai), Ahmedabad: Navajivan, 1932.

10. *Gandhiji's Correspondence with the Government, 1942-1944*, Ahmedabad: Navajivan, 1945.

11. *Gokhale: My Political Guru*, Ahmedabad: Navajivan; 1958.

12. *Hindu Dharma*, Ahmedabad: Navajivan, 1950.

13. *History of Satyagraha Ashram*, Madras: G. A.. N atesan, 1933.

14. *India of My Dreams*, Ahmedabad: Navajivan, 1947.

15. *Letters to Manibehn Patel*, Ahmedabad: Navajivan, 1963.

16. *Letters to Rajkumari Amrit Kaur*, Ahmedabad: Navajivan, 1961.

17. *The Medium of Instruction* (edited by Bharatan Kumarappa), Ahmedabad: Navajivan, 1954.

18. *My Appeal to the British*, New York: John Day Company, 1942.

19. *'My Dear Child': Letters to Esther Faering*, Ahmedabad:, Navajivan, 1956. '

20. *Non-Violence in Peace and War*, Ahmedabad: Navajivan; Part I, 1945; Part II, 1949.

21. *The Rowlatt Bills and Satyagraha*, Madras: G. A. Natesan, 1919.

22. *Sarvodaya*, Ahmedabad: Navajivan; 1951.

23. *Satyagraha*, Ahmedabad: Navajivan, 1951.

24. *Selected Letters*, Ahmedabad: Navajivan, 1962.

25. *Self-Restraint v. Self-Indulgence*, Ahmedabad: Navajivan, 1947.

26. *Socialism of My Conception*, Bombay: Bharatiya Vidya Bhavan, 1957.

27. *Speeches and Writings*, Madras: G. A. Natesan, 1933.

28. *To a Gandhian Capitalist*, Bombay: Hind Kitabs, 1951.

29. *To Ashram Sisters*, Ahmedabad: Navajivan, 1952.

30. *Unto This Last*, Ahmedabad: Navajivan, 1951..

31. *Untouchability*, Ahmedabad: Navajivan, 1954.

32. *Women and Social Injustice*, Ahmedabad: Navajivan, 1942.

Secondary Sources

ANDREWS, C. F., *Mahatma Gandhi's Ideas*, London: George Allen, 1929.

— *Mahatma Gandhi: His Own Story*, New York: The Macmillan Company, 1930.

— *Mahatma Gandhi at Work*, New York: The Macmillan Company, 193 I.

ASHE, GEOFFREY, *Gandhi: A Study in Revolution*, London: Heinemann, 1968.

BONDURANT, JOAN, *Conquest of Violence*, Berkeley: University of Cali-fornia Press, 1965.

BROWN, D. M., *The White Umbrella: Indian Political Thought From Manu to Gandhi*, Berkeley: University of California Press, 1958.

BROWN, JUDITH M., *Gandhi's Rise to Power: Indian Politics 1915-1922*, Cambridge: Cambridge University Press, 1972.

— *Gandhi and Civil Disobedience: The Mahatma in Indian Politics 1928-1934*, Cambridge: Cambridge University Press, 1977.

CATLIN, GEORGE, *In the Path of Mahatma Gandhi*, London: Macdonald & Co., 1948.

CHARPENTIER, MARIE VICTOIRE, *Gandhi*, Paris: Edition France-Empire, 1969.

Chatterjee, Margaret, *Gandhi's Religious Thought* (Notre Dame: University of Notre Dame Press, 1983)

DATTA, DHIRENDRA MOHAN, *The Philosophy of Mahatma Gandhi*, Madison: University of Wisconsin Press, 1961.

DESAI, MAHADEV, *Gandhiji in Indian Villages*, Madras: Ganesan,1927.

— *Gandhiji in Ceylon*, Madras: S. Ganesan, 1928.

— *The Story of Bardoli*, Ahmedabad: Navajivan, 1929.

— *The Nation's Voice*, Ahmedabad: Navajivan, 1932.

— *The Gita According to Gandhi*, Ahmedabad: Navajivan, 1946.

DHAWAN, G., *The Political Philosophy of Mahatma Gandhi*, Ahmedabad:Navajivan, 1951.

DIWAKAR, R. R., *Satyagraha-Its Technique and Theory*, Bombay: Hind.Kitabs, 1946.

DIWAN, ROMESH, LUTZ, MARK, *Essays in Gandhian Economics*, New Delhi: Gandhi Peace Foundation, 1985.

DOKE, J. J., *M. K. Gandhi: An Indian Patriot in South Africa* (introduction by Lord Ampthill), London: The London Indian Chronicle, 1909.

ELWIN, VERRIER, *Mahatma Gandhi*, London: Golden Vista Press,1932.

ERIKSON, ERIK H., *Gandhi's Truth*, New York: Norton, 1969.

FISCHER, LOUIS, *The Life of Mahatma Gandhi*, New York: Harper & Brothers, 1950.

GEORGE, S. K., *Gandhi's Challenge to Christianity*, London: Allen & Unwin, 1939.

GREGG, RICHARD B., *The Power of Non-Violence*, Ahmedabad: Navajivan, 1938. .

HORSBURGH, H.]. N., *Non-Violence and Aggression*, London: Oxford . University Press, 1971.

IYER, RAGHAVAN N, *The Moral and Political Thought of Mahatma Gandhi*, New York: Oxford University Press, 1973. Galaxy Paper- back, 1979. Second edition: Santa Barbara: Concord Grove Press, 1983.

— *Utilitarianism and All That*, London: Chatto & Windus, 1960. Second edition: Santa Barbara: Concord Grove Press, 1983.

— *Parapolitics: Toward the City of Man*, New York, Oxford: Oxford University Press, 1979.

KRIPALANI; J.:B., *Gandhian Thought*, Bombay: Orient Longmans, 1961.

— *Gandhi: His Life and Thought*, New Delhi: Publications Division of the 'Government of India; 1975.

KYTLE; CALVIN, *Gandhi, Soldier of Non-Violence: His Effect on India and the World Today*, New York: Grosset & Dunlap, 1969.

LANZA DEL VASTO, JOSEPH, *Gandhi to Vinoba: The New Pilgrimage* (translated from the French by Philip Leon), London: Rider, 1956. .

LEVS, WAVNE, and RAO, P.S.S. Rao, *Gandhi and America's Educational Future*, Carbondale: Southern Illinois University Press, 1969.

MAURER, HERRVMON, *Great Soul*, New York: Doubleday, 1948.

Merton, Thomas, (ed.) *Gandhi on Non-Violence*, New York, New Directions paperback, 1964.

MUZUMDAR, HARIDAS T., *Gandhi Versus the Empire*, New York: Universal Publishing Co., 1932.

NAESS, ARNE; *Gandhi and the Nuclear Age*, Totowa: Bedminster Press, 1965.

NAMBOODIRIPAD, E. M. S., *The Mahatma and the Ism*, New Delhi: People's Publishing House, 1958.

NANDA, B. R, *Mahatma Gandhi*, London: Allen & Unwin, 1958.

—*Gandhi and his Critics*, New Delhi, OUP, 1985.

NIKAM, N. A., *Gandhi's Discovery of Religion: A Philosophical Study*, Bombay: Bharatiya Vidya Bhavan, 1963.

OSTERGAARD, GEOFFREV, *Nonviolent Revolution in India*, New Delhi: Gandhi Peace Foundation, 1985.

PANTER-BRICK, SIMONE, *Gandhi Against Machiavellism: Non-Violence in Politics* (translated by D. Leon), London: Asia Publishing House, 1964.

Parel, A.J., (ed), *Gandhi: Hind Swaraj and Other Writings*, (Cambridge: Cambridge University Press, 1997).

— *Gandhi's Philosophy And The Quest For Harmony* (Cambridge: Cambridge University Press, Oct 2007).

— *Gandhi, Freedom, And Self- Rule*, Sage publications, 2000.

Parekh, Bhikhu,— *Gandhi: A Very Short Introduction* (Series - Very Short Introductions) Oxford University Press, Usa (2001/06/07).

—*Gandhi's Political Philosophy: A Critical Examination*, University of Norte Dame Press, 1989

PAVNE, ROBERT, *The Life and Death of Mahatma Gandhi*, New York: E. P. Dutton & Co., 1969.

POLAK, MILLIE GRAHAM, *Mr. Gandhi: The Man*, Bombay: Vora & Co., 1950.

POWER, PAUL F., *Gandhi on World Affairs*, Washington: Public Affairs Press, 1960.

PRABHU, R. K., and RAO, U. R. (eds.), *The Mind of Mahatma Gandhi*, Ahmedabad: Navajivan, 1967.

PRASAD, RAJENDRA, *Satyagraha in Champaran*, Ahmedabad: Navajivan, 1949.

RADHAKRISHNAN, S. (ed.), *Mahatma Gandhi: Essays and Reflections*, London: Allen & Unwin, 1938.

— *Mahatma Gandhi-100 years*, New Delhi: Gandhi Peace Foundation, 1968.

RAMACHANDRAN, G., and MAHADEVAN, T. K. (eds.), *Gandhi: His Relevance for Our Times*, Bombay: Bharatiya Vidya Bhavan, 1964.

RAO, V. K. R. V., *The Gandhian Alternative to Western Socialism*, Bombay: Bharatiya Vidya Bhavan, 1970.

Reflections on 'Hind Swaraj' by Western Thinkers, Bombay: Theosophy Company, 1948.

REVNOLDS, REGINALD, *To Live in Mankind-A Quest for Gandhi*, London: Andre Deutsch, 1951.

ROLLAND, ROMAIN, *Mahatma Gandhi*, London: Allen & Unwin, 1924.

ROTHERMUND, INDIRA, *The Philosophy of Restraint*, Bombay: Popular Prakashan, 1963.

SHARMA, JAGDISH, *Mahatma Gandhi: A Descriptive. Bibliography*, New Delhi: S. Chand & Co., 1955.

SHARP, GENE, *Gandhi As a Political Strategist*, Boston. Porter Sargent, 1979.

SHIRER, WILUAM LAURENCE, *Gandhi: A Memoir*, New York: Simon & Schuster, 1979.

SHUKLA, C., *Gandhi's View of Life*, Bombay: Bharatiya Vidya Bhavan, 1954.

SPRAIT, PHILIP, *Gandhism: An Analysis*, Madras: Huxley Press; 1939.

TENDULKAR, D. G., *Mahatma* (eight volumes), New Delhi: Publications Division of the Government of India, 1951-1954.

—*Gandhi in Champaran*, New Delhi: Publications Division of the Government of India, 1957.

WATSON, FRANCIS, and BROWN, MAURICE (eds.), *Talking of Gandhiji*, Calcutta: Orient Longmans, 1957.

INDEX

A

A Critique of the New Left, 123
  Platitude, 22
Abstracted Empiricism, 142
Adult Education Center, 241
Ahimsa, 34
Air Raid Precautions, 3
Alexis Carrel, 14
Appropriate Technology, 293
Arcadian Sensibility, 182
Autochthony, 42

B

Bhagavad Gita, 124
British Colonial, 133
Building, Dwelling, Thinking, 112

C

C. S. Lewis, 213
Canadian Broadcasting Corporation, 7
  Identity, 51
Central Christian Platitude, 135
Collected Works of Mahatma Gandhi, 259
Community Supported Agriculture, 302
Conditions of Attendance, 177
Constructive Program: Its Meaning and Place, 297
Cooperative Commonwealth Federation (CCF), 33
Cultural Capital, 134

D

Dalhousie Review, 120
Deeper Nationalisms, 30
Defence of North America, 43
Defensor Pacis, 223

Dethrone God, 238
Dharmocracy, 102

E

Eastern Orthodox Theology, 217
Economics, Enlightenment and Canadian Nationalism, 82
English-Speaking Justice, 17
Enthralling Fate, 43

F

Faith and the Multiversity, 57
Festschrift, 126
Freedom in Chains, 93
Fusion of the Populations, 261

G

G.M. Grant, 2
Gandhi and Tagore: Visionaries of Modern India, 31
Gandhi Peace Festival, 31
Gandhian Economics, 286
Gandhi's Economic Philosophy, 286
   Idea of Nation in Hind Swaraj, 257
   Religious Thought, 76
   Vision, 72
George Grant, 1
   Grant and the Subversion of Modernity, 127
   Grant Redefining Canada, 203
   Grant's Vision, 73
   Monro Grant, 237
German Vedantic Scholar, 129
Globalization, 133
Gnosis and the Question of Thought in Vedanta, 127
Grand Theory, 142
Great War, 133
Gross Domestic Product (GDP), 303
   National Product (GNP), 295, 303

H

Heidegger, 109
Hind Swaraj, 6, 237, 270
Hindu Wing of Christianity, 120
Hinduism and Christianity, 75
Holy War, 42

I

Imperium Sine Fine, 62
Indian National Congress, 273, 72
Influential National Leader, 72
Integral Humanism, 96
Intimations of Christianity among the Ancient Greek, 130

J

Jacques Ellul, 24
    Maritain, 213
Jawaharlal Nehru, 17
Jnana Yoga, 131
Judeo-Christian-Islamic, 149

K

Knowledge Monopolies, 177
    of Reality, 135

L

Lament For a Nation, 1
Law as Sovereign, 98
    Emanating From Sovereign, 98
Leo Tolstoy, 30
Liberal Education & the Democratic Ideal, 159
Life-Style Choices, 46
Local Exchange and Trading Systems, 302

M

Mahatma Gandhi, 16
Man the Unknown, 14
Mc Master University, 31
Medieval Pre-Scientific Doctrine, 174
Mills' Sociological Imagination, 141
Modern Material Progress, 107
Murray Jardine, 217

N

Nationalisms: Gandhi and Grant, 32
Nationalist Committee, 259
Neo-Luddite Ideas, 174
    Luddite Nationalism, 175
    Vedanta and Modernity, 125
New Democratic Party (NDP), 33
    Sociological Imagination, 138
Non-Cooperation Movement, 72
    Neutrality Thesis, 176
    Violent Resistance, 36

P

Panchayata, 103
Pandit Deendayal Upadhyaya, 96
Parochial Privileged Class, 82
Philosopher of Religion, 238
Philosophies of Heidegger, 109
Philosophy in Canada: a Symposium, 121
    in the Mass Age, 212, 26
Planning For Peace, 42
Pneumo-Pathologies, 61
Poetically Man Dwells, 112

Polarities of Nationalism, 80
Power Elite, 38
Pragmatic Liberalism, 50
Pragmatist Hermeneutics, 140

R

Radical Conservative, 139
  Enlightenment, 137
Red Toryism, 74
Religare, 222
Religion, 222
  and Language, 265
Rethinking Democracy and Beyond, 91
Round Table Conference, 31
Royal Society of Canada, 24

S

Sanyasin, 61
Sarva-Dharma Samabhava, 229
Sarvadharma Sahisnuta, 227
Satyagraha, 15
Science and Technology Studies (STS) Programmes, 180
Secular State, 223
Secularism – A Gandhian Perspective, 222
  in the Indian Context, 225
  of Gandhi and Nehru, 227

Selectivity Imperative in Grant's Work, 190
Semiological Revolution of Claude Levi-Strauss, 132
Sermon on the Mount-Beatitudes, 124
Shastri Indo-Canadian Institute, 207
Sir George Parkin, 2
Social Capital, 134
  Purpose for Canada, 19
Sociological Imagination, 136
Spiritual Quest, 76
Sterile Woman, 94
Superstition, 115
Swaraj, 34

T

Tapasya, 61
Techno Mania, 247
Technology and Empire, 7
  and Justice, 8
  and the Canadian Mind, 83
Terrifying Darkness, 49
The Age of the World Picture, 112
  American Dream, 157
  Autonomy of Technology, 179
  Bhagavad-Gita, 38
  Branch Plant, 196
  George Grant Reader, 125
  Great Ideas Today, 123
  Idiocy of the Village, 298

New Sociological Imagination, 131
Philosophy of Francis Bacon, 120
Religions of the World, 31
Soul of the Person, 150
Spirit of Philosophy, 122
Story of My Experiments With Truth, 240
Technological Society, 24
Theology of the Cross, 58
Theories of Surplus Value, 145
Thinking About Technology, 187

Time as History, 7

U

Universal and Homogenous State, 43
Upper Canada College, 202

V

Vinayak Damodar Savarkar, 60
Vincent Massey, 121
Vita Contemplativa, 121

W

White Man's Burden, 42
William Grant, 3
World Food Crisis, 147

೮೦ ೧೮